"The American dream of freedom and liber fertilized by the blood of warriors, and with the eyewitness, hands-on reminder of courageous U.S. Marine, Terence Sumner Kirk, we have a powerful celebration of the ultimate sacrifices by which our quality of life has been determined. All Americans should fight for the American Dream by improvising, overcoming, and adapting as these brave heroes did."

—*Ted Nugent*

"Terry Kirk repeatedly risked his life to document atrocities against his fellow POWs only to have the country he loved refuse to acknowledge his sacrifice and contribution for nearly four decades. If you're looking for heroes, look no further."

—*Dan Malone, Pulitzer Prize winner and author of* America's Condemned

"Terry's story is a testament to the gallant young men who served the cause of freedom as prisoners of war. The Japanese violated every tenet of the Geneva Convention, forcing the men to work as slaves while imposing horrendous abuse and deliberate starvation. His pictures of the actual physical conditions of starving prisoners, taken by a secret camera, give permanent testimony to their sacrifice. Had the Japanese discovered the pictures, Kirk would have been beaten to death or summarily executed by beheading. An exciting and fitting tribute to the China Marines of 1941 who inspire the men of today's Marine Corps."

—*Roger Mansell, director of the Center for Research, Allied POWs Under the Japanese.*

The Secret Camera

BOOKS BY TERENCE S. KIRK

The Secret Camera

Dragon's Tooth

Magnaway

The Secret Camera

A MARINE'S STORY: FOUR YEARS AS A POW

Terence S. Kirk

THE LYONS PRESS
Guilford, Connecticut
An imprint of The Globe Pequot Press

The Lyons Press is an imprint of The Globe Pequot Press

10 9 8 7 6 5 4 3 2 1

Printed in the United States of America

ISBN 1-59228-826-X

Library of Congress Cataloging-in-Publication Data is available on file.

I thank my editor, Lilly Golden,
Carolyn Noonan, Greg Gran, Tim Day,
and especially my loving wife Millie,
and all the other good people that believed in me,
for their help and encouragement
to bring this forbidden story to the world.

Contents

If dying without a whimper was the mark of a man, there wasn't a boy among them.

1

Issues in Doubt

I awakened with a start. A burly, shadowy form standing at the foot of my bunk was shaking it violently.

"Wake up, Kirk; you have the watch."

I jerked to a sitting position. From the foggy recesses of my mind I recalled that I was a member of the guard. I had the 0400 to 0800 watch.

"Here," the hulk said, holding a large bunch of keys in his hand. I recognized the gravelly voice of Corporal Dedman.

Knowing Dedman for his promptness, I knew the time was exactly 0400, not a minute sooner or later. I also knew it was the eighth of December, 1941.

I took the keys and clutched them to my chest. I was now, officially, the corporal of the guard at Camp Holcomb—the United States Marine Corps Rifle and Machine Gun Range, Chinwangtao, China.

Still clutching the keys and not fully awake, I watched Dedman pass by the dull, glowing potbellied stove and fade into the shadows. The stove was ornate, antique, and occupied the center of the room. I wondered if Dedman had taken the time to stoke the stove before he woke me. If not, that would be one of the first things I'd have to attend to.

I glanced around the dimly lit squad room. Except for "Birdlegs" Brown in the bed next to mine, who was also awakened by Dedman's voice, the rest of the eighteen marines were sleeping peacefully.

I crawled out of bed and began pulling on my clothes. I was tempted, and wanted desperately, to climb back into my sack, but I knew if I did I would go back to sleep, and then there would be hell to pay. To get up in the middle of the night is bad enough when everything is going right, but I was not that lucky. Birdlegs Brown wanted to listen to the radio at four o'clock in the morning. He turned on the multichannel console radio standing between my bunk and his and began spinning the dial. Not slowly, in search of a particular station, but rather aimlessly in pursuit of a strong signal. When he found one, he let it blast for an instant, then he moved the dial to the next and the next. I resisted the urge to turn off the radio, hoping he would realize he was disturbing the peace and go back to sleep.

"Turn that damn thing off," someone yelled from the far corner of the room.

"All right, Brown, like the man said, turn the damn thing off." I, too, had reached the saturation point. "What are you trying to do," I asked, "wake everyone in the barracks?"

Brown looked at me for a moment, then reached for the volume control; instead of turning the set off, he turned the sound very low. With the radio quieted, I did not press my demand.

I finished dressing, and checked the stove to find it was in good shape. Satisfied the stove would hold its heat for at least an hour, I maneuvered through the scattered locker boxes in the aisle to the office, a small room at the west end of the barracks.

Hanging from a cord in the center of the ceiling, a low-wattage bulb scattered a few rays of light through the doorway into the squad room. Bathed in its light was an old oaken desk jammed tightly into one corner of the room. On the desk was the corporal of the guard logbook containing reports of all noteworthy events throughout the day.

There were other books on the desk, pushed against the wall. One, in particular, caught my eye, *The Marine's Handbook*. Its author, Luther A. Brown, was a major in the Marine Corps and the commanding officer of the Marine Detachment at Tientsin, China.

Tientsin had been my duty station—that is, until a week ago, when I was transferred here.

Someone had dubbed the manual "John Brown's Handbook," and the name had stuck. Actually, the handbook was an indispensable guide for marines. Every recruit had one, or should have, to keep out of trouble. The manual covered everything from ingrown toenails to hand-to-hand combat with a rifle butt and bayonet.

I pulled the chair up to the desk, removed a fountain pen from my shirt pocket, scratched the point on a piece of paper to bring out the ink, and began my entry in the logbook: "0400 December 8, 1941. Assumed duties as corporal of the guard, relieved Corporal Dedman who reported the camp all secure . . ."

"Hey, you guys, listen to this!"

It was Birdlegs yelling, and not caring whether or not he woke the whole barracks.

"Listen to this!" he repeated, his voice full of excitement. "This guy says the Japs have bombed Pearl Harbor!"

Brown's hysterics had roused most of the marines. A few were out of their bunks and, like myself, heading in the direction of the radio.

"The Japs have bombed Pearl Harbor!" the announcer screamed just as I arrived. "The United States and Japan are at war!"

Practically everyone was crowded around the radio by the time I got there, and were standing in stunned silence listening to the news. As I stood in their midst, it dawned on me, that I, being the corporal of the guard, was in command of the post. If anything were to happen concerning the war with Japan hereabouts, it was my baby.

The first thing I had better do, I assured myself, was to unload this responsibility where it belonged—in the lap of the base commander, Lieutenant Huizenga. If anyone could start some action before the enemy arrived, it was he.

Having made the decision, I looked around for a messenger and noted Birdlegs Brown was nearly dressed.

"Brown," I said sharply, "go to the officers' quarters, wake the lieutenant, and give him the bad news."

"Why me?" he complained.

"Why not?" I retorted. "You started all this ruckus by turning on the radio. Now don't waste time. Get moving."

Birdlegs donned his overcoat, pulled his fur hat down over his ears, and grumbled something about a lousy corporal before disappearing through the door.

The volume of the radio rattled the windows. The announcer was still at it with high emotion: "The Japs have bombed Pearl Harbor! The United States and Japan are at war!"

The blaring radio had had its effect; everyone who had not turned out with the first wave of news, was now out of bed and collecting his gear. During the confusion, someone found the light switch and now we could see what we were doing. The squad room was stirring with activity; marines who were already dressed were breaking out their combat gear, while others were still looking for their shoes.

If Pearl Harbor had Japs, it occurred to me as I watched the marines preparing to do battle, maybe we have some too. There was a garrison of forty thousand Japanese, more or less, down the road on the other side of Chinwangtao, someone had told me. It was time I went out and had a look around.

I put on my overcoat, my fur-lined gloves and hat, strapped on my pistol belt, and stepped out into the winter night. A gust of frigid air hit me in the face and almost took my breath away. Darkness closed in around me as I moved away from the light streaming from the barracks windows. There was no moon and only a faint illumination from the snow to light my way. The sky in the east seemed to hint of a new day approaching. The horizon showed a pale streak of light.

I took careful note of everything around me. This was no time to get caught napping, I cautioned myself. As I moved farther away from the buildings, I realized the snow was crunching under my feet and making a hell of a racket. It sounded like I was walking through a field of broken glass. I groaned inwardly. *I'll never surprise anyone in this snow; they'll hear me coming a mile away.* I tried walking on my tiptoes, hoping to lower the noise, but it didn't seem to make a bit of difference.

Traveling very slowly, and as quietly as possible under the circumstances, I reached the camp's perimeter. By this time my body was feeling the intense cold and I was forced to squint to keep my eyeballs from freezing. I put my gloved hand to my face so I could inhale part of my own breath to raise the temperature of the subzero air, to protect my lungs from frostbite. Traveling slowly did nothing to help my circulation.

Now, a chill shook me, not from the cold, but from the thought of coming face-to-face with the enemy—a man who might try to take my life, for nothing. The thought was unnerving and difficult to accept.

What would I do? I searched my soul for an answer. Start shooting, or wait to see if he would actually try to kill me?

Waiting to see, I decided, was out. That would be just plain suicide. This was war; Uncle Sam had just declared open season on the Japanese and had issued me a hunting license. I stopped, removed my glove, and drew my .45 caliber pistol from its holster. I knew exactly what I had to do—stay alive.

I stood quietly for a long time, peering into the darkness and listening for a sound, any sound. The silence was unreal; nothing except my own breathing interrupted the stillness. Not even a gentle breeze offered to disturb the hush. The air was so cold and crisp, it seemed that if something were to cause the slightest noise, the whole world would shatter into a billion pieces.

I was so wrapped up in my search for a possible enemy, it was not until I realized my hand was freezing that I came to my senses. I peeled my icy fingers from the pistol grip and returned the weapon to its holster. I tucked my numb hand inside my overcoat under my armpit to thaw it, and continued along the perimeter until I came to the path leading back to camp.

The barracks were vacant except for Corporal Dedman. He was hugging the potbellied stove as if he were still trying to thaw out from his 1200 to 0400 watch. I joined him, my feet like two blocks of ice.

"Where has everybody gone?" I asked.

"They are over at the railroad siding," he growled, "off-loading machine guns and ammo."

As far back as I could remember, Dedman never talked—he always growled.

No sooner had he answered my question when someone tried to kick in the door. I jumped to open it, but Dedman was there before me. Through the portal, the marines came stumbling and staggering, two at a time, under the heavy loads of crates containing machine guns with tripods and all the necessary spare parts.

They were Browning, .30 caliber, water-cooled, heavy machine guns.

The gun crews set to work immediately uncrating the guns, which were coated with cosmoline, a rust-preventative grease. Because of the grease, the weapons were inoperable and in a hell of a mess. They had been packed in cosmoline and crated for shipment back to the States, as part of the slow dismantling of our presence in China. Stored in the boxcars at 40 degrees below zero, the severe cold had hardened the protective coating to the consistency of road tar.

In desperation, we tried many ways to remove the cosmoline. We attempted to slice the grease off with bayonets. Another idea was to set a gun on the hot stove, but when the gunk got warm enough to wipe off the outside, it also dripped on the hot stove and gave off a sickening white smoke.

Everyone agreed that to load and fire one of these guns clogged with cosmoline would not only destroy the gun, but also the gunner and anyone else close by.

At this point, it seemed like an impossible task because the grease was like cement. The operating handles of the guns would not budge, so there was no way to get the bolts open to clean the bore or chamber. We had to devise a way to remove the grease and we needed it fast, or the guns, to us, would be just so much scrap iron.

When it appeared to be hopeless, D.B. Wilson burst into the squad room. "Try the hot water in the shower," he laughed, holding a shining gun over his head. "It works beautifully!"

Each gun crew took a turn in the shower. In short order, all the machine guns were clean and in working condition. The water from the shower was so hot, the guns dried with little or no wiping.

The Browning machine guns were reassembled. The gun crews prepared positions for them by stacking locker boxes on one another and mounting the guns on top of the boxes so the muzzles would clear the windowsills. The guns were placed to cover all approaches.

Standing there amid all the activity, I was not much help to anyone, but as corporal of the guard, I had other duties to attend to. I had better get outside and make another sweep of the perimeter to make sure we were not surprised, or all this work would have been for nothing.

It was still dark outside, but the dawn was at last beginning to show in the east. The cold blurred my vision and played tricks on me, or maybe it was my imagination. I would catch a glimpse of a shadow, then there was nothing. I stopped and listened intently, but all I could hear was the thumping of my heart.

It began to grow light rapidly now. Caught off guard, I realized I was standing in an open field, a perfect target, a silhouette against the snow in my dark uniform. I began walking faster; at least I was a moving target, much harder to hit than a sitting duck. I did not feel at ease until I was back in the shelter of the buildings.

In the barracks, I learned that Brown was still hunting for Lieutenant Huizenga. One of the house boys had told Brown that Huizenga had taken his shotgun and had gone bustard hunting (a bird about the size and weight of a wild turkey) at Shanhaikwan near the Great Wall.

Gunner Lee and Sergeant Bishop were back in camp; D.B. Wilson had driven into town to pick them up. They said there were plenty of Japanese to be seen, but none of them were hostile, nor did any attempt to stop them.

That was strange, I reflected. Another routine day, except for the machine guns peeking through the windows of the barracks and the radio announcer who was still at it, talking about the bombing of Pearl Harbor.

"Chow down," someone called at the door, as if to lend support to my thoughts.

The guns had all been strapped to the bunks with web belts and rope. Ammunition belts hung from each gun and a hose fastened to the water jackets under the muzzles dropped away into water cans beside each gun; spare ammunition boxes were placed close by. All that was needed was to squeeze the triggers and there would be a hail of thirty-caliber slugs spraying the countryside. A few marines were near the stove, but most of them were standing by the guns. Everyone was wearing battle gear and ready for action.

Following the decision as to who would go to chow, the barracks quickly emptied except for a skeleton crew who were left to man the guns. I followed out into the snow for the short dash to the mess hall.

The Chinese cooks were there smiling and bowing, ready to do our bidding. I was surprised; I had not seen any Chinese entering camp while making my rounds. *I'm one hell of a sentry*, I thought to myself.

Their presence also made me wonder—why haven't the Chinese taken off for the hills? They must know by this time that we are at war with the Japanese. Perhaps they had come for one last meal. They had been living the good life; I doubted they would fare as well under the Japanese.

I sat at one of the long mess tables with the rest of the marines and waited for the mess boys to take our orders. Shortly, a Chinese mess boy arrived. "How you likey you eggs?" he asked, grinning broadly.

"Flied," I said, trying to imitate his pidgin English. He grinned even wider, took all the orders and left. He was back with the food in record time, as though he wanted us to eat and get on with the war.

"Flied," he said as he set a plate of ham and eggs in front of me, then backed away, bowing and grinning.

I picked up the fork and was about to stab the ham when a real shocker crossed my mind. This could be my last meal. I shook my head. No, by God, that kind of thinking would certainly get me killed. *I have a long way to go yet; I will do anything to survive.*

I switched my thoughts to the Japanese; I wondered what they were having for breakfast. Fish heads and rice no doubt, I chuckled.

After I finished my ham and eggs, I returned to the barracks.

"Kirk," Huizenga called to me from the stove where he was standing with his arms full of papers, "hang up your pistol, get your field gear, rifle, and bandoleer of ammunition. You'll be my runner until further notice," he ordered.

"Aye aye, Sir." I saluted.

Huizenga was in the process of tidying up the office safe, removing records and depositing them in the potbellied stove where they were being promptly consumed by fire. Sergeant Bishop was checking the machine guns to be sure everything was in readiness.

I went to the office to get rid of my sidearm, but before I returned it to the weapons locker, I stopped at the desk to make an entry in the logbook. "0730," I wrote, "A radio report earlier stated, the United States and Japan are at war."

At once, back in the squad room, I picked up a bandoleer of ammunition from an open case in the aisle and sat on my bunk. I began stuffing five-round clips into the pockets of my cartridge belt. My action was mechanical, as I had done it so many times before on the rifle range when preparing for rifle marksmanship practice.

As I performed the task, my mind began to wander. The Japs are coming. They are garrisoned not far from here. *It's just a matter of time. I wonder what's keeping them. I wonder what my reaction will be when the first bullet comes close and cracks by my ears. This day, there are going to be a lot of Japs trying to kill me,* I shuddered involuntarily. I held up a five-round clip of .30 caliber rifle ammunition and gazed at the sharp, pointed tips. They might try, but I would do my best to make them pay dearly.

I studied the bullets and reflected. *This is what all the training has been about over the past four years. Henceforth, school is out; beginning now and everyday that I'm still alive will be like shooting on record day. If I don't hold 'em and squeeze 'em and get 'em all in the black, I'll have a rotten score. I am also going to be dead, just like Sergeant Tyson, my boot camp drill instructor, promised.*

Even if this was my best day ever, a worry crowded into my mind over the impending battle. It would be one hell of a chore to wipe out forty thousand Japs, even with twenty-two good marines helping me. This was going to be a fearful fight.

"You're gonna be eatin' fish heads and rice," were the parting words of the short-timers, when they left Tientsin for the States or other duty stations.

Stationed in Tientsin at the time, I watched with alarm as our numbers decreased. Marines were leaving, but no one was being sent to replace them. Even some of the barracks were being vacated, closed down and boarded up. The north gate to the compound was locked, leaving only one sentry post. This was the east entrance to the American compound with its double, massive wrought-iron gate.

Encroachment by the Japanese on our freedom to move about the city of Tientsin by setting up barbed-wire barricades was becoming more troublesome day by day. September 1941, they had us bottled up in the British and French Concessions (small areas of the city that had been taken away from the Chinese by the British and French after a "shotgun wedding" type of treaty that was forced on the Chinese back in 1860).

It was not that any part of the city had any more to offer than what was now available—bars, dance halls, and bowling alleys—or that the countryside with its unending expanse of grave mounds were of interest; it was the thought of being held behind barbed wire that was so irritating.

We received newspapers and magazines from the States, but they were always two to three weeks old. The local papers were controlled by the Japanese. There was no way we could look to them for news of a political or military nature that was not all propaganda for the Japanese; however, in spite of the lack of news, it was obvious to the most casual observer that some kind of hostilities were in the offing. With the increasing arrogance of the Japanese and what appeared to be their takeover of China, I was convinced something was bound to happen.

Whatever the reason for the start of the war, it was beyond my power to do anything but take my lumps when it came. What was of concern to me was being caught up in a war out here in China. If I were going to be forced to fight, I would like to at least be able to pick my own battleground with plenty of room to maneuver.

With this thought in mind, I had tried every conceivable means to get out of China, including requesting practically every school the Marine Corps had to offer its enlisted men. The schools, of course, were all in the United States. I was refused admittance to any and all of these schools because I had not completed my four-year tour of duty in the Orient. As a last resort and in pure desperation—seeing that I hate airplanes—I had heard the Corps was hungry for volunteers, so I had requested a transfer to the Marine Corps Paratrooper Training Class. Even though I'd been warned that it was the most grueling training course known to man, I did not care. I was willing to swap my share of fish heads and rice for anything. Unfortunately, my efforts to escape China and its inevitable war had gone awry, and now, here I was, gearing up to do battle on the enemy's terms.

I snapped the last flap on my cartridge belt and looked up just as Huizenga entered the barracks. He had been to the radio shack and back a few times while I was busy stuffing cartridges into my belt. He was trying to contact Colonel Ashurst, the commanding officer of all United States Marines in North China. Huizenga, only a lieutenant, needed to know what to do. Without orders from Colonel Ashurst, he was on his own.

Lareau the radioman was all bundled up in his overcoat by the open window of the little shack, sitting in front of his radio transmitter. He had been trying unsuccessfully to raise the embassy radio station in Peking ever since we'd first heard of the attack on Pearl Harbor.

This time, as Huizenga stepped into the barracks, he caught the tail end of a long tirade by Corporal Dedman. Dedman had not seen the lieutenant enter because his back was to the door.

"So how the hell can the leaders of a country be so damn stupid as to let their troops get caught in a situation like this? We have no chance."

"That will be enough of that, Dedman," Huizenga snapped. "Things are bad enough around here as it is; the last thing I need is a morale problem. Shape up, Dedman, you know better than that. Let's not have any more of that kind of talk."

Dedman was old for a marine; he must have been at least thirty-five. Huizenga was my age, a good ten years younger than Dedman. I am sure Dedman resented being dressed down in front of the troops by a kid, for he mumbled something under his breath and stomped away.

The lieutenant was gone again and did not return until 0745. Fifteen minutes more and it would be time for morning colors. Although Huizenga had told me to discard my sidearm for a rifle, I had not been relieved of duty as corporal of the guard. It was still my job to raise the flag at 0800.

I laid my rifle and cartridge belt on my bunk and approached Huizenga. "Sir," I saluted, "are we going to raise the colors this morning?"

"Can you think of one reason we should not?" he asked in a very even tone, but somehow I got the feeling he had yelled.

"No Sir, I cannot," I snapped back. I felt foolish. Huizenga was getting jumpy. All I had needed was a simple yea or nay.

I drifted into the office to pick up the flag. It was very small, a storm flag, about two by three feet. I felt it was unnecessary to have help raising the colors, so I didn't ask for any.

Five minutes to 0800, I stepped out into the cold and walked the short distance to the flagpole. I was in the open and could see the snow-covered fields sweeping away to the mountains in the direction of Chinwangtao. There was no sign of an enemy anywhere. I snapped the halyard hooks to the grommets at the top and bottom of the flag, glanced at my watch by pulling back the sleeve of my overcoat, and again at the open field.

What a time and a way to start a war—the unnerving thought flashed through my mind—shoot an enemy soldier while in the act of raising his flag.

I watched the agonizingly slow minute hand reach for the hour, and at 0800 sharp I hoisted the flag in record time.

"Raise the colors briskly in the morning," the manual says, "and lower them slowly in the evening." I doubt that any of the authors of the Navy manual dealing with flag ceremonies would have approved of the speed at which I raised it. When the halyard hook hit the block at the top of the flagpole, I secured the halyards with one loop to the cleat, saluted, and was halfway back to the barracks, all in the space of a few seconds.

I remained inside the barracks just long enough to buckle on my cartridge belt and grab my rifle. I found Lieutenant Huizenga stomping back and forth in front of the open window of the radio shack.

"Sir, Corporal Kirk reporting for duty," I said sharply. My rifle was slung over my left shoulder and I rendered a hand salute.

"Stand at ease," Huizenga said returning my salute. "I am going to the officers' quarters for a few minutes. If Lareau makes contact with Peking, bring the message to me immediately."

"Aye aye, Sir," I replied.

As Huizenga disappeared, I looked at Lareau, who seemed to be half frozen. The collar of his overcoat was pulled up around his ears, and a cloud of vapor billowed forth every time he exhaled.

"How's it going?" I asked.

"Nothing," he answered. "This radio has never been so dead." So saying, he reached for the telegraph key and sent something in Morse code.

"I thought there was someone on duty at the embassy radio station twenty-four hours a day," I volunteered.

"There usually is," Lareau agreed, "but there is no telling what has happened in Peking. For all we know, the Japs may have already overrun them."

I stood outside the radio shack for ten minutes or more, stomping my feet to keep the blood circulating while Lareau tried again and again to raise Peking. It was then I heard the footsteps crunching in the snow behind me. I turned to see Gunner Lee . . .

"Japs! Japs!" A sentry near the barracks shouted, and at the same time pumped his rifle up and down over his head, pointing the muzzle in the direction of the enemy.

Across the field I could see the Japanese soldiers for the first time, standing out black against the snow. They reminded me of silhouette targets I had fired at on the rifle range, except these were a lot smaller and they were continually on the move. They bobbed up, moved forward, then dropped out of sight again. They appeared to be coming up out of the ground and were approaching rapidly along a broad front. Each man wore a pair of white gloves that had the effect of doubling their numbers.

I unslung my rifle from my shoulder, flipped the safety off, and pulled the bolt to the rear far enough to see if I had a round in the chamber. Satisfied, I closed the bolt and held my rifle at port arms, ready to fire. A tingling sensation crawled up my spine and into the back of my neck as I watched and waited.

What were General Custer's famous last words? Something like, Where the hell did all the Indians come from?

"All you have to do is aim between the white gloves, you can't miss." Gunner Lee chuckled, interrupting my concentration. I started to comment just as the radio came to life. Lareau grabbed a pencil and began copying the Morse code. The radio transmission lasted for only a few seconds and fell silent again. Lareau worked the key several times, tore the sheet from the pad, and handed it to Gunner Lee. Mr. Lee read the dispatch, then looked up as though he were studying the field before him, rapidly filling with Japanese.

"Sir," I said, "Lieutenant Huizenga instructed me to notify him as soon as Lareau contacted Peking."

Gunner Lee regarded me for an instant, then looked back at the approaching soldiers.

"Was the message from Peking?" I persisted.

"No need to bother him. I can handle it," he assured me.

"Right now, Lieutenant Huizenga is busy." He pointed toward the enemy and continued, "He, Bishop, and it looks like Hinkle, are on their way to intercept a party of Japs coming in to camp under a white flag."

I looked and spotted three marines marching through the snow toward three Japanese who stood in the field at the perimeter of camp under a flag of truce.

The Japanese attack force continued to approach from the direction of the hills. They reached a tentative position approximately 300 yards from camp and halted, except for ten to twelve pairs of soldiers who came about a hundred yards closer and set up what appeared to be mortars.

A flight of aircraft passed overhead, very high. Gunner Lee glanced up. I counted nine planes and watched them until they were mere dots, then passed out of sight. They could not have been ours; of that, I was sure.

Gunner Lee leaned in the window and spoke to Lareau. "Send this . . ." He paused, searching for the proper words, then calmly stated, "We are surrounded—the issue is in doubt."

The issue is in doubt rang in my ears as Lareau expertly beat out the code on the telegraph key. Only a marine could come up with a statement as bizarre as that in a predicament like this. I grinned. He would never have thought of something like, We have no chance, or HELP!! Gunner Lee was just not sure we could take them.

From my vantage point, there were at least 150 Japanese in plain view. There must have been a lot more hidden from our position, perhaps a company or maybe even a battalion, sent out just for drill, to face 23 marines. "The issue is in doubt," to me, had to be the classic statement of the war, at least here in China, in our little war.

I stood transfixed, watching the ever increasing numbers of enemy soldiers pour onto the field. I glanced back toward the radio shack and caught sight of a Japanese patrol approaching the buildings on the other side of camp. Almost at the same time, a marine in battle gear ran from the barracks toward the patrol hidden from view by the intervening buildings.

I started to shout a warning just as the radio sounded off again. I stifled my outcry for fear of interfering with Lareau, who was copying the message from the loudspeaker. The marine disappeared behind the buildings. I looked back at Lareau writing on the pad; as he scribbled, the radio stopped again. Lareau finished writing and reached for the telegraph key, bumped it a couple times, then switched off the transmitter. He tore the note from the pad and handed it to Gunner Lee.

Lee glanced at it, then held it out to me. "Here, Corporal," he ordered, "get this dispatch to Lieutenant Huizenga on the double."

I grabbed the note and took off at a run in the direction of the parley parties. As I ran, I held the scrap of paper up to see what was written on it.

"Comply with demands." Signed, W. W. Ashurst. That was it. The marine party had reached the three Japanese and for some time had been engaged in discussion. I slowed to a walk as I came in close to them. I heard the Japanese officer pleading, "Be reasonable, Lieutenant. I have more than two thousand seasoned troops out there." He sounded desperate.

"They will be of no help to you three if the shooting starts," Bishop growled, leveling his Thompson submachine gun at the trio.

The officer glanced at the sergeant, noted the submachine gun, then turned back to Huizenga. The interpreter on the officer's right chirped, "What are your intentions?" The interpreter repeated himself as if he were not sure he had said it correctly. "What are your intentions?"

"Yes, Lieutenant," the Japanese officer chimed, "just what are your intentions?"

I came up on the right side of Lieutenant Huizenga, who was facing the officer. Hinkle was holding his Browning automatic rifle at the ready on the extreme left side of Sergeant Bishop.

With the note hidden under my hand that gripped the rifle stock, I waited for Lieutenant Huizenga to reply, because I felt it was only right for him to have his say.

"Unless I receive orders to the contrary," Huizenga answered with defiance, "we will stand and fight."

"Very admirable, Lieutenant . . . but why?" the Japanese officer asked with utter dismay. "Twenty-three men . . ."

"Lieutenant," I spoke, "I have a dispatch." I held it out to him. Huizenga accepted the note and read the scrawled handwriting. He seemed to study it as if he did not believe what was written. I think I detected a twinge of pain or sorrow, or maybe both.

Without a word, Huizenga offered the message to the Japanese officer, who held the note close to his face as if he needed glasses. He read it carefully and heaved a sigh of relief and stuffed the message into his overcoat pocket.

The officer uttered something in Japanese to his two companions. Whatever it was triggered the soldier standing opposite me to reach for my rifle. For a split second I almost let him have it because I had seen the dispatch and knew it was all over for us. Then I realized that no one had given me orders to lay down my arms, so I held tight to my rifle and almost lifted the little man off the ground.

"*Baka*," the Jap officer shouted.

My antagonist let go and snapped to attention.

Baka, I mimicked to myself. If I have to learn this language, I may as well start with *baka*—it seems to get results.

The Japanese officer appeared embarrassed by the actions of his soldier, for he turned to him with a few curt remarks. I didn't understand a word of the language, but I got the message even before the soldiers did an about-face and ran back toward their own lines. My guess was that he had told them both to get lost.

The little character I had had the tussle with began waving his arms, indicating to his troops the battle was over. His actions brought the rest of the troops out of their holes. The officer, I recalled, had said he had 2,000 men. It was obvious he was bluffing; from what I could see, there could not have been more than four or five hundred. Even that many was ridiculous, I thought. All these men to whip 23 marines?

Maybe they knew something we didn't.

"Lieutenant," the officer broke the awkward silence, "please stack your weapons in the open space near the large building," he said, indicating a spot near our barracks. Huizenga glanced back and acknowledged with a nod.

"How much time will you require?" the officer asked.

After a brief pause, without waiting for Huizenga to respond, he asked, "Will twenty minutes be sufficient?"

Huizenga nodded again as if he were in a daze.

"Very well, then, I will be back in twenty minutes with a small detail to take possession." With that, the officer walked back toward his own forces who were now lining up into marching formations.

Back at the barracks, while the parley was in progress, a hazardous event was taking place. The marine I'd seen running toward the cook shack, with the enemy patrol moving cautiously up on the other side of the buildings, had been sent out deliberately to bring in a prisoner.

According to Private First Class Ramsey, Dedman felt it was of utmost importance that we have information about the enemy, their strength, weaponry, and so on. To do this, he would need a prisoner.

"Ramsey," Dedman had said, as though he were asking for a glass of water, "go out and get me a prisoner."

Without questioning the motives of his superior, as we had all been taught, Ramsey dashed out of the barracks to do Dedman's bidding, running smack into the Japanese patrol.

Ramsey stopped, rifle held at the ready. The patrol stopped, also prepared. Each looked the other over carefully. No hostile moves were made by either side. Ramsey backed cautiously around the corner of the cook shack and beat it back to the safety of the barracks.

"Damn you, Dedman," Ramsey blurted as he burst into the barracks, "if you want a prisoner, go out and help yourself, there's a million of them out there."

That was curious, I thought, when I heard the story. I could not imagine what Dedman planned to do with a prisoner. He had no knowledge of the language, and neither did anyone else for that matter. If he really wanted that information, it was all there for him to see by looking out the window.

With the parley over, the four of us walked back to camp. Everyone came out to meet us. As we neared the barracks, Huizenga said to Bishop, "Sergeant, assemble the men." He sounded tired.

Bishop planted himself firmly in the open space and commanded, "Fall in on me."

We formed two ranks facing the sergeant, dressed down, and came to attention. Bishop faced about and saluted, still holding the Thompson submachine gun in his left hand.

"Sir, the detail is formed," he snapped.

"At ease," the lieutenant ordered in a controlled voice, and returned Bishop's salute. He stood quiet for a few moments looking in our direction, but not really seeming to see any of us.

Finally, he said quietly, "We have received orders from headquarters to surrender." He sounded bitter.

"The Japs are sending in occupation troops to take over this base in about twenty minutes. Meanwhile, they want all our weapons stacked here, on this spot."

After a pause: "Are there any questions? If not, get on with it."

Huizenga turned abruptly and left us standing as he strolled away in the direction of the officers' quarters, not caring, obviously, if there were any queries.

"All right, move out," Bishop ordered as he stepped up and took command.

A silent group of marines filed slowly in and out of the barracks, carting machine guns, rifles, hand grenades, and whatever else they could find in the way of weapons. In about ten minutes, all our armaments were stacked on the designated spot. After we made sure there were no more weapons, we stayed in the barracks out of the cold and waited for the enemy to show. We did not have long to wait because we had used up part of the allotted twenty minutes standing in formation being briefed by Lieutenant Huizenga.

The Japanese detail marched into camp, right on the dot, doing the goose step. They halted beside the store of arms and ammunition. If they had any idea of using any of the weapons, they were in for a surprise; we had removed and dumped all the firing pins into the cesspool.

Huizenga, Gunner Lee, and Sergeant Bishop all came from the officers' quarters to meet them. The Japanese officer singled out Huizenga and after a short conversation, went back to his men.

Our officers and Bishop held a conference, then Bishop broke away and came toward the barracks.

"Everybody outside for colors," he ordered as he opened the door.

We lined up in two ranks facing the flagpole. Huizenga took his place in front of the small detachment. He glanced up at the stars and stripes. "Kirk and Wilson," he said quietly, "lower the colors."

We stepped to the base of the flagpole, I untied the halyards, and handed one to Wilson.

"Present arms," the lieutenant commanded. The detail of marines saluted smartly, rendering a hand salute, as Wilson and I began lowering the flag.

As I watched Old Glory hanging limp in the still China air and as it slowly descended toward me, my mind became confused about my present predicament. What Dedman had said earlier about someone's stupidity allowing us to get caught out here in China made sense. Then there was the anger for having to surrender to an inferior military force; and worse, having fallen into the hands of people who, by reputation, tortured those they captured. It was unbelievable that this was actually happening to me.

The flag touched my hand. I unsnapped the halyard hooks.

"Order arms," Huizenga said softly.

The marines returned smartly to the position of attention.

Wilson held one end of the flag and helped me fold it. I stuffed the small flag into my overcoat pocket and we both returned to our places in ranks.

"At ease," was our next command. "I want all of you to listen carefully," Huizenga said seriously. "We are being sent to Tientsin. We will be leaving within an hour, so do as I tell you, but do it quickly.

"Each man will be allowed to take only one sea bag with him, no more. I suggest you take your blankets and as much clothing as possible. If you don't, I have a feeling that before this war is over, you will wish you had," he warned. "The rest of your belongings you can pack in your locker box. The Japs say they will store all our excess gear in one of the Godowns [warehouse] here in Chinwangtao. They promised they will return everything to us after the war.

"Sergeant," Huizenga called to Bishop, "take charge."

Bishop moved briskly front and center.

"You heard the lieutenant, time is wasting—dismissed."

We broke ranks and were collecting our possessions in a matter of minutes. I took Huizenga at his word; the first things that went into my sea bag were my blankets. Next, I packed a beautiful bathrobe, handmade by a local craftsman in Tientsin; I had had it made especially for my brother, Art, who lived in California.

The robe was a work of art. It had a huge dragon embroidered in bright multicolored silk thread that covered the entire back of the dark-blue wool garment. Similar, but smaller dragons adorned each sleeve. The pockets had their own little embroidered dragons, and the robe was lined with red satin. The collar, cuffs, lapels, and all four pockets were also trimmed with red satin.

The finishing master's touch was a red satin sash with long, red silk tassels.

Perhaps I should put the robe in my locker box and let the Japs take care of it until after the war, I thought—for only a moment. I noticed some of the marines were packing a few things in their foot lockers. My mind was made up. I remembered how Huizenga had said they would do this for us. To me, he didn't sound as though he was convinced that they were telling the truth.

Why should I worry about storing it, I quickly reconsidered. This war could not possibly last too long.

We had discussed the probable length of the war around the potbellied stove while we were waiting for the Japanese to send in their occupation troops. The general consensus was that if the war lasted two months, we were allowing the Japs an extra two weeks by giving them the benefit of the doubt.

I packed everything into my sea bag that I could cram, but I still had more clothing that I didn't want to leave behind. We'd been limited to one sea bag, so there was only one way to pack the rest of the clothing—wear it. I wriggled into three pairs of trousers, two shirts, a sweater, a green uniform blouse, and an overcoat. I was so bound up I had difficulty walking. Nevertheless, that took care of all my clothing except my dress blue uniform. As much as I hated to part with my dress blues, I had no more room.

We had been told we had but an hour to get ready to move out, and almost to the minute, a Japanese soldier appeared at the door. He said something to us in his language. None of us understood, so no one moved. After a moment, the soldier became irate and began sputtering and screaming at us.

This display unnerved me. I thought to myself, *I know I am going to be compelled to learn this language. They get so damned mad when you don't understand them. If I have to be around them very often, the outcome will be inevitable. Someday, I'm going to get a rifle butt in my face or a bayonet in my guts—just for not knowing what they want.*

Finally, the soldier began beckoning to us. Sign language, we could understand. We followed him outside. There were two trucks waiting. One was for our baggage and the other was our transport.

When we arrived at the train station in Chinwangtao, everything seemed peaceful and normal, as though nothing had happened. Nothing really had, except to us. We were herded aboard the train into a day coach. This was the North China Railroad. I was told that it had been built by Herbert Hoover back in the '20s to haul coal out of Chinwangtao to Peking and beyond. It was not modeled after American railroads. Instead, it had a narrow-gauge track. The boxcars were smaller and so were the passenger cars, but there was plenty of room for twenty-three marines.

Two guards were posted at each end of the car. Each was armed with a rifle with a fixed bayonet. One of the guards at our end of the car was so small his bayonet reached a good foot over his head.

The train started moving as soon as we were aboard. I got the feeling that it had been waiting for us. This was our own special transportation.

The Japanese pulled down all the window blinds to prevent us from seeing out. We were warned not to peek outside or we would be severely punished. I could not understand why. We were told where we were going and we had been there before. I guessed they just wanted to flex their muscles.

The ride was boring, not being able to watch the passing scene through the window. I was tired anyway. My day had begun at four o'clock that morning. The marines were all quiet, and the clicking of the wheels on the tracks lulled me to sleep.

I could have sworn I had just closed my eyes when someone was shaking me. "Wake up—lunchtime. Have a sandwich, compliments of the Chinese mess boys of Chinwangtao."

Minutes passed as I stared at the wax paper-wrapped sandwich. I had no idea what was in it and I really didn't care; I was not a bit hungry.

I asked if anyone cared to take it off my hands. I got no response. No one seemed to have an appetite. I looked up and caught the little soldier with the long bayonet watching me, or maybe he was watching the sandwich. I held it out to him. He accepted and devoured it in a flash, as though he had not eaten for a long time.

After I witnessed his hunger, I became depressed. Perhaps I should have saved the sandwich. If their soldiers are all as hungry as this guy, there can't be too much food left over for their prisoners of war.

2

Tientsin

The camouflaged truck, dirty and squeaking, stopped in front of the huge, double, wrought-iron gate of the American compound. The gateway, known as post number two to the marines stationed in Tientsin, had always been open. Now, for the first time, it was closed, and an armed sentry paced back and forth in front of it. The compound had become a prison camp for the forty-two marines presently stationed in Tientsin, China.

We climbed off the truck and stood in the middle of the street, waiting in the cold wind for the other vehicle carrying our baggage. I was happy to see my bag again; I had had my doubts that I ever would when I tossed it on the truck back in camp at Chinwangtao.

We were ushered inside the compound with our gear to join the marines of the Tientsin detachment. There were no Japanese inside the compound and the marines still functioned as a military unit except for weapons. The barracks we were assigned to were steam-heated, as were all the buildings. A central power plant furnished the heat; it felt good to thaw out. Our new home was a two-story building next to the main gate, post number two. There were no furnishings. We were told that all the bunks, chairs, and tables had been sent to Chinwangtao. They were to be shipped out with us on the eleventh of December aboard the steamship, *President Harrison*.

We were left to our own devices to make the most of a difficult situation. We had no choice but to spread our blankets on the hard wood floors and resign ourselves to the fact that war is hell. It was not the best arrangement, but it beat being outside in the 40 degree-below weather.

Next day, rumors spread quickly throughout the compound that there was a good possibility the North China Marines could qualify for diplomatic immunity under the Boxer Protocol of 1900. This was an agreement signed by all foreign powers who fought to quell the Boxer Uprising back in 1900. In case of hostilities, military personnel of these countries stationed in China would receive diplomatic immunity. The Japanese and the United States were signatories to this agreement.

It was encouraging to learn that we could possibly be considered for diplomatic immunity. That would entitle us to be repatriated as soon as arrangements could be made to ship us home. Needless to say, we were all elated.

Three days had passed since we had arrived from Chinwangtao, and as yet, the Japanese had not furnished us with a scrap of food. On the fourth day they issued us a 25-pound bag of rice. We had been eating, but only from the meager stores on hand that were in the galley at the outbreak of the war. A rumor had it that Major Brown, our commanding officer, had confronted the Japanese and had demanded meat and potatoes instead of rice. This request completely confused them. Not knowing what to do about it, they did nothing.

On the fourth day, Sergeant Jarrett, our mess sergeant, was notified that there were additional rations for sixty-five men waiting for him at the main gate. I accompanied three marines to pick up the food. We received that day one 50-pound sack of potatoes and 20 pounds of onions (give or take a few pounds). It required only one marine to carry the whole issue back to the mess hall.

Seventy pounds of food was not much when I thought of Corporal Dawson and his large appetite. One morning for breakfast, I had watched him put away twenty-eight eggs, just as a side dish. Fortunately for us, we had only one Dawson. Most of our men were young and at an age when eating was one of their favorite pastimes. They could pack away more food than they actually needed to subsist.

Major Brown's demand was partially honored—we got potatoes. That evening, we had potato and onion soup. It was not bad at all after Mess Sergeant Jarrett doctored the soup with all kinds of canned food from our dwindling supplies.

Jarrett estimated he had enough canned food to last three to four weeks, or so the rumor went. I presumed that his conclusion was contingent upon additional help from our captors.

After the first trip to pick up food, I realized they would not need but one man for future details. Such a small amount of food for all these men was depressing. I worried as I took whatever the mess hall had to offer, and soon began losing weight.

The first weekend our captors gave us a pleasant surprise. They allowed us to have visitors. Minnie, my Chinese girlfriend, was among them. I had known Minnie for about a year before the war and had kissed her good-bye when I was transferred to Chinwangtao from Tientsin. At that time I had received orders effective November 3, 1941, for a change of duty station. I thought I would never see her again.

When she saw me, she ran smiling with her arms outstretched to greet me. We hugged and kissed, so happy to see each other again. I never realized how much I had missed her.

Minnie was pretty and petite, along with being independent and stubborn. She was a "sing-song girl," one of the stars in the local Chinese theater. It was a case of boy meets girl, and in no time we became fast friends. We had spent many hours together during the year.

Minnie soberly tried to convince me of how treacherous the Japanese were. She told me many stories of how they had killed her people without mercy and warned me to be careful, never to give them an excuse or they would surely kill me. I laughed and told her I would keep it in mind. When the time came for the visitors to leave, she promised to come back to see me again if she was allowed.

In the Tientsin prison camp, we had very little to occupy our time; we settled for poker, blackjack, cribbage, backgammon, or anything that would help us through the day. During one of these game sessions, a swarm of Japanese doctors with technicians descended on us with stethoscopes and blood-pressure kits. They wanted to test our physical makeup and stamina. Major Brown asked us to cooperate.

The doctors doing the testing asked that we step up on a wooden box, then step down, then step up again, and so on, while each in turn said, *Ichi, Ni*. When they had finished, I thought I could speak two more words of the Japanese language. *Ichi* must mean up, and *Ni* had to mean down, I figured.

After the ups and downs, they took our blood pressure, pulse rate, and respiration. If they expected to find anything other than excellent physical specimens, they must have been disappointed. Marines always keep fit. It's an important part of our training.

The same time the testing was taking place, the Japanese army decided to move into the compound with us. They took over the building which formerly housed the Post Exchange. Their new quarters were on the other side of the main gate across from our barracks.

All the merchandise and money had been removed from the exchange the day after the war started, and was distributed among the troops. The money was divided according to rank: privates received $20 each, PFCs got $30, corporals were paid $50, and so on up. The higher the rank, the more money, just like payday. What it amounted to was a month's pay. I began to invest my money in a few poker games, but backed out because all my luck was the same—bad. The money I had left, about $40, I decided to keep. I knew there was no place to spend it, but it still felt good to have a few dollars in my pocket.

Having given up poker, there was absolute boredom. In desperation, I found myself volunteering for work details. That is one thing a good marine is taught never to do, under any circumstances—volunteer. One afternoon, about two weeks after the Japanese had taken over the PX building, we received a complaint that their water system was not working. I went along with one of the crew from the power plant to check it out.

We entered the double doors of the main entrance and were confronted by a room full of large black kettles. The Post Exchange store had been converted into a galley. The vessels, shaped like basins, were huge, maybe five feet across. Three of them filled the room. They sat on fire bricks built up from the wooden floor. Charcoal fires glowed brightly under each kettle. The fumes from the burning charcoal caused me to choke. Steam billowed from the two pots containing rice, and the other pot was filled with simmering greens. None of it smelled or looked appetizing, even as hungry as I was.

We wedged our way through the pots to the toilet on the other side of the room. I opened the door. The odor that rushed out almost gagged me. All the toilets were filled with feces and running over, as were the wash basins and urinals. I couldn't imagine how they had done it. It must have been difficult climbing on the wash basins to defecate because there was nothing to hold on to, but backing up to the urinals, that was too much—it completely overwhelmed me.

One look told me that plumbing was not one of my specialties, and wading around in all that muck trying to repair their water system wasn't the way to learn. I eased out of the building and hurried back to the barracks. I had had enough volunteering for the rest of the war. From here on, I decided to work under orders. During the third week of December, Major Brown put out a call for all hands to assemble for a meeting. The major, who always looked sharp in uniform, stood squarely in front of us. He was a dynamic personality and had no problems commanding everyone's attention.

Suddenly and vehemently, he launched the meeting, saying, "They are bastards!"

He scanned our faces. He had our undivided attention. I could see he was seething inside. It was not like the major to be anything but in full control of himself. Now, however, he was furious about a certain group of bastards! He took a deep breath, and his normally calm disposition gave way as he vented his innermost feelings. "No, by God, they are not just bastards! They are spurious bastards!"

It took him a full minute to regain his composure as we all waited quietly to learn more about these bastards.

"The Japanese authority," he began, "say they have requested clarification from Tokyo as to our status under the Boxer Protocol. Their story has been the same for the past two weeks. I don't believe they are telling the truth. I suspect they have not done a damn thing," he said with anger.

"However," he continued, "I didn't bring you together to discuss the Boxer Protocol. My purpose is to remind each of you that it is your duty to escape and rejoin your own forces if and when the opportunity presents itself.

"I am not advocating that you do anything foolhardy. I advise that you have a reasonable plan with a fair margin of probable success before you make your attempt. The Japs are not playing games; you could get killed. On the other hand, you may make it back safely to your own lines without so much as a scratch. By all means, do not underestimate your own abilities. Strength in numbers sometimes has very little to do with success.

"One of my favorite accounts that came out of the Great War was the story about a general who was sometimes outnumbered by as many as twenty to one. He was General von Lettow-Vorbeck, the commander of twenty thousand German soldiers stationed in German East Africa at the outbreak of the war.

"With nowhere to run for help, he found himself and his men in a sea of British soldiers numbering more than four hundred thousand men. He had three choices: first, an all-out battle with the British, which he knew would be suicide; he could surrender and sit the war out in a prison camp; or, become a mobile fighting unit. He chose the latter, and abandoned his base to launch hit-and-run battle tactics against the British, causing them to chase him across Africa. He thereby denied Britain the use of her troops stationed in Africa against the Germans in Europe.

"During the four years of war, the British tried repeatedly to capture this wily commander—dubbed 'The Fox'—and his forces, but their efforts netted them only grief and a frantic chase from German East Africa to Portuguese East Africa, then south to Zambesia, north again to the German colonies, and finally, into Northern Rhodesia.

"'The Fox' had a stratagem he used to confound the British. He deliberately left signs to entice his enemy to follow, and then he'd lay in ambush. Part of his armament was a huge mortar which he used with devastating effect. Four or five mortar rounds dropped on the pursuing British column, coordinated with volleys of rifle fire, created pandemonium in the British ranks. As abruptly as his forces attacked, they broke off and vanished into the brush, leaving the English to lick their wounds and bury their dead.

"To patrol the vast area under their domain, the British were forced to set up a series of supply bases at strategic locations. Fortunately for the general, most of these bases were undermanned. For provisions, von Lettow-Vorbeck took from the British that which he was unable to forage from the land.

"At war's end, news reached the general via a British courier that the armistice had been signed. Three days following the cessation of hostilities, the fourteenth of November 1918, von Lettow-Vorbeck marched his troops in parade formation, a contingent of twenty thousand regulars and eighty thousand native volunteers, into British Army headquarters in Northern Rhodesia. Then, and only then, did 'the Fox' surrender."

Major Brown regarded us for a moment. "I am not anticipating that any of you will be a von Lettow-Vorbeck, but who knows? The point I want you to keep in mind is, if General von Lettow-Vorbeck could hide one hundred thousand troops for four years from the British, who were continually searching for him, one man keeping a low profile should not find it too difficult to elude the Japs long enough to get back to his lines."

The meeting dissolved, but I remained seated on the floor, mulling over everything the major had said. Major Brown never struck me as a man who would waste his time on trivia. Could it be that he planned to be the von Lettow-Vorbeck of China, or was it just a story to convince us that escaping was not too difficult?

If Major Brown was planning to organize some kind of mass break, that would be great, I thought; however, guerrilla training was not one of our specialties. Marines are trained for head-on, go, slug-it-out, toe-to-toe type warfare. On the other hand, guerrilla fighting sounded like a hell of a way to fight a war.

The major's talk convinced me—one way or another, I was not going to remain a prisoner of war. I would either go out with the major or I would make it on my own. Having walked through the bitter cold from my barracks to get to this meeting, I was certain that now was not the time to leave our shelter. I would freeze to death before I got clear of the city limits. I would have a better chance in the spring, perhaps in late April when the weather had warmed a little.

There were two problems greater than the weather that I would have to face. First of all, I would need food and water. Secondly, where would I go? There are only two places I knew of; one was to join the Chinese guerrillas (if I could find them); the other was to travel across the face of China to join our forces in Chungking. The thought of joining the guerrillas or traveling across China did not bother me. I was young, healthy, and was not afraid of any man; but food—or the lack of it—was a big worry. When we arrived in China, we were told that over a million Chinese die each year of starvation. With those statistics, it wasn't likely that I would find food laying about for the taking—not with all the poor devils clawing and scratching for every morsel. Perhaps it was fortunate for me that the weather was bad, I thought. Maybe by the time it warmed up enough to travel, I would have solved the food problem.

Meanwhile, as the days passed, with nothing to do except watch the perpetual poker games, I began to weaken in my resolve never to play again. Poker, I finally decided, was the best way to spend my time and the only way to spend my money.

The game I chose was a five-dollar ante. What happened in that game was incredible. In four hands I won $500 and broke up the game. In each of the four hands, I was dealt four queens. The odds against being dealt four of any kind are extremely high—but to be dealt four queens, four times in a row, is astronomical. The ladies were smiling on me that day.

After that, I just could not stand prosperity; I invested most of my money in a gaming wheel that was poorly constructed. It didn't take long for the players to discover the flaw, and in a shorter time than I care to think about, I was relieved of $400. That ended my career as a big-time gambler.

I was still richer by $100 than when I entered the poker game that morning. When visiting day rolled around, I gave the $100 to Minnie along with a camera worth $65. I knew if the Japs found the camera, they would take only one course of action—seize it as contraband. I was sure that Minnie could put the camera to better use. To her, the cash and the camera were a small fortune. The value of the American dollar in China at the outbreak of the war was $16.50 Chinese currency.

Minnie was overwhelmed by this unexpected windfall. A tear trickled down her cheek. "Sho-hoo-za," she whispered (she called me that because I wore a big handlebar mustache), "maybe you need the money." I assured her I had plenty of money, which was true; I had more than I could spend. There was nowhere to spend it.

As the days passed slowly, every hour seemed like a week. We became bored stiff with inactivity. There was no place to replenish our supply of dollars. The shrewd gamblers corralled all the wealth. The poker games were beginning to fade away.

The only high spots of the day were mealtimes. It wasn't that the meals were that good—it was the anticipation and the hopes that the Japanese would come through with some meat or more food. The quality and the quantity were slipping day by day. I ate what the mess had to offer and then wandered back to the barracks to stretch out on the floor and dream of food, home, and escape.

Many times, I contemplated Major Brown's incredible German general and wondered if we could dare such a bold adventure. Our combat strength would in no way match that of 'The Fox's.' That in itself should make it more interesting. One advantage that von Lettow-Vorbeck had in Africa that we lacked in China was trees and brush. All we had for concealment were grave mounds—a poor substitute. It was an impossible dream, but I didn't care. I was ready to try anything.

3

The Train

Late in January, a circulating rumor promised we were to leave Tientsin. No destination or time of departure was given, but we were all warned to be ready and have all our gear packed to leave at a moment's notice.

I had seen a portable shoe-repair kit in one of the many rooms of the theater building. With that kit, I reasoned, I could trade shoe repair for food, or whatever. Perhaps I could work myself into a permanent job repairing shoes. Everyone needed a pair of shoes, of that I was certain.

First, I had to get permission from Major Brown to take along additional baggage—a locker box would be sufficient.

When I put the question to the major, he agreed. "By all means," he said. "I think it is an excellent idea."

I gathered up the equipment, knives, hammers, last, sewing awls, thread, and assorted nails. There were no supplies of soles or heels. I searched a few of the other rooms and discovered a large roll of leather belting. It had been a drive belt for a very large electric motor, but it would make excellent soles and heels. With one of the knives from the kit, I lopped off three good lengths that would fit easily into the locker box. I packed my new enterprise into one of the empty boxes I found in the barracks. I was ready to go.

A few days later, early in the morning, I was awakened by someone yelling, "All right, everybody up. Get your gear and fall in outside. We are moving out in twenty minutes. Anyone not in formation by then will be shot."

Whoever it was that gave us that stupid recital also turned on the lights before he left. His weird sense of humor was not shared by any of the marines who were getting up from the floor, grumbling and packing their sea bags.

I looked up toward the windows; it was pitch black outside.

"What time is it?" I asked aloud.

"Five o'clock," someone obliged me.

"Five o'clock!" another marine groaned. "It's still the middle of the night."

That was how I felt, it was too early for anyone to be getting out of bed, even one made on the hardwood floor.

I must have been slow folding my blankets. When I finally snapped the lock on the top of my sea bag, I found I was alone in the room. Quickly, I shouldered my sea bag, and, grabbing the handle of the locker box containing my shoe-repair kit, dragged it behind me through the door.

In the hallway, blocking my way was a partial case of French dressing. Late or not, there was no way I was going to pass up an opportunity like this. I opened my sea bag and set to work stuffing in as many bottles as I could. I was disappointed that I could not cram in more than five and still close the lock on the sea bag. Convinced there was no more room, I slipped two bottles in each of my overcoat pockets, then opened one and drank as much as I could. It tasted great, even without lettuce.

I must have used nineteen of the twenty minutes allotted us by the time I reached the street. I had no sooner taken my place in ranks when the Japanese began counting us. After the count, they gathered in a small group and began jabbering to one another.

Next, our officers were consulted and they counted us, only to confirm what the enemy already knew—some of us were missing. It appeared as though the major's talk was already working. Stone and Marshall had skipped somehow. No one had seen them, but even if somebody had, no one was saying.

The fact that two marines had escaped did not matter to the Japanese; they seemed to be in a hurry. We were leaving in spite of the two missing men.

We broke ranks and loaded our baggage into a waiting, camouflaged army truck. We got back into formation and marched out of the American compound.

Being small for a marine, I naturally always brought up the rear. I was the last one to clear the gate. I glanced across the street and to my surprise, there was quite a large group of women, the girlfriends of the marines. The women were waving and calling good-bye to their marine friends. I wondered how they had found out we were leaving this early in the morning. We hadn't known this ourselves, until an hour ago.

The temperature was subzero and a brisk wind was blowing, making it seem a lot colder. Why anyone would get out of a warm bed to see off someone they probably would never see again was beyond me. I would hardly have blamed Minnie if she'd stayed home. Nevertheless, I stopped to search the crowd just in case. She saw me first and stepped forward from the group, waving her hand, and threw me a kiss, calling out in her tiny voice, "Bye, Sho-hoo-za."

I waved.

The Japanese soldier bringing up the rear, seeing me hesitate, pushed me. That was my first bodily contact with the enemy. My first impulse was to turn around and smash him in the face. My second, a much stronger urge was, *Do not—your time will come.* The reality of being a prisoner of war began pressing home. It was frustrating and agonizing to find myself, once a free spirit, now confined, suppressed and pushed around . . . I wanted to rebel, but he had the gun. This is what happens when you give up your guns; the people who still have them become downright oppressive. You will do as they say or they will kill you—it's as simple as that.

We arrived at the train station after a few miles' hike. The boxcars we were to travel in were unbelievably small. They looked like packing boxes on wheels. We were stuffed into these tiny cattle cars, complete with straw on the floor, about forty men to each. It was a good thing that Stone and Marshall had escaped or there would not have been enough room for all of us.

Our quarters were so small, there was not enough room for all of the marines to sit down, let alone lie down. On the other hand, it worked out to our best advantage because packed in as we were, the warmth of our bodies kept us from freezing to death.

As we boarded the train, the Japanese handed us a tall bucket with a capacity of about five gallons. It didn't take us long to figure out what it was for. The Japs had anticipated our problem before we knew we had one.

We had changed physically since our capture. Our diet caused a problem. We had changed from bread, meat, and potatoes, to rice and watery soup. There was no bulk in our food since we had become totally dependent upon the Japanese to furnish all our meals. With the content of our food being 99.99 percent water, it was like being on a diet of beer, only not as fattening.

The Japanese officers informed Major Brown once when he had complained about the food that by the Geneva Convention, prisoners of war were to receive the same rations as the soldiers of the forces that captured them. I am sure the major knew the law, but he never quit trying to make life better for us. Every time I saw him heading for a conference with our captors, he clutched his international law book like a preacher going to church with a Bible. A tenacious go-getter, the major. Through his persistence, we received a few favors from the Japanese we would not have been given otherwise. In spite of all his efforts to upgrade the chow, it boiled down to soup and rice. (And the rice contained a good portion of millet—horse food.)

All that talk about fish heads by the short-timers as they were leaving for the States was just that—talk. If the Japanese had any fish heads, they were not sharing them with us.

Millet as a main diet resulted in spending a lot of time running to the toilet. Everyone was affected in the same way: we had to urinate every few minutes. The situation didn't improve any because we were aboard the train; quite the contrary—because of the cold, it worsened.

The train traveled in leaps and bounds all day, all night, and half the next day before it stopped long enough to let us out to stretch our legs. During short stops, one marine was allowed to jump down out of each car and dump the buckets. If it had not been for the mobile urinal that we kept passing around, we would have burst or wet all over ourselves. As a matter of fact, that is how we spent most of our time—relieving ourselves or waiting our turn at the bucket. Sometimes it was downright painful waiting a turn. All the time there was a continual howl for the bucket, but all the screaming and hollering had no effect on how quickly it made its rounds.

After that ride of a day and a half, where no one got any sleep or food, we were told we could get off the train and take a short hike. We formed ranks, but were made to wait until the Japanese soldiers set up light machine guns on the road ahead and trained them on us. We marched into a small town along the tracks. As we passed the men with the machine guns, they picked them up and rushed past us to set the guns up further along the street.

Except for this frivolous behavior by the guards with their guns, the town offered very little activity. If the Chinese we were passing along the street noticed two hundred marines in full uniform marching down their main thoroughfare, they didn't let on. The other occurrence worthy of note was a public address system that blared out martial music; a familiar march, "Under the Double Eagle," by John Philip Sousa. I wondered if the disc jockey knew that Sousa was a United States Marine.

By the time we had marched to the center of town, maybe two blocks, the public address system had ceased playing music; now we were listening to a Chinese orator who sounded like a Fourth of July politician. We were undoubtedly the object of his tirade.

We were ordered to halt and stand at ease. For ten to fifteen minutes we remained where we had stopped, forced to listen to the loudspeaker blasting in Chinese. I couldn't understand a single word, but I guess it was not meant for our ears.

If we were being used for propaganda, I doubt the local people were buying it. If the Chinese were concerned at all, it was probably annoyance that we were cluttering up their main street.

Shortly after the speaker stopped, we were brought some food—a small tin of vegetables packed in water. Each man was given one, but no can opener. Some of the marines had pocketknives which they used to get into their cans. I looked into one of them that had been opened. It contained five or six pieces of anemic-looking vegetables; some of the marines who ate their lunch said the vegetables were tasteless. Since the food in the tin was all water, I decided to abstain. Any additional water would only cause me more discomfort. Not having eaten for the past day and a half, my urge to use the improvised toilet had greatly diminished.

Following that meal, perhaps a half hour later, we were marched back to the train. That was the end of our hike, four city blocks. Within a few minutes we were all packed into the boxcars and rolling again. No one had to tell us we were heading south, as the air was getting warmer, but it felt as though it were almost zero degrees Fahrenheit. Some old China hands said we were traveling the Tientsin-Nanking railroad line. We were going right through the heart of China. That meant little to us; we were locked up in tiny boxcars unable to see out. There were only two small windows at alternate sides and ends of the boxcar that were too high to see out. They would make a good escape hatch, I thought, if it were not for the steel bars on the outside. Finally, someone stood up, and I found a place to sit down after thirty-six hours of standing. I promptly went to sleep.

I awoke suddenly, jumped to my feet and stomped my foot to get rid of a muscle cramp in my right calf. After the cramp abated, I realized it was night. There was no light streaming through the side windows. We were still rolling, the familiar clicking of the wheels sounding louder in the dark. The marines were very quiet. I considered sitting down again, but remembered the cramped leg, and decided against it.

Sleeping on my feet was an art I had never mastered. I leaned back against the wall and tried to get comfortable while I did the next best thing, spent my time daydreaming in the middle of the night. My thoughts drifted back to the German general, von Lettow-Vorbeck, and the amazing yarn the major had spun. If we were to escape en masse, I fantasized, could this country lend itself to that kind of warfare?

Slowly, the truth dawned—there would be no mass escape of any kind. Some of the men were too old and would certainly have to be left behind, but marines, being what they are, would never abandon their comrades. It was obvious that unless we made our breaks individually, we would remain prisoners for the duration of the war. However, I assured myself, that should not be too long. The Americans would certainly kick the hell out of Japan in the next two months. Two months more should be ample time for America to get in shape and get over here. Maybe we wouldn't have to escape after all.

A feeling of comfort settled over me now that I felt sure my stay as a prisoner of war would be of short duration. I became totally unaware of anything until I noticed light coming through the windows. The slowing of the train brought me back to reality. I must have fallen asleep standing on my feet.

We stopped, the doors opened to let us empty the bucket, and we were off again. About noon the cars' braking system went on again. It was too early to dump the bucket—maybe it was the Chinese guerrillas! I held my breath, waiting and listening for the sound of rifle and machine-gun fire. The train stayed where it was for a long time. Nothing happened. Today was not our day. Anyway, what good were we to the Chinese? We had neither arms nor ammunition.

Suddenly, we jolted forward for a short run, stopped abruptly, and jerked backward about the same distance. After another short wait, we slammed forward again. If there had been any room, everyone would have been knocked off their feet. The rails became noisy, clattering like we were running over a junk pile; railroad switches, I guessed.

A tall marine at the far end of the car pulled himself up to look out the window. He yelled, "They are loading us on a barge; this must be the Yangtze River."

The car finally came to a rest. We were aboard the ferry only to sit and wait again. As usual, there was little conversation, not even speculation as to where we were going. The sound of a tugboat whistle brightened things up a bit, and we began to move. It didn't take long to cross the Yangtze. Docking on the south bank of the river was a repeat of the thumping we were subjected to when they loaded us on the ferry. An engine hooked up and pulled us off the barge.

Following a ten-minute run, we stopped again. The car door opened wide, a Japanese soldier motioned for us to get out of the car. We marched over railroad tracks carrying our baggage that had been piled in the cars with us. I was having a hell of a time dragging the locker box with the shoe-repair kit inside until D. B. Wilson grabbed the other handle and gave me a hand. We came upon another train that had been waiting for us. This train was made up of coaches instead of cattle cars. We were going first-class from here on. There was plenty of room for everyone to sit down, and the cars were heated and equipped with toilets.

We spent the next four or five hours of another day waiting, without food. It was late in the afternoon when the train pulled out of the yard. An interpreter came through the cars cautioning us not to lift the window blinds or we would be severely punished.

Remembering an article I had read back in Tientsin about the Rape of Nanking, I peeled back the corner of the window shade just a mite to see if all the Chinese the Japanese had hung on the lampposts during the siege of the city were still there. I had read they hanged their enemies and let them stay there until they rotted and dried. In the gathering dusk, I could see nothing, not even a lamppost.

The coach seats were soft and restful; it was the first time I'd felt comfortable since leaving Tientsin, three and a half days earlier. I leaned back against the seat and instantly fell into a deep sleep. I awoke in Shanghai early the next morning.

We were herded off the train into waiting trucks with canvas tops. Our baggage went into a separate vehicle. Through a drizzling rain, an hour's ride brought us out onto a country road. When the trucks stopped we were forced to get off in mud up to our ankles. It was also raining heavier now. This was not my idea of how to start life in a new home. Somehow, I was sure I was not going to be happy here.

In ranks again, we marched toward a group of low buildings a few hundred yards away. I was not the last man in the rear rank this time because when we climbed off the trucks and lined up alongside them, the direction of our march, for once, put me at the head of the column. I was glad when we reached the side road leading to our destination and finally got out of the hog wallow that was the main road. Some of the ruts were deep and treacherous.

Off the main road we passed through a high gate into the prison camp. On our left was a fence about five feet high enclosing a row of long, low buildings stretching ahead of us, set about twenty feet apart. They were well back from the fence. To our right was an open field dotted with grave mounds, enclosed with the same kind of fence.

As we neared the buildings, many men began to gather along the other side of the wire, but well back from it, to watch as we marched toward them. As we drew within earshot, I heard one yell, "Look, the Japs done captured a bunch of Russians!"

Dressed as we were, with long overcoats and especially our fur hats, I guess we did look like Russians from that distance. From afar, there was no way they could identify us as United States Marines.

We proceeded parallel to the fence, passing five of the buildings, until our way was blocked by a truck parked in the middle of the road. In back of the truck facing us were two Japanese officers. Both were small, one thin and the other fat. After we came to a ragged halt, the skinny one yelled in a squeaky voice, "Look at my commander."

I looked, but was not particularly impressed.

"You are prisoners of war," he hammered home, his fist beating the air, "of his Imperial Majesty, Emperor of Japan. We have rules you must obey, or you will be severely punished," Squeaky promised.

"When you work, you will work hard. When you play, you will play hard. When you theep, you will theep hard." He emphasized each point by shaking his fist.

He went on and on, and the longer he talked, the wilder he became. His English was poor, and in addition, he had a lisp and could not say his es's. Everything he said was annoying. Any infraction of any of their rules, he promised, would be met with dire consequences. I turned him off and began investigating my surroundings.

The wire fence I had first noticed was smooth, not barbed. It didn't appear to be much of an obstacle if someone wanted to escape. The fence across the field to our right was the same; however, a closer examination proved me wrong. The wires were insulated away from the posts, meaning all the fences were electrified. That explained why the prisoners on the other side of the fence kept well away from it.

The group that had gathered to watch us were dressed mostly in civilian clothes, except for a spattering of khaki uniforms that looked like Marine Corps summer issue. Most of them were dirty and unshaven—altogether, a pretty shabby-looking crew.

Next, I took a closer look at the buildings. They were dingy and appeared to be built of rough-cut lumber. Not a dab of paint could be seen anywhere. There were large windowed areas on each side of the buildings, with small windowpanes and asphalt roofs: a combination that almost guaranteed the inside of the buildings would be light and dry, a condition I could appreciate as we stood outside in the rain.

I registered Squeaky again in time to get the full impact of his conclusion:

"DON'T NEVER THAY THERE WILL BE A DAY," he screamed, "BECAUSE THERE WILL NEVER BE A DAY!"

After that welcoming speech, we were escorted through the electric fence to the second building from the north end of camp. The

43

barracks were divided into six bays that were split by one long corridor running through the center of the structure. Two-thirds of the building was for the enlisted men and the rest for the officers. Officers' country consisted of private and semi-private rooms.

I settled down in the last bay on the southwest corner of the barracks. I chose the third straw mat in from the corridor and against the west wall. Between my bay and the one across the hall, a door opened to the outside. There was a wash rack just outside extending the full length of the width of the building. Beyond the wash rack was a "cash and carry" outhouse.

I stood by my mat and looked around. The uncompromising austerity of the place, plus the cold, was totally demoralizing. *Bleak* was a poor word to describe this dismal place. Woosung prison camp: the place that was my new home for God only knew how long.

It was so cold I could see my breath when I exhaled. I sat down slowly on my mat, completely disheartened. I put my hand on the coarsely woven straw mat and pushed. It was hard like a board. Now I understood what Squeaky meant when he said, "When you theep you will theep hard."

4

Woosung

Our first day in Woosung started badly. We were all half frozen. The climate at Woosung was much warmer than Northern China, but that did not help much. Any temperature below freezing is too damn cold for human comfort.

Shortly after we got into the barracks, hordes of visitors descended on us wanting to know where we came from, and so on. We in turn learned that the prisoners we had seen along the fence were Wake Island marines and Wake Island civilians. The civilians were members of a construction company that had been building defense works on Wake Island for the marines. The construction crew had not quite finished their work when the Japanese pulled a sneak attack. They were left stranded on Wake. The marines did not have much to say about their battle, but the civilians told us how the marines had clobbered the Japanese.

After the Wake Island marines and civilians thinned out, we got back to our first priority—trying to keep warm. A few of us crawled under the four stiff cotton blankets we found folded at the head of our straw mats, but when the interpreter discovered what we were doing, he laid down one of his rules.

"No one will be in bed except when thick or it ith bedtime," he squealed out his order as he stalked up and down the corridor.

The Wake Island prisoners had named him "Mortimer Snerd" after Edgar Bergen's dummy before we arrived. It was true, he did sound somewhat like Mortimer; he even looked a lot like him, and there was no doubt in anyone's mind—he *was* a dummy.

Unable to use the cotton blankets to keep warm, we found we had to keep moving constantly or become chilled to the bone. Our most effective method to fight the cold was marching up and down the long corridor, stomping our feet. Stomping kept the blood circulating. To sit down was inviting trouble; our feet would begin to freeze and we would get chilblain. Chilblain causes pain that is hard to explain. The anguish caused by the pain can make a grown man whimper and cry like a baby. We had no alternative; it was either march and stomp, or freeze.

In addition to our cotton blankets, a cloth bag hung from a wooden peg under the shelf locatd above our bunks. The bag contained two aluminum bowls and a pair of chopsticks. I was not fussy about how I had to eat. As long as they gave me something to eat, chopsticks would do just fine.

We had not been given any food since the day before when we were issued that small tin of vegetables packed in water. I still had mine in my pocket. What had kept me going were the four bottles of French dressing I'd picked up in Tientsin. Every time I got a hunger pang, I took a swig from a bottle. I had only one bottle left.

It was still some time until noon and our first meal in many days. I became restless for something to do. I decided to investigate the camp.

A blast of cold air hit me in the face as I stepped out the back door of my barracks. The rain had stopped, but it had turned colder. I pulled my overcoat collar up around my ears and looked down the line of barracks. There were rows of wash racks and outhouses for quite some distance, each barracks laying claim to one of each. Running along the other side of the privies was an electric fence that stretched away until it became lost in a jumble of buildings. The fence was like the one on the east side of the camp where we had entered. There was also a road that ran parallel to the electric fence similar to the road on the east side of the barracks. A sentry armed with a rifle and fixed bayonet was visible patrolling this road.

I strolled over to the outhouse, a very old, weather-beaten shack with a passageway throughout its length. It had sixteen holes, eight on each side of the breezeway. A board had been removed from the floor in each stall. Utilization required an undignified squat over the spot where the board was missing. A note of caution crept into my thoughts as I observed this hazardous situation. A person inexperienced, or not exercising reasonable care, could end up with a broken leg, or worse.

Outside the privy, on the roadside away from the barracks, were flaps resembling the doors over storm cellars in Kansas. They were opened to clean out the deposits. This toilet was nothing more than a concrete tank with a building set on top. By the looks of it, this place had been well used recently by many people. I dreaded the thought of what the privy was going to smell like when the weather turned warm. My bunk was only a hop, skip, and a jump away.

There was another barracks north of ours, but it was only two-thirds the length of ours and did not appear to be occupied. I turned in the other direction to see what life was like further south. The first quarters next to ours housed Wake Islanders, as did the next four. The last three were occupied by the Wake Island marines. Their living space was a carbon copy of ours, and just as cold. There was no heat in any of the barracks—there never had been—and there were no provisions for heating when the buildings were built.

Before I entered any of the barracks, I had no idea that anyone could be colder than I, but I soon learned otherwise. I was shocked to find that most of the marines had no coats, and worse—they were still wearing the clothing they had been captured in, in the tropics. A lot of them were blue from exposure. Most of them had the stiff cotton blankets wrapped around them. That was fine with our captors, as long as they did not lay down. The marines were all doing the same thing back in our barracks, marching and stomping in an effort to keep from freezing.

I had seen enough. These poor devils had something to gripe about, but I heard no complaining; maybe keeping quiet conserved energy. Perhaps they envied me my uniform, but little did they know, in spite of all my clothing, I, like them, was freezing. Never in my life had I been so cold for so long a period of time and not been able to do something about it. My feet were beginning to ache, they were so cold.

I decided to end my tour until a later date. I needed to see this misery like I needed another hole in my head. There was enough in my own barracks. I returned to my squad bay and joined the others, marching and stomping until noon when the call came down for each section to send a man to pick up our food.

The mess shack was outside the electric fence. Our crew passed through the gate beyond our outhouse and walked south along the road to a cluster of buildings off the road to the west of camp. There, they joined the mess men coming from the other barracks who knew the way.

Each man returning picked up two wooden buckets; one contained rice, the other watery soup. As they entered our barracks and passed by our bay, we noticed a great difference in the amounts of rice in each bucket. Some were full, some only half full, but the marine carrying the bucket for our section had a short third of a bucket.

Sergeant Wolfe, the senior man in our section, let out a yell that got everyone's attention. Immediately, all the buckets were brought together and the rice and soup were evenly divided.

The food, such as it was, tasted good; however, by this point, not having eaten for three days, anything would have tasted good. I was ready to eat anything that was not poison, or would not eat me once I got it down.

As for an overall look at the meal, what can you say for rice? The soup, on the other hand, was a different story. Picture white radishes floating here and there in hot water, add little chunks of bean cake (a curd, made from soybeans) bobbing around on top of the water, hold the salt, pepper, and all the other condiments. Rice and gruel like that do not cling to one's ribs for long.

The most benefit I got from the meal was warmth. After the soup was ladled out, the buckets were sent back to the galley for steaming hot green tea. I drank the tea as hot as I could get it past my lips; it was near boiling. A warm glow spread outward from the pit of my stomach and throughout my entire body. Although it lasted for just a short time, it was great, for a moment; even my feet were warm.

I used some of the tea to wash my two aluminum bowls. I dared not use the water from the wash rack. One of the first lessons we were taught when we arrived in China was not to eat any food unless we witnessed it being cooked, and under no circumstances were we to drink the water. We were shown a microscopic slide specimen of a drop of water taken from a tap in Tientsin. The navy corpsman giving us the lecture assured us that 90 percent of the strange wild life we saw swimming in it were harmful to human beings, some of them lethal.

The afternoon of the first day, Major Brown made an attempt to recover our baggage, but the Japanese refused to release it. I do not know why, but every time we turned our belongings over to them, I had a feeling we would never see them again. I was always pleasantly surprised when they returned them. Their holding out on us was not a bit shocking.

The first night in Woosung, about seven o'clock, a Japanese sergeant, an interpreter, and two soldiers armed with rifles came through the barracks to make a head count. The interpreter explained to our officers that roll call would be held every morning and evening. He also pointed out that the Japanese were the victors and the Japanese military had no intention of learning English; the prisoners would have to learn to speak Japanese. The section leaders would report to the roll call party how many men in their section; how many men were present; and where they were if absent. At first, some of the section leaders thought it was comical, but the Japanese were dead serious, and after a few section leaders, called *boontychos*, got their faces slapped, they learned very quickly. Within a week, our *boontychos* were speaking Japanese like natives.

A few days after we accepted the fact that Woosung was going to be our home for some time to come, our doctors, Thyson, Foley, and Pollard, set about doing what they did best—doctoring people. The day they opened their clinic, a Wake Island civilian entered to complain to

Dr. Thyson that he had not had a bowel movement in six weeks or so; anyway, it had been so long he had forgotten when. Naturally, the doctor was skeptical because he had been doctoring people for a good many years and he knew that no one could go that long without making a trip to the head. Of course, the whole idea was ridiculous, so he decided the man was being facetious and told him to come back in a couple of weeks if his problem persisted.

In a week or so it was discovered, as incredible as it seemed, that the man had been telling the truth. Few of us, if any, had occasion to visit the outhouse for that purpose. A quick search for the Wake Islander found and brought him back to the clinic; he did indeed have a severe bowel impaction. Once the doctors became aware of the nature of things, they relieved the man's problem.

This incident held more than just a casual interest for me because at the time, I too was suffering from the same thing. I had not had a bowel movement since I had left Tientsin at the end of January. Here it was the beginning of March.

I asked around and cornered one of the corpsmen who had been in on the cure of the Wake Islander—his name was Davis. I asked Davis to explain what they did to help the civilian, but all he would tell me was, "We used a spoon." He refused to discuss it further.

Everyone had a fork and spoon. We traded our chopsticks to the Japanese for them about the third day after we arrived in Woosung. I went to my barracks, picked up my spoon, and spent the next forty-five minutes of pure torture in the outhouse, relieving my own bowel impaction. When I had finished, I was bleeding, dizzy, nauseated, and weak as a kitten. I had felt that to go to a doctor with something like a bowel problem was too embarrassing—now I was not so sure.

As early spring weather began to warm us, the Japanese thawed out a bit and let us have our personal belongings. I was happy to get the other bottles of French dressing I had stashed away in my sea bag the morning we left Tientsin. Most of all, I was glad to receive my shoe-repair kit. Now, I had something to occupy my time.

I did not wait for anyone's permission; when I got the locker box I went into the shoe-repair business. I was not particular about how I got paid. I accepted rice, food of any kind, and, on one occasion, some postage stamps.

The stamps I received in payment for a half-sole job. According to the Wake Islander, he had picked them up on Wake Island during the battle. On one of the bombing raids the Japs made a direct hit on the post office, scattering sheets of stamps everywhere. The wind blew the sheets about the island, and all those that were not retrieved by the men were blown out to sea. True or not, it was a good story. I had to have a sheet of stamps for no other reason.

At first, I was uncertain about American dollars, but when a rumor started that we were going to be allowed to open a canteen and there would be food and cigarettes for sale, money again was worth something. I felt my little enterprise had not been such a bad idea after all.

A few weeks later, however, the prospects of continued operation of the shoe-repair business became doubtful. I was running out of leather belting and couldn't imagine where I could possibly get more, and had no idea what I could use as a substitute.

One day, I was sitting at the end of my bunk with a shoe on the last in front of me, trimming a new sole I had just put on. I was wondering how I was going to cope with the problem of supplies when Mortimer, the interpreter, stomped into my bay.

"Can you fix booth?" he demanded, glaring.

"That depends," I answered, looking up at him. "What is wrong with them?"

"I get booth," he snapped and departed.

He was back in about twenty minutes, breathing hard. He must have run all the way to the other end of camp to get the boots, then back. He was now standing in front of me holding a pair of riding boots.

"The camp commander booth, Colonel Yoth." The way he said it, I wondered if he wanted me to jump to attention and salute Colonel Yose's boots.

"Can you put bottom on?" He held the boots out to me. I took them and examined them. There was a hole all the way through one sole; the other had only a few days to go before it too would collapse.

"I can fix them," I told him, "if you can get me some half soles."

"What you uth to fix other man booth?" he asked, looking at me suspiciously.

I stooped and picked up a piece of belting from the locker box. "I use this, but it would not be any good for such a fine pair of boots as these," I lied. Actually, the boots were shot. The arches, if there had been any when the boots were new, were completely broken down. The leather tops had deep creases and were cracked in many places. They had never known boot polish or saddle soap. To do anything with them except toss them into the trash heap would be a waste of time and good material.

Mortimer took a piece of leather belting and examined it carefully, then he looked at me, "Thith OK," he said, "I want you tho on."

"Sew?" I echoed in disbelief as I reexamined the rotted leather around the soles of the boots. If I try to put an awl through this welt, I thought to myself, it will fall apart. I should learn to keep my big mouth shut. A fine pair of boots indeed—this is what I get for lying.

"You no can tho?" he demanded.

"No," I answered unbending, hoping a firm negative would send him away.

He stared at me for a full minute and all the while kept puffing up like the lizards do down in Texas. I thought that any minute he was going to burst, but instead, he let out a squeal, snatched the boots out of my hands, and stomped out.

It didn't take Mortimer long to figure out what to do. A half hour later he was back with two armed guards and came at me as though he were going to fight. "We have Japan tholdier can tho. We take toolth," he hissed.

Without further words to me, he ordered the two soldiers to pick up the tools, locker box, and what was left of the supplies. There was absolutely nothing I could do to stop him. I stood by and watched the little jerk and his two gunmen make off with my business. This is the guy who promised us there would never be a day—he was working on it. The day had not been a total loss; in his absence I did get to finish my last pair of shoes.

To the victor go the spoils, crossed my mind as the two soldiers, rifles in one hand and my locker box between them, walked out with Mortimer bringing up the rear. The French have an expression for this; I think it's *C'est la vie.*

Spring had finally come in all its glory, and we could now shed our coats and flex our muscles. Our officers, looking forward to a bountiful harvest, had proposed to the Japanese almost from the time we arrived in Woosung, that they allow us to plant a vegetable garden to supplement our food supplies. Finally, an agreement was reached; we could use the area between the inner and outer electric fence. Another request was also granted—we would not be forced to use the honey, dipped from our outhouses, for fertilizer. Instead, we would use only pure horse manure.

There just happened to be a stable a few miles down the road. The Japanese were delighted to have the Americans volunteer to clean out their horse stalls.

At the time, I heartily agreed with our officers. It seemed like a wise and proper thing to do—to use nothing but pure horse manure. However, after due consideration, I couldn't see where it would make any difference. The Chinese had been farming this land since day one, and have used nothing but human waste as fertilizer from the first time they discovered it helped grow a more abundant crop. I doubted that one application of horse manure or even two, three, four, or five would change the composition of the soil, get rid of the contamination, or do a better job.

A week or so after the gardening got started, I was out in the field beyond the inner fence helping level the Chinese grave mounds. While we were in the process, some of the marines, myself included, decided to dig up a grave, maybe find a buried treasure. The mounds we were working on must have belonged to rich Chinese because we dug as deep as five feet and there was nothing but dirt. The richer the deceased, the deeper he gets planted. The converse is also true. The death of a pauper results in the corpse being laid out on top of the ground, food for the *wonks* [wild dogs]. We finally gave up our quest for buried treasure and finished smoothing out the grave mounds and returned to camp.

I was washing my hands at the wash rack behind our barracks when someone yelled, "Get a doctor!"

A marine came running toward us from the north end of camp where the gardening activity was going on. He passed the outhouse, darted through the gate in the electric fence, and headed in the direction of the sick bay near the middle of camp.

Everyone, including me, dropped what we were doing and headed for the north end of camp. I saw a small knot of people gathered on the near side of the electric fence. As I drew closer, I heard someone in the group call out, "Stand back—give him air!"

The people moved back. I could see a marine lying facedown in the dirt. Another marine was astraddle his back applying artificial respiration. The victim's skin was dark blue. He reminded me of a boy I had seen many years ago when I was in the CCC (Civilian Conservation Corps), shortly after he had been struck by lightning. His skin was the same terrible blue color.

I moved around to get a look at his face, but from what I could see, I still did not recognize him.

"Who is he?" I asked the marine standing beside me.

"A field music [bugler] from Peking," he answered.

"Oh," I said, but not having been stationed in Peking I could not have known him.

"What happened?" I questioned.

"He was tossing onion sets over the fence and touched the top wire," he answered, this time looking at me. I nodded, but remained silent and watched. The fallen marine was deathly still.

Dr. Foley arrived at a dead run. He immediately detailed the four men nearest him to hurry to the galley for buckets of hot and cold water, and another marine to the barracks for blankets and towels. The doctor got down on his hands and knees to feel the marine's neck while artificial respiration continued.

When the men returned with the blankets, towels, and water, Dr. Foley began applying hot and cold packs alternately to the back of the marine's neck. He worked tirelessly, examining the young marine every few minutes for any signs of life. The doctor knelt over him thus for twenty to thirty minutes before he gave up. By then most of the crowd had drifted back to camp. The crew that had worked on him carried the dead marine to the sick bay on a stretcher, wrapped in a blanket.

When I finally returned to the barracks, I learned the dead marine's name was Carrol Butcher, a corporal field music, stationed originally at the embassy in Peking.

Immediately, our officers launched a protest, Major Brown in particular, about the damn fences being charged with 44,000 volts while we had to go in and out during working hours.

Not long after Butcher's untimely end, perhaps a week, I was returning from a visit with an old schoolmate, Art Bennet, a Wake Island marine. We had attended high school together, and we both played on the Mooseheart varsity football team the same year back in Illinois. Art had been one of a crew that manned a six-inch coast defense gun on Wake Island. He and his crew were credited with sinking an enemy destroyer.

I was passing the Wake Island civilian barracks on my way home when a man in white overalls came blindly out of the door and bumped into me. He obviously had something on his mind and was paying no attention to where he was going.

We both apologized for being clumsy and continued on our separate ways.

I had not taken more than a few steps when I heard a guttural, "*Curda!*" [Hey, you!]

The sound came from the sentry standing in the middle of the road on the other side of the electric fence. He motioned to the Wake Islander, apparently wanting him for something. The Wake Islander was heading for the outhouse, but veered off in the direction of the sentry.

"*Denki, denki!*" the soldier shouted at him. The sentry seemed impatient or excited about something as he pointed to the outhouse.

"What the hell does he want?" the Wake Islander called to me.

"Beats me," I shrugged. "Maybe he wants you to change that light bulb. I think they call a light a denki."

He turned away from me and looked up at the light shade on the northwest corner of the outhouse. I looked too; there was a lit bulb in the socket. The Wake Islander faced the soldier again and began making gestures with his hands, trying to make him understand that he did not know what he wanted.

The Jap screamed and jabbed his rifle in the direction of the man as one would make a bayonet thrust. The weapon discharged. The white overalls suddenly collapsed to the ground and began flopping in the dirt as though they were being mauled by a huge dog.

I was stunned, unable to move for what seemed to be the longest time, incredulously watching this nightmare. When I was able to break out of my stupor, I ran to his side and slipped my hand under his head, lifting it out of a pool of blood already forming on the ground. By then he had quit moving and was deathly quiet.

I looked up at the man who was still poised as he had been when his gun fired.

"You lousy son of a bitch," I growled with all the hate I could muster as I glared. I could feel the blood oozing through my fingers. I glanced down at the Wake Islander; there was a hole in his neck. His eyes were slightly open, but sightless. I laid his head gently back into the ever widening pool of blood and as I withdrew my hand, his head flopped sideways as though there was nothing but flesh holding it to his body—as if his neck was broken.

Mechanically, I wiped his blood off my hand on the man's overalls and stood up. A crowd had gathered. I waded through them, not hearing their questions, and hurried into the barracks, not sure of where I was going or what I should do. I found myself standing at the end of my bunk when my knees gave way. I sank down on the mat, clasping my hands while my mind was consumed with rage. The frustration and the hopelessness of the moment staggered my whole being.

Damn! Damn! Damn! were the only words that came to mind, crying out within me until my head ached.

Slowly, the anger and bewilderment ebbed away. I began to realize that there was nothing I or any of us could do to change what had happened or to prevent it from happening again. In the future, if we avoided the Japanese as much as possible, we might survive.

The slain man undoubtedly would be missed after the war. Perhaps he had a brother or sister; he could be a husband and a father. I did not care to find out. I do know I will never forget him or this day if I live to be a hundred, even though I knew him for only a brief moment. To be talking to a person one instant, then watch him being shot to death the next, is a traumatic experience.

Why had the sentry called upon him instead of me? I ask myself and shudder when I think of it.

Major Brown reacted as soon as he heard about the killing. He was in Colonel Yose's office pounding on the desk and demanding justice even before the echoes of the shot had died away. Yose assured the major he would investigate and do what was right.

Hearing all the commotion in the colonel's office, a new interpreter, a surly character, walked in to discover what it was all about. The interpreter, seeing a prisoner talking to his colonel in a loud voice, took it upon himself to discipline this person.

This was not his day. He chanced to err, not once but twice; first, he insulted; then he had the audacity to grab Major Brown by his tunic, jerk him around, then deliver a stinging slap to his face. Without hesitation, the major drew back and smashed the interpreter in the face with his fist. Our major was not into slapping. The interpreter found himself lying flat on his back with a bleeding lip and looking through glazed eyes at a fuzzy ceiling. All in all, the interpreter got just what he deserved for not first trying to find out the problem. To add insult to injury, the colonel did not punish Major Brown; instead, he transferred the interpreter out of the command.

The high mortality rate in camp was beginning to worry me. It appeared that the only way I was going to keep a whole skin was to leave. I made up my mind to slip out quietly on my own, remembering the major's advice that the greater the crowd, the harder it is to hide. My departure would be as soon as I collected a survival kit. I would need food for sure, a weapon of some kind. I might have to settle for a club. I would need a map and whatever else I could find. The most important consideration was where to go in this hostile land.

The two possibilities I'd considered earlier were still my only hope: Chungking, or join the guerrillas. Rumors floating about camp had the guerrillas operating freely south of Shanghai, fifty miles or so. The best bet would be to throw in with them. They were the only friendly forces within a thousand miles. It could be dangerous, but anything would be better than remaining here to be shot down in cold blood.

I solved the problem of a map in a hurry. From my sea bag, I removed a textbook I had used in Tientsin when I was studying the Chinese language, and extracted a map of South China. I drew quarter-inch grid lines on the book map, then transferred the map to a sheet of paper, torn from the book, with three-quarter-inch grid lines. The result was an enlarged version of the original map.

There was no scale on the map, but by comparing it to larger area maps in the book, I judged my grid lines to be about ten miles apart, more or less. I decided to work out the fine details when I got out in the field. The map's primary purpose was to tell me the location of towns to prevent me from stumbling into enemy forces, and to give me a rough idea what lake or river I had encountered to guide me so I would not get lost.

The next step was to start saving food. I figured if I saved enough rice to last me five days, that would be enough to get me where I wanted to go—to join the guerrillas. If I were conservative, I would not need too much. My plan was to begin saving one third of my rice each meal until I was sure I had enough. Five rice balls securely tied in my mess kit bag should do it.

I wasted no time. I began saving immediately, and after the last meal that day, I had a ball of rice in my aluminum bowl on the shelf at the head of my bunk. I slept soundly during the night knowing very soon I would be free.

The next morning, the rice was gone, and in its place was the skeleton of a mouse. There was not a shadow of a doubt in my mind who the culprits were: the damn rats that lived in our attic. One or more of them must have swooped down during the night and devoured everything in the bowl, including the mouse.

A mighty peculiar pack of animals, those rats. In our attic they continually ran through the barracks from one end to the other and back again, all day and all night. They ran like the devil himself was after them. Periodically, there would be a sound like two rat packs meeting head on, and then an awful fight ensued, squealing, scratching and thumping, as though they were tearing one of their members apart. Maybe that is what was happening—they were a hungry bunch.

The thing that bothered me most about the rats was their eating habits. They got most of their food from the outside toilets; occasionally I would see one of the gaunt creatures wading around, deep in the outhouse, helping itself to whatever. After having eaten their fill, they would come back in the barracks to benefit from the body heat in the attic generated by the POWs. They tracked filth and disease with them. No one seemed concerned about them. If any effort was being made to get rid of them, it was kept quiet. I consoled myself with the thought that in a few days I would not have to worry about them. I would be gone.

Now that I knew I was going to have to fight the rats to keep them from my food, I devised a new plan to keep the rats from winning.

The next day, I saved another ball of rice, but instead of leaving it in the bowl on the shelf, I tied the drawstring of the cloth bag that encased the aluminum bowls to the mosquito netting wire that ran across the bay at the foot of our bunks.

This time, I did not sleep as deeply. The loss of the rice the night before was still fresh in my mind. About midnight, I was awakened by a sound coming from the foot of my bunk. I looked up at the cloth bag just in time to see it fall with a big rat wrapped around it. The rat must have walked the wire to get to the bag, then gnawed the string. Before I could untangle myself from the mosquito netting to retrieve my food, the rats had scattered it all over the floor, each grabbing a mouthful before escaping up the wall and through one of the many holes into the attic.

This last foray by the rats convinced me that I had a serious problem: The rats had joined forces with the Japanese to keep me from leaving Woosung. There was no way to cope with the rats; no matter where I tried to hide the food, they were sure to find it. It was a perplexing dilemma.

I knew that leaving Woosung without food would be suicidal. I'd be stepping into a country where the consumption of every scrap of food is preplanned. The farmers throw their youngest girls on the dung heap after the harvest when it is determined that there is not enough food for the family to last until the next harvest. I wouldn't know how to compete.

In camp, things were not much better; except for the food issued to us, there was none that could be bought, sold, or traded for.

I was so annoyed by the rats that I was becoming difficult to live with. Unfortunately for me, I chose a sergeant to loose my wrath upon.

Sergeant Wolfe was suffering from a case of piles, and his behavior was becoming obnoxious. He had been to the clinic, but the doctors were unable to help him for lack of medical supplies. They sent him back to the barracks for bed rest. His bunk was next to the window on the same side of the bay as mine. All day and all night he lay on his mat, venting his pain by groaning and pounding on the wall with his fist. I endured his agony for days until in one of my weaker moments I cut loose at him. "Wolfe," I said sarcastically, "nobody could hurt as much as you are putting on—give us a break."

"You lousy, two-bit corporal," he blurted, coming out of his bunk like a tiger, unmindful of his pain. "What the hell do you know? If it wasn't for the Corps passing out warrants like confetti, you would still be a private."

I could not see what my rank had to do with what I'd just said, but as long as he started it, I knew how to play the game.

"Wolfe," I retorted, on my feet and facing him, "the only reason you are a sergeant is because of your old age; the Corps felt sorry for you and gave you a sympathy warrant."

Wolfe was in no mood to banter words with me. He hobbled past me into the corridor, but before he left he shook his finger. "Kirk, you have a big mouth; we will see what the colonel has to say about this."

Of course, I didn't believe he would put me on report for something as stupid as this. Bickering was a way of life that went on all the time among the troops. I laughed to myself. Even if he does, what could the colonel possibly do to me in prison camp? Yet, I wondered.

Twenty minutes later, Sergeant Major Davis came into the bay. "Kirk," he beckoned, "come. Major Brown wants to see you."

As I walked along the corridor beside the sergeant major, he asked, "What's up, Terence?"

I was so angry I couldn't answer him.

Why, I asked myself, would the major call me on the carpet for telling Wolfe he had been given a sympathy warrant? Why would he waste his time over a squabble between two non-coms?

We entered officers' country and stopped before one of the private rooms. Davis knocked on the door. We heard, "Come in."

Major Brown was seated behind a small wooden table. I halted three paces in front of him. Wolfe was standing off to the side, very quiet; there were no signs of moaning or groaning.

The major came right to the point. "Corporal Kirk, did you make a statement that all officers and non-commissioned officers in the Marine Corps were a bunch of shitheads?"

"Sir," I began, not quite prepared for what I had been accused of, "I did not say anything like that."

"Corporal," he continued, "it does not really matter what you said." He looked into my eyes.

"You were disrespectful to a superior officer. Do you deny that?"

"But, Sir," I complained, wanting to explain that it was Wolfe who had started the downgrading.

The major stopped me right in the middle of my protest, speaking in an even tone.

"Countercharges are not accepted; do you understand?"

"No, Sir," I answered with indignation.

Again, he repeated, this time enunciating each word clearly and distinctly as though I were a four-year-old child:

"Counter—charges—are—not—accepted. Do—you—understand?"

Putting it to me in such a way left me no alternative.

"Yes, Sir," I answered dubiously.

Major Brown asked Davis and Wolfe to leave the room. When they had gone, he looked at me with a puzzled expression and asked, "Kirk, what's the matter, this place getting to you?"

I made no comment. The major shook his head. "It's obvious that we're going to be stuck here for some time. I recommend that in the future, if you have any derogatory opinions concerning your superior officers, I won't deny you that privilege, but keep them to yourself. We are a military organization and I intend to see that we remain one. To do that, there must be discipline. Don't you agree?"

"Yes, Sir," I concurred.

"I gave you credit for being made of sterner stuff." He eyed me with concern. "Kirk, I can't ever recall your being on report before—make sure this is the last time. Now get out of here and act like a marine. While you're at it, shave off that mustache."

"Sir, shave off my mustache?"

"You heard right, shave if off," he stated flatly. "Perhaps that is your problem—you think that mustache makes you special."

I didn't like the idea of shaving off my mustache. I had had it for a long time and had become rather attached to it, so to speak. It was a handlebar and required a lot of attention. What a shame, I thought, as I put the scissors to it and cut off one side then the other.

A few days after I got rid of my mustache, I became ill. I had no idea if it was from the filth in the water, the outhouse just outside the door with all its flies, now that spring was here, or the rats walking through my mess gear with their shitty feet. All I knew was that I had a bad case of the runs. I hoped it would subside so I could get on with my plans, but day by day, my illness got progressively worse.

A week passed, and I was not any better; I went to the sick bay to see if our doctors had a cure. I was given a handful of paper packets containing charcoal. That was the cure for diarrhea furnished to us by the Japanese. I took all the packages at once, thinking that if a little does a little good, taking it all ought to cure. The charcoal did absolutely nothing except color everything passing through me—black.

My illness persisted for many weeks. I spent as much time in the outhouse as I did in the barracks. There were times I would make as many as eight trips an hour. Rest was out of the question. As soon as I returned from the toilet, my stomach would begin acting up and I would find myself having to go again. I put it off each time until I could no longer endure the pain; then with great effort, I'd get back to my feet and stagger back to the head.

Everything I ate passed straight through me with no sign of it being digested. I trailed away from 150 pounds to less then 90. What bothered me most was the loss of sleep; I was so tired.

Many, many prisoners were suffering from diarrhea, but it afforded me little comfort to know I was not alone in my misery.

One morning in the spring, I was sitting on the end of my bunk between trips to the toilet and enjoying the nice warm weather. Except for marines like myself who were too sick to work in the field, the barracks were empty. This was the type of weather I had been waiting for to make my escape. Now it was impossible for me to go anywhere. It was all I could do to travel the short distance to the toilet and back. If I tried to escape, I doubted whether I could travel 100 yards—and besides, I would easily be caught by my trail of diarrhea.

Three officers—Cunningham, Wooley, and Smith—a Wake Island civilian named Teters, and a Chinese houseboy had made a break for freedom two weeks earlier. That was about the second week in March. They were caught the evening after they escaped and were brought back to camp the next day. They were paraded through the stockade to impress upon us that escaping could not be done. They were taken to Shanghai and locked in the local jail. At least, that is what we were told.

Yet, only a few days back, four marines had escaped. They were enlisted men, North China Marines—Story, Brimmer, Stewart, and Battles. I would have given anything to have been able to go with them. So far, there had been no word of their capture.

Suddenly, I was shocked out of my depression by a hellish racket at the back door. First one Japanese soldier and then another burst into the building and went ricocheting along the hallway, each being dragged by the meanest-looking dogs I had ever seen. Their enormous fangs were bared, and saliva dripped from their pointed jaws. The dogs were black with light brown streaks along their legs and feet, with pointed ears and stubby tails. I would guess they weighed 90 to 100 pounds each, maybe more. The dogs were as heavy as the soldiers trying to hold them. They had very little control over the animals. Wherever the brutes went, the soldiers were dragged along. The interpreter ran after them trying to catch up. I crawled back into my bunk knowing that sooner or later, someone would tell me what was happening.

In about a half hour, a marine came by laughing. He said the Japanese were trying to make bloodhounds out of Dobermans. They let the vicious dogs smell articles of clothing belonging to the escaped marines, then turned them loose outside the back door to track the escapees. The dogs ran straight for the galley. Everyone, except the Japanese, thought it was funny as hell. The big bad dogs turned out to be chowhounds.

During the following weeks soldiers scoured the countryside in search of the escaped marines. They were never found.

Meanwhile, back in Woosung, because of failing health, I had a slight touch of amnesia. That is the only way I could account for waking up in the bay across the hall from where I normally bunked. To say I awoke was not exactly true, either; I was in a semiconscious state and knew what was going on about me, but was not part of it, nor did I care. What brought me around was someone standing at the foot of my bunk massaging my foot and holding out his hand to me, saying, "Here, take this."

I shook my head to clear the cobwebs and when my eyes came into focus, I recognized Dr. Thyson. I plucked the brown capsule from his extended hand and held it tight to my chest.

"Take it now," he ordered. "That is opium. It's hard to get, and I wouldn't want you to lose it. It will cure you."

I popped the capsule way down my throat and swallowed. In spite of its large mass, it slid down easily.

"How many times have you gone to the head today?" the doctor asked.

"I don't know, I didn't count them." I tried to speak, but could only whisper. "A bunch, I think."

"I want you to keep track of your trips from now on until I see you again tomorrow. Do you understand?"

I nodded my head yes. The doctor moved on to the next bunk.

It was close to three o'clock in the afternoon when the doctor gave me that pill. It began to take effect about six in the evening. Around seven, I went to sleep, the first real sleep I had had in months. Sleep to me had been a series of catnaps for as far back as I could remember. I slept until breakfast the next morning. Even then I had no urge to make a trip to the toilet.

Shortly after breakfast, my rest came to an abrupt end with a vengeance, as though I had to make up for lost time. The doctor came for his daily visit about four o'clock, and by then I had made seventeen trips to the head.

The next capsule sustained me until ten o'clock the following morning. Each succeeding day the medication prolonged my period of relief. The day I managed to contain myself for a span of twenty-four hours, Dr. Thyson handed me one more capsule. "This in the end of your treatment, son. I am sure you will make it from here on, but if it starts up again, let me know immediately."

"Aye, Sir," I answered. "Thanks a lot, Doctor."

I was feeling great, considering the shape I was in after he gave me that final pill. I weighed 89 pounds, and most of it was bones. In a few days my intestines and kidneys began to work properly again. I even gained weight, I think. I know it was a lot to expect from a diet of rice and watery soup, but there was nothing else to eat. Perhaps it was because I had no bowel movement for a few days.

I was placed on the permanent sick list that exempted me from all work details—that is, except one. Everyone, including the sick, had to turn in five flies—dead, of course—and five dead mosquitoes each day to our captors.

There were swarms of flies now plaguing us by day since the weather had turned warm. The land around us was a semi-swamp; the mosquitoes attacked us at night. Our officers complained and requested an insect abatement program from the Japanese. We got one immediately.

"Each man will catch and kill five flies and also five mosquitoes each day and turn them in to the main office," was the order that came down to us. "Anyone who does not turn in his quota each day will be severely punished."

Of course, the whole idea of each man in camp catching a quota of insects was just plain ludicrous. This had to be the most ridiculous idea the Japanese had come up with yet, but it was typical. There was nothing we could do but comply.

Very shortly the fly population began to diminish. In a couple of weeks it was noticeable. In a like period it became difficult to find enough flies to fill one's quota. The enemy had evidently faced this problem before with their own troops and had used this method to cope with it. Taking a broader view as they had, I had to agree that the system was not as stupid as it first appeared. Consider the fact that there were 200 men in our barracks, multiply that by five, and add the rest of the camp with as many men in each barracks, all turning in five flies apiece. No matter how prolific the flies are, they could never survive that kind of slaughter. The method was primitive, but effective.

Flies were no problem to catch at first, but mosquitoes were a different matter. When I swatted a mosquito, all I had left were bits and pieces. A solution was not long in coming. One marine solved the mosquito quota for all of us. He hung a jar over a lightbulb. At night the mosquitoes, moths, and a lot of other bugs were attracted to the light and became trapped in the jar and died. When the other barracks learned of this, they did the same. No one in the main office cared to count the thousands of dead bodies; they took our word for it that the count was right.

There was an advantage to being confined to the barracks: I usually heard all the rumors first. One in particular raised a glimmer of hope. The news was that a repatriation ship was headed for Shanghai to pick up everyone considered to have diplomatic immunity, to take them back to the States.

The rumors had it that the ship was Swedish and named *Gripsholm*. Later, it was an Italian ship, *The Conte Verde*. Whatever the ship, it was not for me and the 200 other North China Marines, because the Japanese still refused to honor their agreement with regard to the Boxer Protocol. It was strange that we were allowed to keep all of our belongings where they stripped all the other prisoners of everything. I always had a feeling that there would be another ship. At first, the North China Marines were treated with kid gloves, for the Japanese knew that sooner or later, the United States would demand the return of their embassy and legations guards—but our government never did.

As it turned out, only a few members of the American and foreign prisoners of war got to go home. The four marines left behind by the 4th Marines (when they pulled out of Shanghai shortly before the war began), were among them. These four had been attached to the American consulate in Shanghai.

Summer came early, hot and muggy. With it the Japanese were jubilant and making it a point to let us know of their victories. They furnished us with newspapers published in English from Shanghai and Japan. They furnished the *Nichi-Nichi Shimbun*, one of Tokyo's newspapers, to make sure we knew that our armed forces were being "clobbered." I would have considered the newspapers more of their propaganda had it not been for a smuggled radio, brought in in pieces from Peking.

Pierce, one of Peking's radiomen, rewound the coils in the radio to receive transmissions on short wave from San Francisco. It was depressing to learn, and hard to believe, that what we were reading in their newspapers was true. Places like Singapore, Malay, the Philippines, and Corregidor had all fallen to the enemy. All the news from the radio was bad. In addition, we were fighting in strange places I had never heard of, such as the Solomons.

The future of the prisoners of war was beginning to look mighty bleak. Maybe the war would last a lot longer than we had figured.

Summer was passing, and with it my hopes to escape were also fading. I couldn't get enough food or the right kind of food to rebuild my body back to where I could survive. To survive, I may be forced to run long distances or fight in hand-to-hand combat. In my present condition, it would be difficult winning a fight with a four-year-old child.

The four marines who had escaped in the spring were still at large; I was sure we would have heard about it if they had been captured.

Then, in mid-October, a situation developed that precluded me from ever escaping. The Japanese posted a list of what they called technicians who were going to be sent to Japan to help with Japan's war effort. Needless to say, Major Brown made a strong effort to stop the transfer on grounds that it was against international law for prisoners to work in war industry, but to no avail. I was on the list; my occupation was welder.

At the first opportunity I cornered Mortimer. "How come you are sending me to Japan as a welder?" I questioned him with concern. "I know absolutely nothing about welding." I tried to convince him, but he turned a deaf ear.

"Your book thay you welder, you welder, you go Japan," he grinned like an idiot.

"What book?" I demanded.

"Your record book," he answered, "your Marine Corps Record Book." Then he stomped away leaving me with my mouth open.

How the hell did the Japs get a hold of my record book, I wondered. Somebody must have goofed. All those records were supposed to have been burned.

One of the first things we were taught in boot camp was that in case of capture, give only your name, rank, and serial number. My boot camp instructor, Sergeant Tyson, instilled in me that any information, no matter how insignificant, could be of value to an enemy. The more I thought about it, the more furious I became. How could anyone be so unthinking as to let a whole set of record books fall into enemy hands? The enemy knew as much about me as did the Marine Corps, and without having to ask me one damn thing—because of someone's stupidity or negligence. Now I was being shipped to Japan as a welder, and to what else, only God knew.

I had good cause to worry because when I got to Japan, they were going to find out something about me that the Marine Corps was not aware of—I am not a welder; I never was. I knew little or nothing about welding. What worried me was whether they would think I was holding out and beat hell out of me until I could weld.

The question of my ability to weld started when I joined the Marine Corps, the day I walked into the recruiting station in the downtown post office in Chicago, Illinois. The recruiting sergeant, a stickler for filling in every blank on the enlistment papers, insisted that everyone had an occupation. I told him I had just graduated from high school and had not been around long enough to learn a trade. He rejected my explanation and after a series of questions, he found I had had vocational training as a blacksmith. He discounted blacksmithing as a trade because, he said, the Marine Corps had no horses. His interrogation revealed a mere mention of forge welding. He held up his hand: "That's it, you are a welder." He filled in the blanks and from that instant, background or training notwithstanding, I was a welder.

My knowledge of forge welding was limited to heating two pieces of iron in a forge to a sparkling white heat, placing one on top of the other on an anvil, and hitting the two with a sledgehammer, thereby causing them to be fused together. Because of that the sergeant pronounced me a welder. Any resemblance of forge welding to welding with either a gas or electric welder is remote indeed. I couldn't convince the recruiting sergeant back in Chicago, and now that the information was in my record book, there was no way to dissuade the Japanese. I wondered what they would do to me once they found, after bringing me all the way to Japan, that I wasn't a welder.

The afternoon of the day we left for Japan, I gave a marine the flag I had lowered on the first day of the war at Chinwangtao. He promised he would raise it over Woosung at the end of the war. I was afraid to take it to Japan with me for fear it would be found and confiscated.

The rest of my belongings I brought along, including, of all things, my Woosung escape map.

On November 2, 1942, thirty-six prisoners—consisting of sixteen North China Marines and twenty Wake Island marines and civilians—were taken by truck to the docks in Shanghai and put aboard what appeared to be a Japanese cargo ship.

Sending marines to Japan as technicians did not make much sense, especially when they had a veritable storehouse of talent right under their noses. The Wake Island civilians were construction workers—not kids like the marines, but craftsmen. Old heads who knew their business. It is amazing that no one was smart enough to see it.

We boarded the ship and stowed our gear under a canvas on the weather deck and were escorted to the after cargo hold. When my turn came to go below, I climbed into the open cargo hatch and clung to a ladder attached to a stanchion. One by one, each of us went down into total darkness. After feeling my way, rung by rung into nothingness, I finally reached the bottom. I backed away from the ladder carefully to avoid tripping or smashing into something. When the last man entered, the hatch was closed and a small light came on up near the entrance.

When my eyes became accustomed to the semidarkness, I discovered the hold was about 40 feet square and totally empty of anything except for the thirty-six of us and a handful of huge rats. They were afraid of us because they knew we were hungrier than they were.

We sat or laid down on the cold, steel deck plates. Our furnishings consisted of a single wooden bucket, which we were to use as a toilet; the same kind of bucket we received our rice and stew in, in Woosung.

5

The Transport

In an effort to keep warm on the cold, steel plates, I rolled into a ball. Chilled as I was, I dozed off into a fitful sleep. Sometime during the night I was awakened when the ship's screws began turning and churning the water. Someone, somewhere in a remote corner, voiced the thought that was on my mind.

We were under way; the vibrations of the ship's engines had a numbing effect, and shortly, perhaps before we even cleared the harbor, I had fallen back asleep.

The following morning, two buckets were lowered on ropes from the hatch above. One was full of rice and the other had aluminum bowls and a wooden paddle to dish out the rice. Not one of us had any eating utensils; we had turned in our forks and spoons to the soldiers before we left Woosung. We ate with our hands, which was not very sanitary. Each of us got an equal amount of rice, but that was all—no soup.

That evening they gave us another bowl of rice, and that was our ration for the day; it amounted to two teacups of rice.

The next day was a little different. About noon the Japanese yelled down to us to come up on deck, ten at a time. When my turn came, I got my first glimpse of life aboard a Japanese transport, not a cargo ship as I had first thought. As we moved along the gunwales following our guide toward the forward part of the ship, I noticed a lot of confusion and congestion brought on by the large black cooking pots set up in the passageways. Each pot had a paddle-wielding man, stirring the rice, or whatever. The paddle was wood and looked very much like a canoe paddle. Other soldiers were on the move, carrying wooden buckets full of rice in all directions.

All this I noticed in passing, but what impressed me most were the many sailors stationed along the lifelines with powerful field glasses, completely engrossed, scanning the ocean. Realizing what they were looking for, I became flushed with mixed emotions. Having this ship torpedoed with me aboard was not my idea of how to get even with the Japanese. On the other hand, I was glad that someone had them worried.

Anyway, I thought, they weren't doing as well as they wanted us to believe in Woosung by showing us those newspapers. Otherwise, why would they need all these lookouts?

Our group arrived on the forward weather deck, and lined up facing an officer wearing a white smock. Beside him on a small table was an array of test tubes and glass rods, plus a large flask filled with what I assumed to be water or alcohol.

The officer motioned for us to pull down our trousers. One by one we moved forward to the table. When my turn came, the officer had me bend over, and he inserted a glass rod into my rectum momentarily. Next he removed the glass rod and placed it in one of the numbered test tubes. Before he would let me pull my trousers up, he dipped a swab into a bottle of Mercurochrome and painted the same number that was on the test tube on my butt.

None of us knew what it was all about, but we did a lot of speculating. The general consensus was that we were being tested for amoebic dysentery. What they would do with any of us who turned up positive was anyone's guess. To hear so much chatter in the hold at one time was unusual, but everyone was toying with the idea of what would happen to them if they were unlucky enough to have the bug.

"It's simple," volunteered a voice that seemed to echo from the bulkheads of the hold. "The Japs want to keep the disease out of their country. All they have to do is pick out any of us that have it and push us over the side with the garbage; the sharks will take care of the problem."

There was no rebuttal to that remark. Everyone fell silent, perhaps all agreeing that that was pretty close to the truth.

The sea began to get rough toward the end of the second day. The stern of the ship raised and the screws came out of the water; then the stern slammed back down on the surface of the ocean with a hell of a bang that would send a shudder throughout the ship. The noise and jarring made me wonder if the old tub would hold together. The bulkheads and deck plates were cold and damned uncomfortable. Now with the storm brewing, we were being buffeted around like dice in a cup, which made sleep out of the question.

Staring wide-eyed at the tiny lightbulb overhead near the hatch cover, I thought of what I had seen on deck. All those sailors searching the ocean with powerful glasses were not there because they had nothing better to do. The Japanese must have lost some ships and were afraid of submarines. If a submarine sent a torpedo into this old rust bucket—I shuddered to think—we would be on the bottom in a couple of minutes.

The prisoners' biggest concern was the way the Japanese detested us as human beings for having surrendered. I doubted if they would have bothered to open the hatch if the ship was hit. Whether they opened the hatch or not was immaterial. The hatch door was only wide enough for one man at a time to pass through. It would have been impossible for all of us to get out before the ship went down. Undoubtedly, there would have been a dog-eat-dog scramble to reach the hatch. In the condition I was in, I would be stepped on like so much cow manure as everybody made a break for the hatch. Another thought popped into my head: What if a torpedo smashed into this compartment? I considered the possibility, then concluded: I would never know it. There had been times in the past few months when the future had not looked too promising—this was one of them. I would keep my fingers crossed and pray that our subs were hunting for bigger game in other waters.

The next day began with the dangling bucket from the open hatch. The ship slowed down during the day and finally stopped. It was late in the afternoon. Shortly after we stopped dead in the water, they let down our bucket of rice.

Time passed slowly as we sat in the dark hold waiting for anything to happen. It was hours before the prison guards came for us. When they did, it was dark outside. It was a relief to vacate the stinking hold of that ship for the waiting trucks. The trucks were equipped with canvas tops to prevent us from seeing where we were going. Our trip took three-quarters of an hour, more or less, before we came to a stop in the center of a residential district.

We were herded into a narrow street and almost immediately, the street began to slope upward. With every step the ground became steeper. Carrying my sea bag was becoming a struggle.

Tiny houses lined both sides of the road. They appeared to be made of wood. By the light streaming through their windows, I guessed that the windows were made of rice paper like so many in China.

Dogs barked or growled at us from the shadows of almost every home. They sounded as though they would like to tear us apart. The tone of their voices told me there were a lot of large dogs. Big dogs, to me, meant there was a lot of food here. Perhaps we would not be so hungry here in Japan.

We finally reached our destination, a large, three-story concrete building set into the side of the mountain. My first impression, even in the dark, was that it looked like a prison, a fortress, a citadel. It was as good a place as any, I decided, as long as I could lie down and rest. The climb up the mountain had been a good half mile.

We entered the prison by climbing up a long, narrow fire escape from the road to the top floor, into a well-lit corridor. We passed along the hallway, moving straight in. On our left were many closed doors; on our right was a solid wall of windows making a light well in the center of the complex. At the far end of the corridor we made a right turn into another long hallway.

Here we halted, lined up two abreast, and counted off in groups of ten. Each ten-man detail was assigned to one of the vacant rooms along the hallway.

Our room was equipped with ten steel bunks about three feet wide and six feet long. There were five on each side of the room. The head of each bunk butted against the wall, with no clearance there or between the bunks. A narrow shelf over the bunks spanned each wall. The center aisle was wide enough for two men to pass, as long as they turned sideways. The entrance was in the middle of the wall leading from the hallway, and directly across from it was a wall of windows reaching from bunk level to the ceiling. Each bunk had the familiar straw mat and a pile of stiff cotton blankets.

We were ordered to go to bed immediately. Without any coaxing, I spread my blankets, thanked God for my safe deliverance to somewhere, and fell into a deep sleep.

6

Y a w a t a

"*Tinko, tinko!*"

I heard a yell in the hallway and sat up.

"What the hell is *tinko*?" I asked the obvious question aloud.

"Tinko is muster." My answer appeared in the doorway, an American sailor by the looks of his dungarees.

"The tinko party will be here in about ten minutes," he warned. With that he disappeared.

It was still dark outside. There was no light coming through our windows. Everyone crawled out of bed, folded and replaced the blankets at the head of the bunks, the way we had found them the night before. With that done, we wandered out into the hallway and followed the lead of the sailors a few doors from us. We lined up two deep against the wall to the left of our doorway.

Shortly, we heard the tinko party turn the corner at the far end of the hallway, the same direction we had come in last night. I marked their progress by each succeeding room leader as he sounded off to the party, reciting his roll call in Japanese.

When they confronted our room leader, Corporal Sawyer, a North China Marine, he had difficulty with his recitation. This was the first time Sawyer had been called upon to perform the duties of a boontycho.

We had all listened to our section leaders spout Japanese every morning and evening at roll call in Woosung. I had heard it so many times I could recite the speech in my sleep.

The tinko party was made up of three Japanese: one very small interpreter about the size of a half-grown boy; a sergeant, regular army; and another uniformed man with an insignia over his left breast pocket that bore five stars.

The interpreter listened for only a matter of seconds before he lost his temper. Without warning, he jumped off the floor and slapped Sawyer a resounding blow across the face.

"Next time you learn Japanese or you will be severely punished," he sputtered.

I watched the tinko party move on to the next room as I contemplated Sawyer's dilemma. This place was not going to be any better than Woosung—maybe worse, if that last exhibition was any indication of what our future held. One thing about Woosung: at least the Japanese were all outside the wire. Here, they were living in the same building with us. I was afraid that this kind of familiarity would breed contempt.

Following tinko, the word came down the line to send two men to pick up the food. The galley was on the floor below, accessible via the stairway, through the double doors, at the end of the hall, on the main corridor where we had entered last night.

The men returned with two buckets of rice and one of soup. We divided the rice among the ten men, and each received approximately one packed teacup full—about the same as we were accustomed to, perhaps a dab more. The soup was good compared to the swill they had fed us in Woosung. This soup was laced with tiny bits of meat, plus a scattering of egg noodles. The second bucket yielded a like amount of rice for each of us, but we were instructed to put this ration in our *bento* [lunch] box, which we found on the shelf above our bunks. The lunch boxes were made of wood with a tight-fitting lid, also wood. This box of rice was to be our noon meal. We were going to work in the factory.

It was getting light outside as we finished our breakfast. The Japanese were in a hurry to get us to our new jobs. We were herded out of the building into the narrow street and made to line up four abreast. With our bento boxes tucked under our arms, at a command, we straggled down the hill through the hundreds of tightly packed Japanese homes. The neighborhood dogs greeted us again with a howling protest as we passed.

The night before I had been mistaken. I thought all the houses were made of wood; instead, they were built of bamboo with straw roofs. I was right about one thing—they did have rice-paper windows.

If one of these houses were to catch fire, I would have been willing to bet that half the town would burn to the ground before they could stop it.

The hike to the factory was all downhill. The soldiers led us deep into the heart of the Seitetsu Steel Company of Yawata, Japan. This industrial complex was no small operation. We crossed a maze of railroad tracks that fanned out in all directions. The switch engines puffed back and forth drawing trainloads of coal, scrap iron, ingots of steel, steel plates, and many other materials and products.

The soldiers halted us after we were well into the factory grounds. There they split us into smaller groups to be sent to different parts of the plant. Each group was turned over to a Japanese civilian who was to be the pusher. I marched away with a detail that finally stopped on the shipping docks.

This was to be our first job as technicians, I thought—to unload a lousy ship?

There in front of us had to be the filthiest ship in the Japanese fleet. The civilian who was to be our foreman confirmed my fears by telling us in pantomime that that was exactly what we were expected to do. He went through the routine as though he had a shovel in his hands.

"This is technical work?" I mentioned to the prisoner beside me. "They brought us all the way from China for this kind of technical work. I wonder what kind of work their laborers do?"

Presently, a truck pulled up and dumped a load of scoop shovels in front of us. Now I understood why the ship was so dirty; it was carrying a load of coal. While we waited to go on board, each man in turn stepped out, picked up a shovel, and returned to his place in ranks.

Everyone, with a shovel in hand, was standing quietly, and with nothing better to do, we were watching a bevy of young Japanese girls strolling along the pier toward us. Suddenly, one of the young women stopped directly in front of us, pulled a string at her waist which caused the rear flap of her pants to drop, and bending slightly forward, she relieved herself over the edge of the dock into the bay.

This sort of behavior came as a shock to all of us, never having seen this kind of carrying on ever in our lives, but when her friend beside her, perhaps through the power of suggestion, did the same thing, that was too much. One of the prisoners let out an uncontrollable guffaw that set the rest of us off, roaring with laughter. A guard standing nearby discovered the object of our hilarity and got mad as hell. He ran to the women and ordered them away, then turned to us enraged, and commanded, "*Ki-o-ski.*" [Attention.]"

We remained at attention for only a few minutes because our labors were needed to unload the ship. We began to move up the gangplank, but were stopped, and half our detail was led away to work at some other job.

What was left of our group climbed down into the hold of the ship, each dragging our scoop shovels with us. The compartment was only half full of coal. The winch operator, in a hurry to get started, dropped a large steel box into the hold, almost on top of us. The box had a capacity of about two yards. We were all of the same mind—that was, not to kill ourselves filling it. There were fifteen of us and it took as many minutes to fill the box. When the winch operator hauled the full box out of the hold, we sat on the coal and rested until the box returned.

Ten o'clock, we were in the act of filling the box again when our pusher yelled, "*Ya-sa-may,*" [Rest], then added, "to-bah-co."

None of us had any cigarettes, but he must have known that, for he removed a pack from his shirt pocket and passed it around.

What a crazy-looking cigarette, I thought, as I extracted one from the pack. It was twice the diameter of a regular smoke, about half again as long, and for its size, weighed almost nothing. One-third of it was a cardboard tube and the rest was packed tightly with what looked like finely shredded tobacco. The pusher lit a piece of rope and passed it around to light our cigarettes.

I took the rope, held it to the end, and drew in hard, expecting a lot of resistance in the fine tobacco. Half the cigarette vanished in a flash. I gagged; it tasted like the rope smelled. Two more easy draws and all I had left was the cardboard tube.

"Want to know what you just smoked?" an American sailor laughed at my dismay over its rapid disappearance.

"It couldn't be tobacco," I assured him. "Hell, when I was a kid, I smoked corn silk that tasted more like tobacco than this stuff."

"It is tobacco," he chuckled. "To stretch a point, you could call it that. They strip rice paper into shreds, let it soak in nicotine, dry it, then roll it into these things. We call them stovepipes."

I decided, in the future, if there was anything else to smoke, I would pass up the stovepipes. If it were not for the long cardboard tube acting as a cooling chamber, a careless smoker could easily fricassee his tonsils.

At noon we knocked off for a half-hour lunch break. The rice was beginning to taste good. Again, at three o'clock we were given a ten-minute smoke break. Finally, at five we quit for the day and started the long trek back up the mountain to the citadel.

I had entered my room and sat down on the end of my bunk to catch my breath when the word was passed: everyone wanting a bath should fall in at the stairwell in the north corridor. I could not remember the last time I had had a bath. In the entire year-and-a-half in Woosung, we had not been offered a bath. Needless to say, we all needed one badly.

Each prisoner, with only a pair of shoes and a towel wrapped around him, gathered at the head of the stairwell. There was no heat in the building, and it being November, we stood waiting and shivering in the cold. Everyone was decked out with a good case of goose pimples.

The guard led us down three flights of wide stairs to the bottom floor and into a community bath. We stepped into the bathroom and there before us was a huge sunken concrete tank filled to the top. The water had a gray tinge and a definite odor of sulphur, as though it had not been changed in a long, long time. A steam pipe coming straight down from the ceiling into the center of the pool was making an ear-splitting racket, popping and banging. The live steam being injected into the water was heating it. The water vapor rising from the pool testified the steam was doing a good job; the water looked as if it were boiling. Dirty or not, it was so hot I was sure it was safe. No bugs could live in it at that temperature.

The bath was occupied at the time by a number of nude Japanese men and women. The guards made us back out and stand in the hallway, after which they closed the double doors and held us there in the cold until the Japanese had all been chased from the bathroom.

When our turn came, I thought I would never be able to get into the water because it was so damned hot. However, with persistence, I managed to ease in slowly. I settled in until only my head was above water. The bathing pool was only about four feet deep, so I was in a squatting position.

Since the war had begun, which seemed a thousand years ago, this was the first time I had been truly warm. It felt good, so soothing. I would have liked to have remained in the hot bath for hours, but fifteen minutes was all the guards would allow us. We were ordered out to make room for another group of prisoners who were waiting, shivering in the cold hallway. I crawled out of the bath, my body as red as a boiled lobster. I retained the heat I had absorbed from the bath for hours.

That night after supper, I met some of the sailors from down the hall. Some were survivors of a United States submarine, *Grenadier*, and others were merchant seamen taken from sunken merchant ships. The merchant seamen had had their ships sunk in the Atlantic Ocean by a German raider who fished them out of the water and brought them halfway around the world to Japan. Also, there were merchant crews, Hindus, and Chinese who were captured along the China coast.

I was also introduced to a means of survival—wheeling and dealing with the Korean and Japanese civilians in the factory for food. The prisoners had bags of parched soybeans they received in trading with the factory workers. Any article of clothing was good for trading, especially T-shirts.

When our detail had been stopped as we were boarding the coal ship, and half the men were taken away to another job, they were assigned to unload an iron ore ship. While unloading the iron ore, they found copra, or coconut meat, wedged in the framework of the ship. All of them brought pockets full of copra back to the citadel. The copra, undoubtedly, was left there from the days when the ship plied the South Seas, trading in coconuts. The copra was dirty and rusty from the iron ore, but by cutting away the outer layer it became quite edible. Some of the men took their chunks of copra into the bath with them and washed the dirt and rust off in the filthy water.

Without a doubt, we had enterprises in full swing here in camp. The people with the beans, after eating their fill, tried to trade the rest for cigarettes or rice. As hungry as I was, I could not bring myself to trade away a meal later for a few beans now. Everyone was not like me, and there were some trades made.

The next two weeks were spent unloading coal and iron ore ships. The routine of work did not change, but there was a change of room leaders. I took over the job as room leader from Sawyer when he quit in a huff.

It happened one evening, about two weeks after we had landed in Japan. A call came from the office for all room leaders to come pick up razor blades for the men. Sawyer went for them, but was back very shortly with no blades.

"Sawyer," I asked, "what happened to the razor blades?" I could see both of his cheeks were beet red from being slapped.

"To hell with the razor blades," he growled. "I'm not going to stand up there and let that dirty little bastard pound the hell out of me, not for a few lousy razor blades."

"We sure could use some razor blades, Sawyer," I needled him. "How the hell are we going to shave?"

"I couldn't care less if you ever shave," he exploded. "Here's some more news for you: You're never going to shave again if you depend on me to go back there and get the shit beat out of me for a couple of lousy razor blades. If you want those damn blades, go get them yourself—and you can have this stinking job too while you're at it."

"I got it," I said. Without an instant's hesitation, I was on my feet heading for the office.

I stood outside the office for a second. Hasigawa, the boy-sized interpreter, was seated behind the desk. Behind him were two file cabinets and a wall full of windows. The door was open, so I knocked on the doorjamb. Hasigawa looked up.

"What you want?" he sneered.

"I have come for the razor blades for room twenty-three."

"Send boontycho," he snapped.

"I am new boontycho," I assured him.

I had a feeling I'd better not tell Hasigawa that Sawyer quit. Under those circumstances I doubted if Hasigawa would let him. He would probably harass Sawyer to death.

"I will make a better boontycho than other man," I declared.

"You make a better boontycho?" he echoed, and got up from behind the desk and marched deliberately to face me.

"*Ki-o-ski,*" [Attention] he barked.

I had no sooner come to attention when he swung his arm back and jumped off the floor and belted me across the face in one motion. Before I could recover, he delivered another stinging blow to my other cheek.

I was furious. I wanted to reach out and strangle the little bastard. I was beginning to understand Sawyer's point of view, but I couldn't back out now. I had committed myself. I braced myself, expecting him to clout me again, but he held back. He stood in front of me looking contemptible with an insipid grin on his face. Momentarily, he returned to his desk, picked up two packages of razor blades, and brought them to me.

Had there been any choice in the selection of room leaders, undoubtedly someone would have volunteered for the job. Or perhaps, he would have been selected by drawing straws. In the military, there is no option; as long as the man is healthy, the senior man takes command.

Both Sawyer and I were corporals, but his date of rank was prior to mine, and being senior, it was not only his right to take command, it was his duty.

Sawyer had done what was expected of him for a short time, but from his actions, I presumed he didn't feel obligated to abide by any military regulations as a prisoner of war. He had stepped aside, and at his invitation, I had taken over as room leader.

I wanted the job because I felt if I were in a position of authority, no matter how insignificant, someday it might allow me some measure of control over my destiny and that of the men in my command.

As room leader, I had full control of all supplies, food, clothing, and whatever issues came into the room. Up to now, there had been very few issues.

On random days, once or twice a month, the Japanese issued us bite-sized cookies, a sort of shortbread with powdered sugar all over them. There were usually three or four cookies per man. I made sure that over the long run, each man received an equal number.

During the first month in Japan we received a large, heavy Japanese Army-issue overcoat, a pair of split-toed sneakers, and a suit of work clothes, consisting of a jacket and a pair of trousers. The material in all the garments looked and felt exactly like burlap. In addition to the clothing, they issued us an aluminum mess kit with a tight-fitting lid. The metal mess gear was much better to haul our rice to and from work and was easier to keep clean.

All in all, things did not look too bad. For a start, the food was a little better than we had had in Woosung, and they seemed interested in keeping us clothed. Maybe all my worrying was for nothing.

7

The Yoheen Gang

O ne month and a day after we arrived in Japan, our work patterns suddenly changed. It must have been decided that it was time to put their new crop of technicians to work and stop wasting their talents unloading ships and working on labor gangs. This morning, when the column halted, a new interpreter began calling men by name and designating that each stand with a particular group. I was called out to join the welders.

Our group, about fifteen strong, was escorted to one of the nearby factory buildings. We were ushered into a far corner of the building. Immediately, the Japanese foreman got down to business. He singled me out and beckoned that I come forward. Beside him, his assistant, with a helmet in one hand and an electrode in the other, held them out to me. I took the helmet and electrode. The foreman handed me a welding rod and indicated that he wanted me to run a bead on the boiler plate at my feet. I noted the plate had beads all over it where many before me had tried to prove they could weld.

I decided that now was the time to let them know I was no welder. I shrugged my shoulders, shook my head, and tried to convey that I didn't know how to weld. The foreman was bewildered. I suppose he had been told we were all welders. I knew what he wanted, and he must have known what my head shake and shrug meant; however, he refused to accept it. Finally, I gave up trying to beg off and decided to show him.

I donned the helmet, bent down, dropped the shield over my face, and jabbed the welding rod at the boiler plate. The foreman and his assistant moved closer with their helmets in place to observe the master at work. The rod stuck to the plate; I wrenched it free and tried again and again, with the same results. After six tries, the foreman tapped me on the shoulder and took away the helmet and electrode.

I stood aside while the rest of the prisoners were being tested. It seemed that everyone, except me, was a welder. As soon as the testing was completed, the new crop of welders was whisked away to some other part of the factory. I was left standing beside the test stand, alone. It was still early in the day. I expected someone to come for me. Noon came, but that was all. Everyone quit work for lunch. Like them, I ate my rice, too. In a half hour the workers all returned to their jobs. I was still ignored. I began to wonder what dire circumstance I had gotten myself into this time—now that they knew I couldn't weld.

It was late in the afternoon when I spotted the interpreter who had called us out of ranks the first thing that morning. He and two Japanese civilians were approaching.

"I understand you had a little difficulty with the arc welding this morning," he said, extending his hand. "Just call me Nishi." His grip was firm.

"My name is Kirk," I countered. "Where did you pick up the English? You sound like an American."

"I should hope so," he laughed. "I was born and raised in the States. San Francisco, to be exact. I still think there's nothing better than beefsteak, apple pie, and motherhood." He smiled. "Getting back to welding," he questioned, "what happened?"

"Nishi, I have been trying to tell these guys, starting back in Woosung, that I know absolutely nothing about welding, but they got hold of some bum dope and refused to believe anything I say," I explained. "Actually, the only welding I know is forge and gas welding, and very little of that. I brushed across them when I worked in a blacksmith shop when I was a kid. I never mastered either of them."

Nishi turned to the two Japanese who were listening intently to our conversation as though they understood what we were saying. Nishi said something that made them laugh, then nodded to me. "Have you ever used a cutting torch?"

"Once or twice," I answered dubiously.

"That's good enough—you'll do all right. Everything is going to be OK," he promised.

With that, the trio walked away. The whole Japanese race had lost interest in me, it seemed, now that they had discovered what I'd been telling them was the truth—that I was no welder.

It was not until quitting time, when I saw the prisoners leaving, that I quit my stand and followed them out of the building.

The following morning at the factory, myself and another marine, Tony LePore, of Wake Island, were called out of ranks and assigned to the Yoheen [scrap iron] gang. We two made a total of twenty men; two marines, and the rest appeared to be civilians. Two soldiers with fixed bayonets marched us through the factory and a mile beyond in a westerly direction.

The scrap iron pile covered many acres. It had been located on a section of reclaimed land. Slag and cinders from the factory were used to fill in the bay. As we walked, I could see a train of slag pots being dumped.

We were well into the scrap pile before we reached our destination, a small, corrugated-iron building. Two Japanese civilians were there to meet us. One was small and possibly in his forties. He wore a khaki uniform, a blouse, breeches, wrap leggings, and split-toed sneakers. His assistant, a big man for a Japanese, was much younger. He also wore wrap leggings and split-toed sneakers, but no uniform.

The smaller of the two was the number-one pusher. He immediately began giving orders. The other members of the Yoheen gang filed into the shed and out again carrying their hoses, cutting torches, and goggles.

Tony and I waited until the head pusher beckoned to us. Inside the equipment shed he issued us each a set of hoses, a cutting torch, a pair of goggles, and a small tool kit. Outside again, we formed two ranks and followed a set of railroad tracks deeper into the scrap iron pile. The soldiers with the bayonets remained behind by the equipment shack.

At the work area, all the prisoners and Japanese civilian workers began setting up their burning equipment. The little pusher came to

Tony and me and introduced himself as Cawashima. The big pusher also came forward to shake our hands and let us know his name was Tacashima.

Our first instructions from Cawashima were to build a stove to heat the oxygen bottle. He spoke enough English for me to understand that the oxygen in the tanks was in liquid form. To get the most burning time out of each bottle, the oxygen had to be heated. He suggested each of us borrow a torch from one of the prisoners to build our stoves first.

All the men burning scrap iron had built stoves from material taken from the scrap pile. I copied one of the stoves and filled it with coal I found laying about, the remnants of a coal storage pile from sometime back.

With the oxygen bottle against the the newly built stove and the hoses both connected, one to the carbide generator and the other to the oxygen tank, I remembered Cawashima's first rule—no burning until the oxygen was hot. I sat comfortably warm on the tank in spite of the chilly November weather and whiled away thirty to forty minutes. During this time, I disassembled the torch to see how it worked. It was simple. As near as I could remember, it was like the one I had used a few times in the blacksmith shop back home.

When the tank began to feel warm under me, I was sure it was hot enough to start cutting. Cawashima came over to check me out when he saw me light my torch, to make sure I knew what I was supposed to do. Satisfied, he walked away and left me alone.

My first opportunity to meet the rest of the prisoners came when we quit for lunch. We all retired to a corrugated-iron shack that had been built from material found in the scrap pile. It also had a stove in the center and was warm and cozy. It was just large enough to accommodate all the prisoners.

They were all merchant seamen except Douglas Blessenger, who was a naval gunner's mate detached from the United States Navy on temporary duty aboard one of the ships that had been sunk. They were all Americans except Dennis Lee, of Southampton, England. All were victims of the same German surface raider that preyed on shipping in the Atlantic Ocean.

After fishing the survivors of the five ships from the water, the German warship had hauled the eighteen crewmen around Cape Horn, across the Pacific to Yokohama to be imprisoned by the Japanese. When they arrived in Yawata, for reasons known only to the Japanese, they were all assigned to work on the Yoheen gang.

They told of their shipmates being killed or lost at sea as they were forced to abandon their ships, which were under heavy attack from the German raider. Their ships were set afire by shells, and bulkheads were ruptured, spilling burning fuel on the ocean and engulfing their vessels. What was worse, after being picked out of the water, they found themselves trapped belowdecks on the raider. Each time the Germans encountered an enemy ship, a gun battle ensued. The fights were all short because the German raider was more heavily armed than any merchant ship. Most merchantmen were outfitted with small deck guns, primarily used for taking potshots at submarines. Nevertheless, their constant fear was that one of those small deck guns from our allies would accidentally find a vulnerable spot like a magazine and send the German raider with all hands, straight to hell.

Tony LePore came to see me during the afternoon break. "I didn't want to say anything to those guys who lost their friends, but at least they died in the line of duty. The three sailors—along with the two marines who were murdered on the Nita Maru one day out of Yokohama, as we were being shipped to China—were not that lucky."

"What happened?" I asked with deep interest.

"It was sick—I mean, really sick," he began. "A Jap officer came down into the hold and picked six guys at random: Master Sergeant Hannum, Technical Sergeant Bailey, Seaman First Class Lambert and Seamen Second Class Franklin and Gonzales. I forgot who the other guy was because he didn't get killed. They brought him back after it was all over.

"They tied this one guy to the hatch cover so he could watch while they hog-tied the other five men, and propped them up on their knees. The officer read something from a paper in Japanese, and then with their samurai swords, five officers chopped off the five men's heads. In seconds the deck was awash with blood.

"The officer in charge of the butchery then ordered the Jap sailors to throw the bodies and heads overboard. Later we learned that the decapitations were reprisals for the Japs that were killed taking Wake Island," Tony explained.

I agreed with him—the Japs were nothing but a bunch of murdering bastards.

The day marking the fifth week in Japan, we were informed that we would not be going to work that day. At last, I thought, we're going to sleep all day and get some much-needed rest.

After breakfast, we formed ranks outside our rooms as ordered, to wait for what we thought was an inspection party. It turned out to be a search detail. For four hours we stood in the cold hallway while a group of soldiers went through everything we owned in search of contraband. No one knew what they were looking for, but whatever it was, it was not hidden in anything we had because they took nothing. Following lunch we were ordered to assemble on the roof of the building. Hasigawa was there, standing on a large wooden packing box and waiting for us as we straggled out onto the roof. He talked like Mortimer in Woosung, warning of severe punishment if we broke any of his rules.

"You are prisoners of the Imperial Japanese Army. If you try to escape, you will be shot. You will work or you will not eat." He emphasized each point with the clenched-fist routine.

"When you are sick and cannot work, you will receive only half rations." He paused to let it sink in, then continued, "Because you are working for the Seitetsu Steel Company [now Nippon Steel], you will get paid one yen a day for every day you work. We will save ninety sen for you and will allow you ten sen with which you may buy cigarettes and other things from the canteen we will open for you someday. If you work hard, one day we will set you free so you may find a Japanese wife and raise a family."

Hasigawa droned on. My mind was ten thousand miles away, not listening to a word he was saying, until he said the magic words, "Red Cross packages." He was still talking, "One package will be divided between two men. These gifts from the Red Cross contain food," he pointed out, "so we will reduce your normal rations. Too much food is not healthy for anybody; we do not want to see any of you get sick."

At this point, Hasigawa had run out of things to say, so he dismissed us with one final instruction: "Go back to your rooms and get some hot water and rags to wash the bedbugs out of your bunks."

We worked on our bunks for a couple of hours, digging out the bedbugs and their eggs from the crevices and smashing them. Hot water? There was no hot water—not that it would have done any good anyway; it probably would have stimulated the bedbugs' reproductive organs and hatched the eggs. As for rags, he must have been joking—any rags in Japan are used strictly for patching clothes.

At four o'clock we received the call to come to the office to pick up the Red Cross packages. I took four men with me so each man could carry two packages apiece. The packages were heavy, and by the time I got back to the room and passed them around, I could hardly wait to find out what was in them. It was like Christmas a few days early; there were cigarettes, candy, cheese, butter, canned meats, cookies, jams, jellies, chewing gum, and almost everything a starving man could hope for.

After we sampled a little of this and a little of that and enjoyed a good cigarette for a change, we went downstairs for our daily bath. There, we got more good news. At least 10,000 Red Cross packages were neatly stacked in a large room off the bath. The room was filled from the floor to its twelve-foot ceiling. Everybody rejoiced—there was enough food in those packages to keep the prisoners in this camp for a year, maybe more, even if the Japanese never gave us another grain of millet.

Hasigawa was true to his word: for supper that night our rations were cut by a third. We were all living high with our Red Cross goodies; no one seemed to care. With all that food down by the bath, we had no need to worry.

A week went by, but there were no more issues of Red Cross food. The boxes remained in the room where we had seen them for better than two weeks, then they were gone—vanished. The packages were all taken away while we were at work.

I was disappointed, but not surprised. Philosophically, I considered, half a Red Cross package was better than none at all. The thing that bothered me most about the Red Cross issue was that our food rations were never fully restored to what they were before the Japanese so graciously gave us a taste of what we knew we were missing.

A few days later it was Christmas, but Christmas was no different than any other day working on the scrap pile. Except for one small thing: On the way to work, Philip Elliot, a stocky young man with a shaved head and a very serious disposition, from Caldwell, New Jersey, spotted some sweet potato peelings on a garbage pile as we passed close by one of the buildings. He was a practical individual, and could see the possibilities even in a trash heap. Quickly, he scooped up the peelings in his hat and brought them along to work. As we were having lunch in our cozy little hut, Elliot spread his peelings out on top of the hot stove. He parched them. They smelled good. He invited everyone to have a taste. I tried one; it was not exactly like eating at the Waldorf, but it was edible. What a Christmas.

After that day, all of us were constantly on the lookout for anything edible in the garbage piles, or anyplace. We were not particular; food was food. Once we cleaned it off and cooked it on our stove, it couldn't hurt us, and it might do us some good.

Herschel Langston, who hailed from Van Buren, Arkansas, was the first to make a lucky find. One day he fished a chicken's head out of the bay as it came floating by. Gingerly, he deposited it in his aluminum mess kit, and with enough water to cover it, he set it on the stove to cook. Presently, the water began to boil. The chicken's head released all its pent-up odors, completely filling the shack from corner to corner.

"Langston, what the hell are you going to do with that stinking thing?" I gagged.

"I know you are not going to believe this, but I am making chicken soup," he said with mock seriousness. "If you stick around, you shall be the first to taste it."

"No, thanks," I begged off as I got up to go outside for a breath of fresh air. "I am not ready for chicken-head soup, especially with the feathers still on it."

8

Tragedy

It was one of the many foul days in January. It had been raining all day. We crawled up the hill soaked to the skin. The prisoners who worked in the factory buildings were more fortunate than the Yoheen gang. Most of the prisoners only had to be in the rain while going to, or returning from work. The Yoheen gang had to work in the rain the whole day, except for a short half-hour lunch period.

The hot bath was again a lifesaver. After I thawed out and absorbed as much heat as my body would take, I wrapped myself in my Marine Corps woolen blanket and kept warm until bedtime.

This particular night, I had just settled myself for a comfortable sleep on my rock-hard straw mat, when a terrific commotion brought me out of bed to look down the corridor. Approaching was a large group of soldiers led by two five-star Japanese officers. The soldiers were clad in blue-green uniforms. The hallway was filling rapidly as they poured around the far turn, advancing three and four abreast. Their uniforms were unkempt, dirty, and dripping wet, as though they had spent the last few days in foxholes.

Those who were able to walk under their own power were helping their buddies through the last few steps. They looked sickly; a lot worse than most of us.

Following their assignments to rooms and the quieting of chatter and confusion, they went to bed. I lay on my bunk, reflecting. I could have sworn one of the soldiers they dragged past me was dead.

Who were they and where did they come from? I wondered as I dropped off to sleep.

Next morning, we learned the blue-green soldiers were Javanese, with a sprinkling of Dutch corporals and sergeants in command. Better than half of them were sick. I had been correct the night before; some of them were dead. They were either brought in that way or they had died during the night. Those few dead were just the beginning. Every day thereafter, the soldiers died at the rate of three to four a day. It was almost two weeks before the dying slackened off. The rumors were that the soldiers were dying from pneumonia. That was not difficult to believe. They had been brought out of the tropics into a winter climate, just as the Wake Island marines and civilians had been. I was amazed that more of them did not die. Any time of the year would have been a better time to come to Japan than now, in the middle of the winter.

The real tragedy was that they were only boys, fifteen to seventeen years old, and some appeared even younger—all of them too young to die. I got the impression from their uniforms that the Japanese had captured a military academy. In spite of their tender ages, they seemed to be bearing up bravely. If dying without a whimper was the mark of a man, there were no boys among them.

The Japanese disposed of the dead by cremation. The bodies were stacked on a two-wheeled cart like cordwood, and four men were assigned to pull the rig to the nearest crematorium. Once there, the prisoners performed the task of committing the bodies to the ovens.

Urns containing the ashes of the deceased, cremated the day before, were placed on the cart for the return trip to the citadel. Each urn had a white ribbon wrapped around it and tied in a bow at the top to hold the lid in place. A label on each crock gave the dead man's name, rank, and serial number.

A special room was set aside for storage of the urns. They were placed side by side on shelves that lined the room from the floor to the ceiling. There was enough space on those shelves to store the ashes of everyone in camp. The little crocks were mute witness that many young men had died before their time. It was the only room in the building that was locked. Weird, I thought, the only people who definitely can't go anywhere are locked up.

We were fortunate that the Javanese who died had not had a contagious disease, or there would have been one hell of an epidemic. It was a fact that most of us in the prison camp were not exactly in the best of health.

Death was not reserved exclusively for the Javanese, even though toward the end of February they still had the highest mortality rate. A British soldier brought in from Singapore died of pneumonia. While all these new arrivals were dropping dead, our first casualty was a merchant seaman who was struck down with a heart attack as he reached the top of the hill, returning from work. His buddies picked him up and rushed him into the sick bay, but there was nothing the Japanese doctor could do for him.

In memory of the dead seaman, the long climb home each night was thenceforth referred to as "cardiac hill."

Following the fatal steps of the merchant seaman, "Big Red," a submarine sailor of the United States Navy, was next to go. With death and dying all around me, I tried to dismiss the nightmare as fantasy. These people were not real, those who were dying. It was all a bad dream from which I would soon awaken.

However, there was no way to hide from reality. I found it all too true. "Big Red" did exist. He was young like the Javanese, and had it not been for the war, a long and fruitful life would have been his. Unfortunately, because of poor and insufficient food and for no other reason, he had no chance to survive.

The day the U.S. submarine, the *Grenadier (SS-210)*, was sunk in surface action in the Bay of Bengal, off Malaya in April 1943, "Red" would have been spared a lot of misery and suffering if he had gone down with his boat. He was a big man, but in issuing rations, the Japanese made no allowance for a man's size.

I had first noticed Red in one of the rooms off the sick bay where patients were usually isolated when the Japanese gave them up for dead. We passed by his cubicle each day going to and from work. He was always sitting up on his cot to watch what little part of the world there was left to him pass by his doorway. Red would call out to us and we would respond with words of encouragement.

The lack of proper food resulted in a very bad case of beriberi. Everyone in camp had beriberi to some degree, but because of Red's size, he had a lower tolerance to the disease than most of us. In spite of his strong will to win, the disease got the upper hand. Liquid accumulated in his body, causing his abdomen to swell and his skin to become as tight as a drum, resulting in pressure and pain. The Japanese doctor finally punctured his stomach and inserted a rubber tube to drain off the water to relieve his distress and suffering. As much as a gallon of fluid was taken from him every day.

Red's tenacious grip on life was admirable. He hung on where lesser men would have long given up. He survived weeks beyond the time predicted by the Japanese doctor.

During his last days, even the day he died, he would call out to passersby, "I'm going to live. I know I'm going to make it."

Early in March, when the buds of spring were beginning to burst and everything that had slept through the long winter was awakening to a new life, the last delicate thread holding Big Red snapped. He slipped away with a murmur on his lips, "I'm not going to die . . ."

Red was not the only prisoner who died at that time, but he fought harder than most to exist. His body was taken to the crematorium the following day. Added to the misery of his drawn-out suffering and death, his body was denied the dignity it was due. Because he was too large for their ovens, one of the prisoners was given the grisly task of sawing off his legs to allow his body to fit into the small space to be cremated.

9

Poke Salad to a Whipping

As the last echoing notes of the Japanese bugle call to reveille ricocheted through the corridors, I braced myself for the inevitable.

"There will be a better day tomorrow if we live to see it," said "Foots" Anderson. It grated on my nerves.

"Foots," aptly named because of his tremendous foundations, was a country boy before he joined the Marine Corps. He would greet each day with a thought of tomorrow.

My point of view was in direct opposition to the first part of his statement. There was no way that tomorrow would be any better. In retrospect, the yesterdays were the "good old days." I remember the meat in the stews and the extra rice we were served when we first arrived in Japan, and I will never forget that half of a Red Cross package. Now, the only ingredients in the soup were *daikon* [white radish] and hot water. Rice rations had been drastically cut and millet had been substituted.

The second part of Anderson's soliloquy was really annoying. With all the deaths we had had during the last few months, I could do without being constantly reminded that today could be my last. There was no way to shut him up. In spite of all the growls, groans, and grumbling each morning, he popped up like a robot and recited his piece.

This day started not unlike all the yesterdays. We rolled out of bed, lined up in the hallway for roll call, and when that was over, we had breakfast. Breakfast was not ham and eggs; it was a teacup filled with a mixture of rice and millet and a teacup of watery soup. Anyway, we got ready to go to work, but as we were waiting for the call to start our daily grind, Foots sat gazing out the window into the courtyard below. The time was early April, and the weeds were beginning to grow everywhere.

Foots raised up and put his face against the windowpane. "Well, I'll be darned!" he said in amazement. "That's poke salad!"

Sawyer jumped up and ran to the window. "Where?" he demanded.

"Right there in the middle of that wall yonder." Anderson described its position, feeling proud for making what he thought was an important find.

Sawyer searched the area indicated for a familiar plant, then remarked, "I see what you mean, but that ain't poke salad; that's just a weed."

"The hell you say," Foots reacted. "I know poke salad when I see it. I have eaten it all my life. I was raised on poke salad back in Bastrop, Louisiana."

"If you have been eating that stuff all your life, it's a wonder you ain't dead. I am telling you that ain't poke salad." Sawyer was angry, and backed away from the window facing Anderson.

The argument on the identity of the plant in the courtyard changed into name calling, and just as quickly, Anderson and Sawyer were standing toe-to-toe, slugging each other. Except for the men close to the action, who moved to give them room, no one seemed concerned.

The fight was brief. After the exchange of two or three punches, it was all over. With their arms hanging slack at their sides, the two stared wide-eyed at each other, gasping for air. Both were completely exhausted. Without a weapon of some kind, like a club, there was no way they could have harmed one another. In their physical condition, together, they could not have whipped a well-fed five-year-old boy with one hand tied behind his back.

Under different circumstances, a fracas like this would have been hilarious, with long, tall Foots towering over scrappy, little, freckle-faced Sawyer; however, nobody laughed or cared. I shook my head, amused, and wondered where they got all the energy. When the call finally came a few minutes later, they seemed to have completely recovered. I envied their vigor.

I had only been watching, but still, I felt like I had just gone ten rounds. A gnawing in my guts told me I was about to be sick again with malaria. I first got the disease in Woosung when we lived in the swamp.

Sure enough, that evening I staggered up the hill with a high fever. I went to bed praying I would still have the fever in the morning when I showed up for sick call so I could take the day off from work. Working every day, day in and day out, without a day's rest, destroys one's body. It is a break to lie down and rest, even if it is necessary to get sick to do it.

I was in luck. My fever held until I was able to register it on the thermometer in the sick bay after breakfast. The doctor told me to go to bed and to inform the boontycho to cut my rations in half.

There were no half rations in my room. I was the boontycho, and although it was my responsibility to enforce the half-ration rule under threat of great bodily harm, I had an understanding with all my men that as long as I was their leader, sick or otherwise, no one would have their rations cut. What little food there was in a half ration, spread around to the other men, did not amount to more than a few grains of millet. On the other hand, that half ration was enough to keep a sick man from starving to death.

During the day my fever subsided and I was forced to return to work the next morning. By noon my fever was back. Cawashima could see I was very ill. He made me return my equipment to the shed and crawl under a piece of scrap iron, out of the wind and out of sight. When I returned to the citadel that evening, I was burning up with fever. The next morning when I reported to the sick bay, I still had it. The doctor remembered me from two days before and ordered me back to bed, this time for five days on half rations. I had no chills with the fever. The doctor said it wasn't malaria; it was dengue fever.

On the third day of my encounter with the disease, the doctor sent for me. I arrived at the sick bay to find him waiting with a huge hypodermic syringe in his hand. He motioned for me to sit on a stool facing him. I noted the hypo was filled with a clear liquid. He took my arm and without the benefit of an antiseptic swab, jammed the needle into a vein. As he emptied the syringe into my bloodstream, I became alarmed; there was an air bubble at the top of the syringe. Immediately, I pointed it out to him, but he grinned, nodded, and continued to depress the plunger. I became terrified for fear he would inject air into my vein. I had heard that an air bubble in one's bloodstream could be fatal.

The doctor perceived the reason for my anxiety, but this did not deter him a bit; his grin became even broader. At the last instant, when the medicine was virtually gone, he stopped and withdrew the needle. I heaved a sigh of relief, broke out into a cold sweat, stumbled back along the corridor to my room, and collapsed on my straw mat.

When the day rolled around for me to go back to work, I still had the fever. The doctor sent me back to bed for another five days. The fever lasted two more days and when it broke, the sweat poured off me like a river. At that point I only had three days to recuperate. In two days I was back on my feet, a little unsteady, but walking nevertheless. That was my ticket to go back to work. My appetite had returned, although I had not stopped eating, even when I was feeling my worst.

Dengue (backbone fever), like malaria, is caused by mosquito bites. It drives the victim's fever up as high as 105 degrees, and has a tendency to constipate—which is not too bad, if at the time, the person has a bad case of diarrhea. The worst fear of the disease is that it leaves its victims weak and vulnerable to pneumonia.

I had only one more day to get all my strength back, because with no fever and being able to stand, there was no way I could get out of going to work. I was sitting on the end of my bunk, worrying about how I would be able to navigate that damn hill tomorrow in my condition . . .

"Ki-o-ski!" Hasigawa was standing in the doorway. I had not heard his catlike approach in his split-toed sneakers.

I eased off the bunk as quickly as I could and assumed the position of attention.

"Is it true, you are shoemaker?" he questioned.

He surprised me, but I quickly assented with a nod.

"Follow me," he ordered, and led the way to a windowless room at the southeast corner of the building. The room was across the hall from the office, but around the corner from its entrance.

Stacked against the right wall of this room were many anodized five-gallon containers, perhaps twenty or more. Each one had a tight-fitting lid. I was certain they were the cans from which Hasigawa issued us the cookies.

Piled high on the left side of the room were many pairs of Jap military shoes. Directly in front of me, opposite the door, was a shoemaker's bench with a last in front and a drawer on the side under the seat.

"Can you fix shoes?" he pointed at the pile.

"Yes," I said with certainty, not knowing the condition of the shoes.

This is what I need to stay away from that damned hill, I told myself. If I could stretch this job into a week, I would have my strength back. I couldn't afford to let this opportunity slip away; even if I couldn't fix all of them, at least I could spend a lot of time repairing some.

"How long will it be finished?" Hasigawa wanted to know, as though he were reading my mind.

I stepped over to the pile of shoes, picked up two pair, and examined them. The two pair needed their soles tacked down and a few hobnails, nothing more.

"If they are all like these two pair, it will take a week or ten days at the most," I answered with apprehension, fearing I might be outside his predetermined time frame.

"Good—now work," he ordered.

I picked up a pair of shoes with an inward sigh of relief and sat down behind the last. With the shoe in place, I opened the drawer on the side of the bench and found a few nails to secure the sole tightly to the insole. I removed the shoe from the last and felt inside the shoe to make sure all the nails were crimped. Once more on the last, I replaced the missing hobnails, then handed it to Hasigawa.

Hasigawa had been standing very close, watching my every move. He took the shoe, examined it carefully, then slipped his hand into it as I had done to feel for nails.

"Ten days." He held the shoe out to me. I accepted it as he turned to leave. At the doorway, he spun around and stated clearly, "Ten days."

How did Hasigawa know I knew how to repair shoes? I sat still for some time, pondering. There is only one answer, I mused. Mortimer must have passed the information along with that stupid idea that I was a welder. Maybe he felt guilty for stealing my shoe-repair kit, or perhaps he thought his tip would help the Japanese war effort. No matter how Hasigawa got his information, at a time like this, I couldn't have asked for a better break. I would be well enough in ten days to run up that hill. This good fortune could only be an act of God, I thought.

Each day when I entered the room to my shoe-repair job, I checked all the cookie canisters in hopes of finding one of them open. Not until the eighth day did I find a lid on one of the cans that had not been properly seated.

I had my fill of cookies every time I felt it was safe to dive into the cookie jar, so to speak. Periodically, I ran to the door to make sure there were no soldiers in the hallway. With their split-toed sneakers, it was difficult (if not impossible) to hear them approaching. Satisfied that the coast was clear, I returned to remove the lid and stuff as many of the bite-sized cookies in my mouth as possible. Quickly, I replaced the lid exactly as I had found it, making sure there were no telltale crumbs, then hurried back to my seat and began pounding on a shoe. While I pounded, I chewed and swallowed the cookies as fast as I could. It would have been disastrous if I had been caught with a mouthful.

I made an untold number of trips to the cookie can that day, but paid for it the following day by making the same number of trips to the toilet. Since the first time we had been issued cookies, which happened on an average of twice a month, they had had an ill effect on me. The sugar, or whatever it was in them, soured my stomach, and the result was always a bad case of diarrhea. Each time we got an issue, I knew what was going to happen, but food was food, and I ate them, regardless.

I completed the shoes on the tenth day as I had promised, but I could have done the job in a lot less time, five or six days at the most. It was necessary for my health's sake to stretch out the job.

The following day I was back at work on the scrap pile. It was then I decided to start trading some of my clothing for food. There wasn't much to trade for except parched soybeans, but soybeans were better than nothing. The only difficulty in trading was finding a Japanese or Korean with enough guts to take a chance. Most of them were afraid that if they got caught, the soldiers would kick the hell out of them.

In spite of the danger, a big burly Korean, who worked nearby loading coal into gondola cars with a *yoho* pole (a pole carried across the shoulders with a bucket hanging from each end) made his desire known that he wanted to do business. At lunchtime I offered him my Marine Corps green woolen blouse for beans. During the afternoon break, he was back with a white cloth filled with beans. It must have weighed at least five pounds. I gave him the blouse, which he tucked under his coat; he briskly walked away, looking very pregnant.

A five-pound bag of beans was too bulky to conceal in my clothing from the scrutiny of the guards. The soldiers made a point of inspecting the prisoners returning from work each day for contraband. Whenever they suspected someone, the prisoner was jerked out of ranks and searched. If anything was found, there was the usual slapping around, but the beatings were only the preliminary. The real punishment for having contraband was assignment to the "dead run." If there was no dead run the next day, which was unusual, then he would run the next. His name would be placed on the list. When his name came up, he went. For some, pulling the two-wheeled cart one day on the dead run meant being a passenger on the next day. The prisoners were forced to run all the way to the crematorium and all the way back up-hill. Every so often, the run proved too strenuous, and some of the prisoners, because of their weakened condition, collapsed and died.

To prevent the loss of my soybeans and possible punishment if I were caught, I took all the beans I could carry safely without making my pockets bulge and hid the rest under the scrap iron pile. The next day I went for another helping, but much to my chagrin, the rats had beaten me to them. They left the bag with a hole in the side, but not a single bean. It was small comfort to know that now I need not worry about getting caught with contraband.

I had no time to fret over a few beans. I had to get out and do some more trading, or look for another source of food. It was shortly after I returned to work that I found something far better than beans. We were lined up in the stairwell outside the bathroom when I noticed a stack of straw sacks piled against the wall where some of the Red Cross packages had been stacked months ago. I eased over to them and moved along the bags, looking for some clue as to what was in them. I kept one eye on the five-star guard standing in the partially open bathroom door. At last, after covering nearly the full length of the sacks, I was rewarded to find a hole that looked very much like a varmint hole. I reached in and removed a few pieces of whatever it had to offer and slipped back in ranks.

I glanced about cautiously to make sure no one had been watching me. No one seemed to be aware of my little exploration. I brought my hand up to see what I had captured from the enemy. It was a joy to find I was holding a handful of raw noodles. Without hesitation, I popped them in my mouth.

The next evening, I came prepared. I brought along my metal mess kit with the tight-fitting lid. I edged over to the rat hole, reached in, and got a big handful of noodles. I dropped them into my mess kit— then froze in terror! The noodles hitting the bottom of the mess kit sounded like nails dropping on a tin roof. Expecting at any second to be clubbed from behind, I braced myself and waited, but nothing happened. I looked around sharply to see the soldier standing in his usual place by the bathroom door watching the bathers. The noise from the steam pipe used to heat the water must have drowned out the clatter of the falling noodles.

I had noodles in my soup for the next few weeks. Each day, as long as the noodles lasted, I brought a mess kit full of them back to the room and stored them in my sea bag. Unfortunately, this food source was doomed to a short life. Other prisoners learned of the booty, and each, in his own way, liberated some of the noodles. The Japanese discovered the pilfering, and soon removed all the bags.

As with the Red Cross packages, I was disappointed that our supply of noodles was cut off, but the next turn of events made me concentrate on the present unpleasantness.

The month of May was well under way when one evening, a great hulk of a man with a shaved head and wearing a fixed sneer planted himself in our doorway. My first impression was, *He's no ambassador of goodwill.*

"My name is Ras," he boomed, looking around the room into all the faces to make sure everyone was paying attention.

"There is one thing I want all you people to understand. Whenever everyone else is doing without, Ras is going to have his," he growled, holding his cram-packed sea bag in one hand. His sneer turned to a scowl, and he set his feet apart as if to challenge anyone—or everyone—in the room to defy him.

"Who's in charge here?" he demanded.

"I am," I shot back at him with hostility to match his. I was sitting on my bunk by the door, a few inches from him.

To flaunt his physical power, he growled, "I am taking this bunk," indicating the bunk opposite mine on the other side of the door.

"Ras," I tried to explain, "we got the news a few days ago that your group was on its way here from Hokkaido. We were told that each room would have to put up two men. As you can see, there are only ten bunks. Everyone has agreed to take turns sleeping on the iron rail between the bunks. You might say we have all agreed to share the misery."

"You don't hear very good," he snapped at me. The veins in his neck bulging, he then turned and faced the other prisoners. "And that goes for the rest of you people.

"I will say it once more. When everyone is doing without, Ras is going to have his. That ought to be clear enough. I am not sharing my bunk with anybody." He glared at the other men who returned looks of hatred and bitterness.

I was angry and frustrated, but there was absolutely nothing any of us could do about his arrogance. Ras was over six feet tall, healthy, well fed and must have tipped the scales at well over two hundred pounds. If all the prisoners in the room tried to jump him at once, he was powerful enough to destroy all of us.

The next day after work, Ras went directly to the galley. He was seeking a job as a mess cook because he had worked in the galley while a prisoner in Hokkaido; this accounted for his excellent physical condition. The Japanese sergeant in charge of the kitchen was nicknamed "Bull" by the prisoners because he was a big man, a giant according to Japanese standards.

Ras said or did something that set the "Bull" off, or maybe it was just being his charming self that caused the big man to chase him out of the galley and up the stairs with a club. After that, Ras was not so aggressive, but his personality remained obnoxious.

May wasted itself away, and as it came to an end, another incident occurred: Sergeant Robert Smith, a North China Marine, lost his Marine Corps fair-leather belt, the belt marines wear with their winter greens and summer khaki uniforms. It was a wide, thick leather belt with a heavy brass buckle.

While Smith was at work, a five-star guard wandered into his room and stole the belt from his belongings. Robert missed the belt immediately, and everyone helped search for it, but to no avail. A few days later, someone noticed the five-star guard wearing a Marine Corps belt. He passed the information on to Smith, who went straight to the office and reported the theft to Hasigawa.

The guard was called in and confronted by Hasigawa. Of course, he denied having anything to do with the theft. The guard was wearing the belt at that time, and Smith pointed out the fact to Hasigawa. Smith also explained to the interpreter that on the inside of the belt near the buckle, his name and initials were stamped in ink. If he would have the guard remove the belt, the matter would be settled.

Hasigawa refused to order the soldier to take off the belt to verify that it really was Smith's. If he had, both Japanese would have lost face. To be caught red-handed as a common thief by a *furyo* [prisoner of war], whom they regarded as the lowest form of human life, would be an unbearable shame.

The two of them were cornered like rats. Hasigawa did what came naturally. He branded Robert Smith a thief, a cheat, and a liar. To make matters worse for the sergeant, he turned him over to the five-star guard for punishment, adding injury to insult.

The guard made Smith bend over and grab the iron rail that protected the floor-to-ceiling windows overlooking the light well in the center of the building. It was a very public flogging. The five-star removed the stolen belt from his waist and proceeded to whip Smith's behind severely. Although the whipping was short, Robert undoubtedly never forgot the irony of being beaten with his own belt.

The affair did not end there. Two days later, on our once-a-month day off—which was not particularly for our benefit—we were ordered to assemble outside the main entrance in the courtyard and on the road below the fire escape to see and hear our commander. Hasigawa and the Japanese colonel appeared at the head of the fire escape as though it were a pulpit.

Hasigawa began translating the colonel's words: "I have called you together to tell you it has been reported to me that there are thieves among the United States Marines."

Of all the unmitigated gall, I fumed. They did the dirty work and then blamed us.

"You are a disgrace to the Marine Corps and not worthy to be called marines . . ." Hasigawa paused, looked puzzled for a moment as his colonel continued, ". . . the greatest fighting force the world has ever known."

I was amazed to hear him say that, but those were his very words. A rumble started up in the ranks with speculation that the Japanese must have taken a hell of a beating. His statement set me to thinking. Up to now, they claimed to be the world's best combat soldiers. The only logical conclusion had to be that the marines must have beaten their best somewhere.

I promised myself, then and there, that when I got back home I would find out what happened on or before May of 1943.*

The colonel's speech told me more how the war was going than anything I had heard up to now. He convinced me we were winning—at least, the marines were.

---

* A six-month campaign beginning August 1942, which ended February 1943 on Guadalcanal. The marines won, but lost 2,000 men (compared to the Japanese loss of 25,000 men).

10

The Race

One morning in early June, while we were lined up for roll call, I could hear Hasigawa telling each boontycho down the hallway from me that we would not be going to work today. He repeated the words "Field day" to each room leader.

When he got to me, I knew what he was going to say, but the way he said it made me wonder. He was overjoyed about something. For him, that was a novelty. Most of the time, whenever he confronted a prisoner, he was usually scowling.

Field day, I thought; *if it is anything like the field days I remember in the Marine Corps, no thanks.* I'd rather go to work. A Marine Corps field day meant being armed with scrub brushes, mops, and buckets to spend the whole day polishing the barracks. I could not share Hasigawa's enthusiasm.

We prepared to leave for work as we did every morning after breakfast. This day, instead of rice for lunch, they gave us two hamburger buns each. No one was sure what Hasigawa meant by field day. He didn't explain, so we prepared for work. It was then that a call came for all room leaders to report to the office. Hasigawa was bubbling, actually dancing with glee.

"Today," he informed us—with a tone in his voice I had never heard before, an exuberance that was completely out of character— "today we are going to run races." He paused, with a smile from ear to ear, trying to rally us to join in his enthusiasm. Our response was one of perplexity, but that did not slow him one bit.

"I want a member of every nation that we have here in this prison camp to compete against the Japanese soldiers who will run in the races. There will be two races: one will be the hundred-meter dash, and the other will be a relay race. After you have picked who will run for your country, bring their names to me and I will give you all a big surprise. We will not leave for the field before nine o'clock; that will give you plenty of time to choose your runners. Now go," he said with a big grin, after giving us what he considered good news.

There were quite a few Americans in camp—marines, submarine sailors, and merchant seamen. There was also a lot of indecision. Finally, the marines volunteered to represent the Americans. No one professed to be a sprint man, so I offered to run the 100-meter dash. Nobody objected or cared who ran what, so I had the job.

Competing in sprint racing was not new to me. As a student at Mooseheart High School, in Mooseheart, Illinois, I had run the 50-yard, 100-yard, and 220-yard dash.

In 1934, while vying for honors in the national high school relay races that year, there were so many contestants entered in the races, I had to win three eight-man heats to qualify for the final 100-yard dash. In the final race, I took fourth place out of six runners, but the first, second, third, and fourth places all crossed the finish line in almost a dead heat, at a time of ten seconds flat.

A few years later, as a member of the Civilian Conservation Corps, I competed in a number of athletic events, won a few races, and brought home some first-, second-, and third-place medals. Still later, I ran in a meet sponsored by the French military in Tientsin, China, in 1941. A white Russian nudged me out by a step.

Following a brief discussion among the marines, the relay runners were chosen. Their names were given to me to give to Hasigawa. Most of the room leaders were already at the office when I arrived, and shortly thereafter, the rest reported. It was then that Hasigawa went to his office and returned with a handful of three-by-five-inch cards. He held them up for us to see.

"I will let all of you send a postcard to your family," he said, smiling. He passed down the line giving each of us twelve cards and a typewritten copy with two sentences thereon. I glanced at it: I AM IN GOOD HEALTH. I AM WORKING FOR PAY. That was it.

"Look at the message you are to write," Hasigawa said seriously, standing in front again.

"Do not add words to the card, or it will not be posted and the man will be severely punished. All you must do is copy the message in your own hand and address the other side of the card to your family. Are there any questions?" Hasigawa waited, but got no response.

"You may go and give out the cards to the other men. I want the cards all back before nine o'clock, or they will not be posted," he promised.

I passed out the cards with Hasigawa's instructions, and cautioned the men that failure to carry them out to the letter would mean their card would not be mailed, plus they would get a few lumps. As for my part, I did exactly what Hasigawa prescribed, because I had to let my mother know that I was still alive.

It had been better than a year since anyone back home knew of my whereabouts. The last message the Japanese said they sent for me was from Woosung. For all my family knew, I could have been long dead.

I read my message again as I returned all the cards to the office.

"I am in good health." Two months earlier I could have argued with that, but now, my bout with dengue fever and a round of malaria behind me, and since I had stopped eating those damn cookies, I felt fine. To keep from getting sick, I traded my cookies for rice or a bun. Discounting the fact I was 40 pounds underweight after my sicknesses, I had since traded my woolen blankets and all my T-shirts for soybeans, and I had gained a little of that weight back. I must have weighed at least 120 pounds. I'd never felt better. It felt great to be alive.

"I am working for pay." That part of the letter I could disagree with wholeheartedly. We were paid ten sen a day, three yen a month. The only thing we could buy was ground chili pepper in small cylindrical boxes. At first I poured the pepper on my rice so thick, tears would roll down my cheeks. Each meal I added a little more, until eventually, I could eat a whole box of chili pepper on one cup of rice without shedding a tear. After I reached that point, it was like nothing. I could have spread the three yen over my rice and gotten the same effect. We were not required to purchase cigarettes. The Japanese issued everyone twenty "Golden Eagle" cigarettes a week. When you inhaled it felt like the eagle was ripping your throat out with its talons. To say we were working for pay was ludicrous. From an economic standpoint, there was nowhere to spend the money; therefore, it was worthless. Even the local Japanese and Korean workers refused to take military script.

It was not far from the citadel to the field Hasigawa had mentioned. Before us was an athletic stadium, similar to any that can be found at most high schools in the United States. It was complete with two sets of bleachers, one on each side of an oval cinder track that looked across a center of turf resembling a football field.

The stands were already filled to overflowing with Japanese civilians—men, women, and children. Everyone, it seemed, even the tiny babies, were waving small Japanese flags.

All the prisoners who were taking part in the races were allowed to break ranks to examine the track. I wandered out on the field where I spotted "Moose" Kirkpatrick, a North China Marine. He was gazing at all the people who had come to see the races. He had volunteered to run anchorman on the American relay team.

"Moose," I interrupted his contemplation of the crowd, "there must be two to three thousand people here—what would you guess?"

"Easily that many," he remarked.

"It also looks like we have no friends in this crowd," I offered. "There is not one American flag anywhere."

"That would be interesting to see," Kirkpatrick chuckled, then nodded toward the west end of the field where the prisoners of war were gathered. They were obliged to sit on the ground because there was no more space left in the bleachers.

"We're not alone, Terence. We brought the best damn rooting section in the world with us, practically every nation on earth." He was right, of course; to a man, the prisoners had no other loyalties at this time but to each other—we were all brothers by ordeal.

While waiting for the races to begin, some of the prisoners were out on the track running back and forth—warming up. It seemed like a good idea.

Directly in front of me, on the track, was a hurdle set up to its high position. I tried to jump over it, but failed miserably. I ended up in a heap on the ground, then had to struggle to untangle myself from it. I got back on my feet and limped away with a slightly wrenched back. That was enough warming up for me. I was ready to run my race before another trick like that hurdle turned me into a cripple.

As the delay continued, I took the time to ponder how passing strange it was that the Japanese would want to risk competing against such despicably wretched human beings as prisoners of war. That was their true feeling toward us: we were the scum of the earth.

Why make a big event out of it? Someone was not thinking clearly. At present, the general physical condition of most prisoners was very poor at best, which was easy to see by the most casual observer. If the Japanese won the races, that was to be expected, but—if they lost—for shame!

I was sure the whole spectacle had been planned. The Japanese had no intention of losing. The soldiers we were to compete against were undoubtedly ringers—probably the cream of all the athletes they could muster.

The more I thought about them bringing us out here before the local peasantry to make fools of us, the more disgusted I became. In spite of my anger, I had to concede that, if they swept the day, they would have a morale builder. It would make damn good propaganda.

I was soon to find out how fast the Japanese were. Hasigawa, at the east end of the field, calling through a megaphone, ordered all prisoners who were to compete in the 100-meter dash to assemble near him.

No sooner had we lined up on the starting markers than did Hasigawa walk away, leaving us standing there.

I had chosen the position on the inside of the track. While I waited for Hasigawa to return, I dug a pair of starting holes and tried a few starts. Not quite satisfied, I modified the holes and tried a few more starts. I then returned to my position and waited.

None of the other men in line were using starting holes except myself and the Japanese runner. The way he dug out on his starts verified my earlier suspicion that he was a ringer. His starting stance and his breakaway were too pat to be that of a beginner. He not only looked fast, but he had at least one advantage over the rest of us: he was wearing track shoes with spikes. Despite his apparent speed and track shoes, the one thing about him that really bothered me was the fact he was wearing his army uniform. I was sure he could run a lot faster if he wore shorts. Maybe he felt he had enough speed, especially against a bunch of tottering prisoners, and that being encumbered by a uniform was of no consequence. He would win no matter what. I peeled off my jacket to take every advantage I could get. All I was wearing were my green burlap trousers and a pair of split-toed sneakers.

The Japanese runner was short, dark-complexioned, and his head was shaven. He had just satisfied himself that his holes were right and took his position on the outside of the track, next to the stands. A stockily built British soldier, in a khaki shirt and shorts, was waiting quietly next to him. He caught me eyeing him and winked. I nodded. Beside the British soldier, clad in a bedsheet which he wore like a diaper, was a Hindu who appeared to be starving to death. He was nothing but skin and bones. Then a Javanese, who, like the Japanese, was dressed in full uniform, red piping and all. He was a tall boy with a square jaw and looked more Dutch than Javanese. A Chinese representative was next to him, rather old to be running anywhere, let alone a foot race. Actually, he had been a cook aboard an American merchant ship before it was sunk. The next four men all wore shorts and were stripped to the waist: a Filipino, a Guamanian, a Dutchman, and next to me, a Malayan. Of the four, the Dutchman was the only one that had any size, and except for him, they all had their heads shaved and looked very tired. There were ten contestants in all.

The Japanese civilian in the center of the field attracted my attention. He was yelling through the megaphone, first addressing one set of bleachers, then the other. At the same time I caught sight of Hasigawa on the track walking toward us with another Japanese civilian in tow. The other man was carrying a pistol. Hasigawa and his companion stopped in front of us.

"This is the hundred-meter race," Hasigawa announced, "and this man is your starter. He will count, *ichi* [one], *ni* [two], then shoot the pistol. Anyone who starts before the pistol shoots is not in the race." He paused to let it sink in. "Are there any questions?" he asked hopefully.

There was a time in the past months when a few serious men did ask for a clarification, only to pay for it by nearly getting their teeth slapped out. Recently, no one had given Hasigawa an opportunity to ply his sadistic traits, at least, not that way.

A few moments later, the starter, standing on the turf beside me, called out, "Ichi."

I nestled down in my holes.

"Ni."

I raised myself slightly, shifting part of my weight onto my hands—which I had placed on the ground in front of me—and tightened all my muscles in my legs, back, and arms, making ready to spring forward.

Bang! The gun fired.

I was away . . . away and out in front. There was no one within my vision to the left. A surge of power passed through my body. I felt that there was no limit to the speed I could attain. I ran faster and faster at will. Never before had I felt so in tune with the universe. This was my day. No man, past, present, or future, could outrun me in a race this day.

With ever increasing power and speed, I crossed the finish line, still accelerating. I swung off the track and into the infield, turning back toward the oncoming runners to see the Japanese was leading with yet ten meters to the finish line. The rest of the field trailed in a group by five meters. As the Japanese crossed the finish line, the crowd roared and waved their flags. As the last man finished, crossing the line, the officials rushed out to congratulate the Japanese soldier on his outstanding victory.

They marched him past me and out to the center of the field. Through a megaphone, one of the officials made an announcement to the crowd that caused them to cheer. The ceremony continued for about five minutes.

Meanwhile, dumbfounded, I sat down in the grass on the spot where I had stopped and watched in disbelief. I could have sworn I had won that race fair and square, but I was being treated as though I did not exist. Maybe it was because I'd run off the track into the infield.

With the backslapping completed, the group of Japanese retired to the bleachers. Kirkpatrick approached me as they passed.

"Terence," he grinned, "that was a pretty stupid thing you did. You were so far out in front, you were out of the race. Nobody can run as fast as you did—at least, not against the Japs." He laughed as he reached down to pat me on the shoulder.

"Better luck next time."

I knew there would never be a next time; I had had my chance and had somehow blown it.

"Moose," I questioned, "did I jump the gun back there?"

"Absolutely not, Terence. I was right there on the line; you were like a stone until after the gun went off," he assured me.

"I wonder why they counted me out?" I said aloud. "Do you have any idea, Moose?"

"It beats me," Kirkpatrick said. "Maybe they have some rules we never heard about."

Following that short conversation, Moose moved away, leaving me even more confused. Maybe it was like he said—I overdid it, but I could not help myself. In the many races I had run in the past, there was always a burst of speed in me that peaked somewhere along the track, and from there on to the finish line, sheer guts kept me running. But here, today, I had never peaked. There was still plenty of reserve even after I crossed the finish line.

Shortly, two Japanese dragged a small platform out to the center of the field. A few minutes later, a group of dignitaries followed, all dressed in the traditional Japanese kimonos. Each in turn mounted the platform and delivered his own brand of oratory. Having been taught only the gutter language by the soldiers, all this babbling of the upper crust went over my head. I really didn't care what they were saying. I got up and drifted over to join the prisoners of war at the far end of the field.

I had my lunch—two hamburger buns—while I sat on the grass and relaxed, waiting for the relay race to begin. I was thankful at least for this one day of rest, my first since I'd arrived in Japan.

Even though I'd lost my race, after Kirkpatrick had told me I hadn't jumped the gun, I felt I had won and was at peace with the world.

An hour passed; finally the call came for the runners of the relay race. Kirkpatrick came trotting across the field toward the prisoners. He called out, "Kirk, front and center."

I got to my feet, waved to him, and yelled back, "Me?"

He beckoned.

"Terence," he said when I reached him, "everyone wants you to run as starter for this relay race. Will you do it?"

"You bet I will, Moose; nothing would make me happier," I answered with enthusiasm.

"Just one thing," he cautioned. "Don't let them count you out again for jumping the gun. Wait until everyone is off their marks, then do what you do better than anyone—run like hell."

"Good thinking, Moose—I'll do it just like that," I agreed, in high spirits.

Kirkpatrick reached out and patted me on the shoulder like I was some kind of puppy dog, then he grinned. He had done the same thing to me so many times before when we worked together in

Tientsin as communication linemen. He knew it griped me, but he did it anyway. He was much bigger than I, and he would laugh when it made me angry. That was the only mean streak in him, however, and on this day I wasn't bothered in the least. I would tolerate anything to be able to run once more, on this, the day I could run like the wind.

Kirkpatrick trotted across the field to take up his position as anchorman. Somehow, I had the feeling that it was he who had arranged the switch. He must have talked the original starter into letting me take his place.

I reported to the starting line and picked up my baton. I chose the outside of the track this time, near the bleachers, to avoid tripping over someone or getting boxed in when everyone would be fighting for a pole position along the inside of the track.

Again, only the Jap had dug starting holes, but this runner was not the same soldier that had raced in the 100-meter. This guy was taller, with longer legs.

I felt that starting holes would be unnecessary because I had no intention of breaking away fast this trip. I could not afford to be scratched again.

Hasigawa stepped up and went through the same instructions he had given us in the earlier race.

When the gun fired this time, I hesitated, but only for an instant, just to make sure that all the runners were off their marks.

Satisfied, I sped forward, and within twenty-five meters I had overtaken and passed everyone, including the leading runner, the Japanese soldier. I stayed on the outside of the track instead of angling over to the inside curb, and went into the turn still on the high side until I was halfway through, and only then did I begin to drift to the inside. Halfway to the inside curb, I realized what a damn fool trick I had just pulled. I had lost precious ground because I'd wanted to show off.

Now, perhaps, I thought with dread, I had lost the race for the American team. A pang of shame shot through me for my indiscretion. I tried to atone for my sin by giving every ounce of strength I had in me for the little time and distance there was left.

I passed the baton to Westmorland, a swarthy, stocky marine from the Wake Island detachment. He started in good form and was far down the track when the Japanese passed their baton. Before their second runner could pick up his stride, Westmorland went pounding into the turn going away. Through the turn and into the straightaway, he pulled further and further ahead of the Japanese with every stride. The gap was also widening between the Japanese runner and the rest of the pack.

Wes passed the stick to Salay, a North China Marine, about the time the Japanese was three-quarters of the way through the turn. The rest of the runners were stretched out behind one another entering the turn. Salay took the baton and started moving out. From my vantage point he appeared to be running stiff-legged. I groaned inwardly, but as I watched intently, he seemed to be traveling at a good clip. I was afraid that with his peculiar style of running, he would tire or pull a muscle. As he came around the turn and down the backstretch toward me, I realized my worry was for nothing. He was coming on strong. If he was weakening, he did not show it. His pace remained unchanged and determined. He was actually moving away. The ever-widening distance between him and his nearest competitor, the Japanese, was becoming awesome.

Kirkpatrick grabbed the baton from Salay long before any of the runners had cleared the turn into the backstretch. He was away in a burst of speed. Kirkpatrick was six feet tall and more, a regular Adonis with the physique and looks to match—broad shoulders, narrow waist, well muscled, and handsome.

Moose had a great advantage over the rest of us on the team. He was not suffering from malnutrition because his job was in the galley where he got plenty to eat. He was up to full strength, and right now he was using it to our best advantage. His powerful strides carried him along, covering seven to eight feet at a bound. I watched spellbound as he completed the turn and entered the homestretch.

I glanced behind me in time to see the Japanese runners pass their baton. Their anchorman was none other than the one who had been credited for having won the 100-meter dash.

A pall had fallen over the stadium. When it had happened I wasn't sure, but after I had passed the baton and stood in the infield watching the race, I felt the crowd was strangely quiet.

The Japanese was a good twenty meters ahead of his nearest rival going into the final turn as Kirkpatrick, running like a demon, crossed the finish line.

I sank to my knees, completely awash with emotion—that we could have beaten them so badly! The glow of victory caused a lump to well up in my throat; my eyes filled with tears and I uttered a sob. I could not help myself. Even though I tried to fight it, I could not hold it back. We had done it! A rout, a complete and utter disaster for the Japanese team. We had destroyed their plan to show the Japanese people how great they were, I chortled.

Hasigawa called the American team together behind the bleachers, not out in the middle of the field as had been the case of the winner of the 100-meter dash. Here he said, "You have won the race. For that you will receive a prize." And so saying, he handed each of us a package of cigarettes and at the same time delivered a stinging blow to our cheeks. After completing the awards, Hasigawa stepped back, scowling. "Winners must also have humility," he said hotly.

Suddenly, my cheek no longer smarted. I wanted to shout, *We spoiled your day, you little bastard!* I also wanted to keep on living, so suppressed that impulse.

The next week, Hasigawa called a meeting of all boontychos to inform us that there was going to be a change in the amount of food we were to receive from here on out. Winning the race may have had something to do with it.

"All Japanese are conserving food," Hasigawa told us. "Prisoners of war must also have a cut in rations. In the future, prisoners of war are to receive five hundred calories a day instead of seven hundred and fifty."

I had no idea what he was talking about until the next day. I discovered the Japs had replaced all the rice in our rations with millet. This worried me because it was hard enough to climb that damn hill on 750 calories. How could we possibly do it on 500?

Maybe they thought if we could outrun their best athletes, we were being fed too many calories. Whatever the reason, our future looked mighty bleak.

1 1

Kokura

All my worries about scaling the hill on short rations suddenly vanished. Three weeks after the cut in rations, just as everyone was preparing to leave for work, Hasigawa called all room leaders to the office. We waited in the hallway for a long time, perhaps an hour. It was past time that we should have departed for work. Most of the men were in the corridors milling about, coming by and asking what was happening.

Finally Hasigawa came out of the office to spring the surprise—that our future was about to change.

"Today," he announced, "you are moving to a new camp. It will be your new home. There are new buildings that were built especially for you. It is a long way from here, so you will go by train. There will be no transports. Tell your men they can take only what they can carry, no more," he cautioned.

"I am not going with you; you will have another interpreter at your new camp." He saved that choice bit of information for last. He said it as if we should grieve that he was not coming with us.

I explained to my men what I had been told. Of course, they wanted to know more—Where are we going? How far? And so on. I promised them they would all find out when we got there.

I had but few worldly possessions left to pack. I had eaten almost everything I owned; that is, I traded what I had to the Japanese civilians and Koreans for soybeans. My wardrobe and incidentals consisted of one green burlap work suit, a cap similar to a baseball cap, a pair of split-toed sneakers, and a heavy overcoat. All these articles were furnished by the steel company and the Japanese army. I had also managed to save my brother's bathrobe. Last but not least, I had a double handful of toothbrushes and many cans of tooth powder. The Japanese were overly generous with their dental supplies. There was one thing certain: If we were killed, accidentally or otherwise, or died of starvation or disease, they were going to make sure we left this world with a clean set of teeth.

We cleared the citadel within an hour after being notified we were to move. I looked back as we started down the hill for the last time, thankful that my tour of duty in that miserable, cold, concrete hole had finally ended. Any place would be better, anywhere away from that damn mountain.

We took the same route to the factory that we used everyday, but instead of splitting into our respective groups as we had each morning for the past six months, we remained in one column. The guards marched us until we were halted beside a train of ten or more open gondola cars. The guards motioned for us to board the train. We tossed our gear into the cars and climbed the ladders at either end, then jumped down into the beds. We were told to sit down on the steel floor plates.

Our range of vision was greatly restricted at this low position. We could only see what passed overhead. Presently, with neck-snapping jerks, the train moved forward and we passed over a short suspension bridge. Next, we entered a tunnel that was about a mile in length. Out of the tunnel and in the open again, there was nothing to see but blue sky. The train proceeded on for half an hour or so, then surprised us with a very rough stop.

Out of the cars, we found ourselves in a railroad yard. The soldiers moved us away from the tracks along a dirt path in an easterly direction. The countryside was different than that of Yawata. Here there were absolutely no people, no houses, and best of all, there were no hills. Farming was nowhere in evidence, at least not to the casual observer. All around us the fields were overgrown with high weeds. The best word to describe the area was—neglect.

North of us was a great body of water that stretched away to the horizon. The general consensus was that it was the Inland Sea or the Sea of Japan.

A huge hydroelectric plant sat like a beacon on its shore. In spite of the Japanese effort to camouflage the tremendous complex by dabbing it with green, brown, and white paint, it remained conspicuous by its solitude and huge smokestacks belching black clouds of smoke into the clear sky.

As we proceeded, keeping the hydroelectric plant on our left, we came upon an enclosure with walls too high to scale without the help of a rope and grappling hooks. This had to be our new home. Atop the wall I could see two machine-gun towers. As we passed the corner of the compound under one of the towers, I noted a guard looking at us through the sights of a light machine gun.

Further along the wall we came to a pair of huge doors, opening into the enclosure. As we entered, to our right was an open guard room filled with soldiers watching us. On our left was a single-story building with a lot of windows facing the street. It looked like an office.

Beyond the guardhouse, on the right side of the street, were six two-story buildings; on the opposite side of the street, beyond the office, were four more. All of them were built of wood with windows on the south and north sides of the buildings from the ground to the eaves. Another single-story structure blocked the far end of the street.

The prisoners, standing four abreast, stretched the full length of the street. If I were a betting man, I would lay odds that our prisoner count was well over a thousand men.

All the North China Marines were assigned to the second barracks from the office on the west side of the street—barracks number two. The barracks consisted of four sections, of approximately thirty-six men each. The marines were placed in section two, the forward half of the north and south upper tiers. The other three were made up of a section of Hindu sailors, one of Javanese soldiers, and the last, of British soldiers.

As soon as all the marines were in the barracks, I stood on my mat near the edge of the tier and called for everyone's attention. I waited until the noise abated and most of the men were looking at me. "I am taking the job as boontycho of section two," I declared emphatically.

"If there are any objections by anyone who outranks me, you are invited to come up here and take my place. If not, forever hold your peace."

There were no comments or attemps to oust me from my new, self-appointed position. I couldn't blame them for not wanting the job, if it turned out to be anything like the room leader's role at the citadel. As for me, I still felt that any control—no matter how small— over my destiny and that of the men in my charge, was better than none. I did what my conscience dictated.

The first challenge to my authority came with the evening meal. Each section had sent a man to the galley, the building at the north end of the street. When the food arrived, the Hindu was first to enter with a full bucket of rice and go scooting past toward his section. The Javanese did the same with another full bucket of rice. The Britisher stopped just inside the door with two buckets of soup. Our marine entered last with a half bucket of rice and two empty buckets.

I could see immediately there was need for supervision. I jumped to my feet and yelled to the Hindu and Javanese, "Hey, bring that goddamned chow back to the front of the barracks!" And without taking a breath, added, "All section leaders get your asses down here on the double. We have a chow problem. Make it fast—we're hungry!" I shouted above the din.

The Hindu and Javanese both stopped dead in their tracks, did an about-face, and started back toward the entrance.

Well trained, I mused.

On their heels and in a hurry came the Hindu chief wrapped in a white cloth. Behind him, a Dutchman in a dark-brown woolen uniform and wearing a tam-o'-shanter. The Limey in charge of the British section stuck his head from under the tier directly below me. "Who dah yah tink yah are, Yank?" he protested. "Tah hear yah talk, yud tink yah was the captain o' dis bloody billet."

I crawled down off the tier and faced the Englishman. He was a sergeant, a big man, and wore a scowl, which did nothing for his looks.

"I just took charge of this bloody billet," I snapped. "Someone has to establish order out of all this chaos. What's more, I'm going to remain the top kick of this outfit until the Japs say otherwise," I informed him. "If I am unable to handle this job by myself," I added, in case he was wondering where I came by my authority, "I have thirty-five marines who would be only too happy to back me." I nodded toward the upper tiers.

The marines were all standing along the edge of the tier looking down on us. With all the noise in the barracks, they could not possibly have heard what we were saying. They were probably curious to see what was holding up the chow. Their hunger, I was sure, brought them to watch.

The sergeant glanced up into the solemn faces, then turned back to me. "Ah guess yah could say might is right, aye, Yank?" he grinned.

"If that is what it takes to get the job done," I agreed.

I turned my attention to the Hindu and the Dutchman. "Do you guys understand English?" I asked.

They both nodded assent.

"OK, I will lay out a plan. If you have a better idea, we will take it from there.

"We now have seven buckets, but we need another to divide the food so there will be a bucket of rice and a bucket of stew for each section. If you agree, I will send to the galley for another bucket to make this idea work.

"I propose that we divide the rice first. We will use one of our aluminum bowls to dish out the rice. Beginning with the half bucket of rice, we will divide it bowl for bowl into the three empty buckets. When the half bucket is empty, fill it from one of the full buckets to match the first three. The rest of the rice will be divided equally into the four buckets until there is less than four bowls left. Next, and most important, so everyone will receive an equal amount of rice over the long run, the remaining rice will be dished out in fully packed bowls, beginning with section one, then section two, and so on. If there is not enough rice to make a fully packed bowl, what there is will be scattered, as equally as possible, among the four buckets.

"I will keep a record of who gets the next full bowl of extra rice. Within a few meals the quantity of rice will balance out so each section will, in time, get the same amount.

"Dividing the stew should pose no problem. We will have two buckets of stew and two empty buckets. Make sure that all sections get an equal amount of daikon." [white radishes] I paused, waiting for a comment, but got no response.

"Well, how about it?" I demanded. "Does anyone have a better idea?"

"I like it," the Hindu was first to speak. "There is no reason I can think of why it should not work."

"Good plan," chimed in the Dutchman.

I looked at the British sergeant questioningly.

"Wud yah mind repeatin' that again, Yank?" he grinned.

"Not on your life," I growled. "This is a hell of a time for levity. Get serious. We have all these people waiting for food. You will just have to trust me," I said soberly.

"Jolly good, Yank, as long as we're getting the grub, but the first time it stops, watch out." He shook his finger at me as he ducked under the tier and out of sight.

In a few minutes we had the extra bucket and the crisis was over. Everyone had settled back to eat the lousy chow we had been enduring ever since we won the race.

The mess men who brought the extra bucket from the galley informed me that the single-story building blocking the end of the street was not only a galley, but also the prisoners' bath—the west half of it. In the center was a smaller bathroom for the Jap soldiers.

Our captors felt that we must not waste any more time than necessary in our new home. The next morning, we marched back to the railroad yard and boarded the open gondola cars for a ride back to the factory. Our jobs were the same—only our address was different. We now lived a half-hour's train ride north of the factory. Most of the prisoners worked near the train's terminus, in the machine and auto repair shops. Only the Yoheen gang and one other group had any distance to hike from the train station. The scrap iron detail had two to three miles to walk, and the other group that worked in the rolling mills had a mile or so to get to their jobs.

This day, except for the train ride, was like all the others—until morning break. We had gathered in our corrugated-iron shed for rest and relaxation when Henry Hahne of Turlock, California, a great big country boy, standing in the doorway, spotted a little girl holding a leash being dragged across the field by a large German shepherd on the other end. He called everyone's attention to the fact that she and the dog were heading our way. Henry watched them for a moment, then turned to us and said in a hushed voice, "If you guys can keep the girl occupied for a few minutes, I will get her dog and we will have meat for lunch."

This is crazy, I thought, *but it should prove interesting, no matter how it turns out.*

Joe Walker, of Clearwater, Florida, a tall, bony, hawk-faced individual with a whimsical grin, as though everything was a big joke, and Langston, the chicken-soup man, both got up and went outside to help in any way they could. The rest of us followed to see what was going to happen.

Walker called to the little girl and when she came near, he offered her a lot of gibberish that sounded like Japanese. Between Walker and Langston, they managed to gain her undivided attention. Meanwhile, Henry began petting the dog, and when the girl let go of the leash, he stealthily led the animal behind the iron shack.

The girl was still trying to make some sense out of what Walker and Langston were saying when Cawashima and Tacashima returned from the equipment shed; both of them bade the girl leave at once. She protested and began calling her dog, but the dog did not come. Cawashima insisted she leave, and she began to cry, and tried to tell him something. I am sure it was about her dog, but Cawashima did not want to listen. He made her leave.

It was pitiful to watch. She would walk a short distance, turn back and call her dog. Cawashima would yell at her and she would move a little further, then turn around again and call her dog. Finally, after five or six tries, she gave up and disappeared. Before I returned to the scrap pile, I went into the shack and opened my mess kit. Hank had not been kidding; there on top of my rice was a slab of fresh meat, red with blood. I quickly buried it under my rice and poured some boiling water into the mess kit from our can of drinking water. We always kept water boiling on the stove. I took the mess kit with me out to the scrap pile and put it on my oxygen bottle stove so the meat would cook by lunch time.

In two hours, we knocked off for lunch. I could hardly wait to sink my teeth into that big hunk of meat. I opened my mess kit after finding a comfortable seat, dug up the meat from under the rice and for the first time in what seemed like years, I gazed at all that meat and actually drooled. The instant I bit into that piece of dog, I blurted, "Damn, that is the most god awful meat I ever tasted!" My taste buds turned inside out and told me I had just bitten into the north end of a southbound skunk.

"What the hell did you expect?" Henry chuckled. "Filet mignon?"

The meat and all my rice tasted like a wet dog smells. There was no way, now that I had gotten myself into this situation, that I would ever think of wasting all my food by throwing it away. I did what everyone else was doing, bad taste and all, and gagged it down.

"Hank," I asked, in the middle of my dog dinner, "how the hell did you kill, gut, skin, and butcher that dog in less than ten minutes, and what happened to the head and the rest of it?"

"In the first place," Hank laughed, "I only killed the dog and cut off its hind legs. Bernstein and Williams took care of the remains."

"Oh," I exclaimed. "Tell me, what did you cut it up with, and how did you do it so fast?"

"Easy," he said, holding up a good-sized pocketknife, a real toad stabber. "I worked on my father's ranch most of my life before I became a merchant seaman. We raised all kinds of animals for market and did most of the slaughtering ourselves."

"No disrespect intended, Hank," I remarked, "but that was the foulest meat I have ever had the misfortune to have eaten. This is one time I regret you ever knew anything about butchering."

"Now, what the hell did you expect," he rebuked me. "A dog is a dog is a dog."

Silence followed our little tête-à-tête. No one had anything to offer. A thought popped into my head and for the hell of it, I broached the question. "Is there anyone who feels for the little girl?"

Instantly, I was showered with epithets and a few choice abusive and scurrilous remarks, all of which told me they *did* care and were angry because I had brought it up. I had to laugh aloud.

"You might consider that a Japanese dog has just become a casualty for aiding and abetting the enemy," Walker volunteered.

Everyone chuckled at that.

"The Japs owe us a lot more than one lousy dog," Hoyt Williams of Beaumont, Texas, spoke up, "but if that is all we can get, it beats digging in the garbage piles. As vile as that dog was, I am sure I got more food value from that hunk of meat than I ever got from the garbage heaps."

Most of us felt the same way; at least, that kind of rationalizing made us feel better about the whole affair.

Weeks after the dog incident, the smell of the animal still persisted in and around my mess kit. I tried many ways to eliminate the odor, but scrubbing the mess kit with sand, ashes, soap, or boiling water was all to no avail. There was nothing I could do but let it wear off.

The problem of getting rid of the dog smell faded when I found myself faced with an even greater worry—malaria had come back to pester me once again. Sergeant William Killebrew, a North China Marine from Peking, also contracted the disease and was having an attack at the same time. His bunk was four mats away from mine. We both drew ourselves into the fetal position under our pile of blankets and shivered and shook. Our teeth chattered in unison while the sweat poured off us in rivulets. My attack lasted three days as usual, with a series of chills and fevers that came at eight- to ten-hour intervals, with a respite between each seizure. When it was over, I could hardly stand. On the third day, Killebrew was taken to the hospital because he developed a very bad cough. The hospital was merely a place where the Japanese put the terminally ill prisoners. There was no more medicine or care there than there was in the barracks. I take it back—there was a greater abundance of charcoal.

Following my three-day bout with malaria, I was given two days to recuperate before I would again be forced to return to work. On my second day, I was lounging on my mat and trying to figure out a letter I had just received from a person in Glasgow, Scotland, who claimed to be my Aunt Bessy. It was two pages long and told of bad weather and two sick kids. Until I received the letter, I hadn't been aware that I had an aunt anywhere. It seemed that not only did I have an aunt, but she lived in Glasgow, Scotland. It must have been true because the letter was addressed to Terence Sumner Kirk, a name not too common. I wondered if she was my mother's or my father's sister. My meandering thoughts were suddenly interrupted.

"Hey, did you guys hear the good news?" a prisoner yelled as he burst into the barracks, "we won the battle of Midway Island!"

That news was old to me. I had heard rumors of our victory in some kind of skirmish at Midway when I was in Woosung; however, it was all hush-hush because it was supposed to have come from a radio that the marines had hidden away. Everyone was to act as though they knew nothing; that way the guards would not go looking for our source of news—in this case, the radio.

I crawled to the edge of the tier. "Where did you get that information?" I asked.

He looked up at me from the floor, his face flushed with excitement. "A merchant seaman by the name of Rodgers in barracks five just got the letter this morning from his brother," he said jubilantly.

It was good news. I lay back on my bunk and began pondering Bessy's letter, but my mind kept wandering back to our victory at Midway. It seemed weird that the Japanese would let something like that slip through without censoring it.

In a few minutes my curiosity got the better of me. I had to see Rodgers. With nothing else to do, I drifted over to barracks five.

Rodgers was not too difficult to find. The guy that brought the news said he was redheaded with lots of freckles. He also had a crowd around him, discussing and speculating on the size of the battle.

"My name is Kirk," I introduced myself. "I am from barracks two. I heard about your letter and the battle of Midway. Is it true your brother was able to get that information to you through the Japs?"

"Sure," he answered with exuberance. "Would you like to see the letter?"

Without waiting for me to answer, he took a folded piece of paper out of his shirt pocket and handed it to me.

"Wait," he cautioned, "before you read the letter there are a few things you must know; otherwise the letter will fool you, just as it did the Japs. Without knowing the key points, the letter won't make sense."

"Oh?" I questioned, raising my eyebrows.

"First off," he explained, paying no attention to my skepticism, "the letter was signed by my mother. I regret to say, both my mother and father are long dead. They were both killed in an automobile accident ten years ago. There are only two left in my family, my identical twin brother John and myself. I knew he was the one that wrote the letter. It was like I wrote it myself when I realized he did it.

"He mentioned my eastern cousins. To my knowledge I have none, at least none that John or I know of. The eastern cousins had me puzzled for a bit, but finally it dawned on me he meant the Japanese. The halfway house he talked about was Midway, and the reception or party was the battle. My father's brother Samuel threw me for a while, because my father was an only child. Then it dawned on me what he was trying to get across. To me, my father's brother would be my uncle—Uncle Sam, of course.

"That's it. You have all the key words. Read it," he urged. I unfolded the letter. It read:

Frank,

I hope you are well. This short note is to let you know that a lot of your relatives had a planned reception at the halfway house. They invited many of your eastern cousins, the ones that you are not too fond of.

I would liked to have been there, but I was busy elsewhere at the time. Your father's brother, Samuel, was there and he said that in spite of your eastern cousins, the party was a howling success.

Love, Mother

I looked up from the letter. Frank beamed with a grin from ear to ear. "What do you think? That brother of mine is a slick one?"

"He convinced me," I assured him. "It looks like he put one over on your eastern cousins too. I had heard rumors last year about Midway when I was in Woosung, China, but this is the first real confirmation."

I returned to my barracks and Aunt Bessy's letter that I had left lying on my mat. A thought struck me as I gathered up the letter to hide under my blankets. Maybe this letter is in code like Rodgers's letter. This one makes no sense either, unless there is a key somewhere. I was not ready to try to decipher it, not then. I put the letter under my pile of blankets at the head of my mat to work on at a later date. I lay back on my mat and relaxed, dreaming about the end of the war. At least we were winning once in a while. My spirits began to rise as I was sure the war must be coming to an end. That evening, when the prisoners were back from work and the news permeated the camp, everyone was elated.

The high spirits carried over into the next day at work. The Yoheen gang could talk of nothing else. At noon, while we were sitting in our little shack eating our millet, someone suggested we all help Uncle Sam with his war effort. It was proposed that we bleed our oxygen tanks during the night. Instead of turning the bottles off tight when we secured for the day, we were to crack the valves just enough so they would leak, but not so much that they could be heard. Each morning, with no oxygen, we would kill time doing nothing while waiting for the next shipment of oxygen. In the discussion, it was theorized that this kind of sabotage would cause the Japanese to work overtime to provide oxygen for us that they would not normally be required to do.

I sat listening, but made no comment until it had been hashed over and agreed upon; then I spoke to Walker, the instigator. "How long do you think you can get away with a dumb trick like that?"

"A dumb trick, is it?" he boomed. "What are you, some kind of traitor?"

"Let us not be stupid," I rebuffed him. "Think of it. They don't need us. Look around you—all the scrap we have ever cut up since we started working on this scrap iron pile is still here. They haven't used one bit of it," I said angrily. "Why the hell should they keep furnishing us with oxygen?"

"You missed the point," he said, lowering his voice. "We know we can't win the war by leaking oxygen, but we can put an additional strain on the Japs. It may be small, but nevertheless, it will hurt them somewhere."

"Small," I echoed. "*Infinitesimal* is the word you are looking for."

"So," he looked wide-eyed at me, "does that mean you are not with us?"

"No, that doesn't mean I'm not with you, but either way, I'm damned if I do and damned if I don't," I growled. "I'll go down swinging with the rest of you, but I still think it's a stupid idea, wait and see."

"I would have been willing to bet you would see it our way," Walker said with a grin.

That evening, we left the site with all the oxygen bottles leaking quietly.

Back in camp, I received the sad news that one of my men had died. Sergeant Killebrew had succumbed to pneumonia. I couldn't help thinking of the statement made by Cordell Hull, the Secretary of State, to President Roosevelt: "If we don't get the flower of the American youth out of China, they'll be nipped in the bud."

Killebrew was a good marine, young, healthy, and handsome. He was too young to die. A minimal amount of medical care would have saved his life, but we had nothing. The Japanese, who controlled the world's supply of quinine, refused to give us any help.

The following morning, the sergeant's remains were loaded on the dead-run cart with the bodies of two other prisoners who had died the same day. The dead run moved out to the crematorium at the same time the prisoners left for work.

We arrived at the scrap pile to find all the bottles we had left cracked the night before—empty. As Walker had predicted, after the tanks in the reserve pile were used up, we rested and waited for the next delivery. The following day was like the day before, except for a longer period without oxygen. That was because there were fewer reserve tanks to draw from. Though I had had misgivings about the whole idea in the very beginning, I was enjoying the rest and relaxation. On the third day, there was absolutely no oxygen in any of the tanks. Even the Japanese cutters were sitting idle.

All the time, Cawashima never let on that he knew what we were doing. I was sure he must have known. No one could be that stupid. Nevertheless, he was his congenial self through it all, always smiling.

The weather was exceedingly warm for late August, and most of us were taking advantage of the shade offered by the overhanging steel plates jutting from the scrap pile. Most, that is, except Jack Bernstein of Kansas City, Missouri. He was sweating in the sun, moving his carbide generator. Although he was stocky and appeared to be having little or no trouble moving the 30-gallon tank full of water, I wondered why he was doing it the hard way. It would have been much easier to dump the water, move the empty tank, then refill it. I didn't have the energy to call that to his attention, so I leaned back quietly and watched him work as he positioned the tank beneath a power pole.

With the prospect of a long delay in the next oxygen shipment, none of us bothered to charge our acetylene generators. However, Bernstein began loading his carbide basket (the stuff that makes acetylene gas when dipped in water). Next, he hung the basket on a hook inside the bell and set the bell into the water in the bottom half of the generator, causing the unit to begin generating gas.

By one o'clock the gas pressure within his bell and the heat from the sun had caused the bell to rise out of the water by two-thirds its length, about two feet.

Shortly thereafter, the oxygen arrived and we all set to work charging our acetylene generators. I had just dropped the bell of my generator into the bottom tank and turned to hook up my oxygen . . .

A terrific explosion burst on my ears! The shock wave almost knocked me down. I quickly regained my bearings and turned back in time to see the top half of Bernstein's generator sailing high into the sky, some thirty or forty feet. I watched as it reached its apex and began falling back to earth.

Cawashima came running toward us along the railroad tracks from the direction of the equipment shed. His smile was gone now and when he sized up what had happened, he ordered Bernstein to pick up all the pieces, plus the rest of his equipment, and return all of it to the equipment shed.

Cawashima looked up at the broken cross arm dangling by its insulator on the wire and swinging back and forth, bumping against the power pole. The top of Bernstein's generator was a crumpled mess where it had smashed into the cross arm on its upward journey. Cawashima shook his head and uttered something that sounded like *Exso*.

Cawashima was distraught and angry with Bernstein. For the rest of the day, he put Bernstein to work moving and stacking scrap iron.

That evening on the train, I was sitting beside Bernstein. After the train began to move, I asked him, "What were you trying to do this afternoon, knock down the power line?"

"You betcha," he laughed.

"Why?"

"I figured if I could knock out that power line, a lot of motors would stop, there would be a lot of people in the dark who would have to stop working, and who knows what else."

"Good thinking. Too bad you missed," I offered.

"I think that was damn good shooting anyway," he boasted.

"I have seen better," I said sarcastically, as long as he was taking an ego trip. "The wire was still intact. Next time let us know what you are trying to do. Someone could have been killed by that generator top."

"That's war," he said with complacency. "In war, somebody always gets hurt. That is what makes war hell."

"It's the enemy you are supposed to hurt, not your friends," I reminded him. "By the way, what was the idea of wrestling that generator tank full of water when you could have dumped it and moved it empty?" I asked, puzzled.

"Simple," he turned to face me. "If any of the pushers at the shack where we get the water, or the Jap workers, had seen me going back for a second helping, they might have become curious and spoiled the whole plan."

"I can appreciate your wanting to help the war effort, Bernstein, but all you succeeded in doing was to break one cross arm, mess up your equipment, and scare hell out of a lot of people. Next time, let us in on it, will you? So at least we can take cover." I implored.

"I'll have to give it some more serious thought," he said absent-mindedly.

1 2

The Broken Block

The morning following Bernstein's explosion, instead of our usual routine of picking up our hoses and cutting equipment, we marched past the equipment shed with Tacashima leading the way. Cawashima, who always accompanied us from the train to the job, on this day stopped at the scrap pile to oversee the Japanese crew and left us in Tacashima's hands.

We tried to question Tacashima as to our destination, but all we could get out of him was, "No burn."

We followed him along a railroad track for a half mile to a group of tall, dilapidated, corrugated-iron buildings. We entered the first, where there were sheets of corrugated iron missing from the sides here and there and half the roof was gone. Strewn about in piles were deteriorated straw sacks, like the ones I stole noodles from a while back in the citadel. These were full of chrome ore. That is, the bags were bursting at the seams and the ore had spilled out all over the ground. There was a huge pile of new straw sacks just outside the entrance that I had noticed when we entered the building. It didn't take a genius to figure out what was in store for us.

Tacashima set us to work filling the new sacks and stacking them neatly in piles. One bag, when filled, weighed about 200 pounds. It took four of us to lift it in place.

During our lunch break, Tacashima encouraged us to look in the other buildings. He was delighted to inform us that tidying up the first building was only the beginning. All the other sheds needed the same kind of treatment. The only difference between the one we were working in and the others was the type of ore they contained, which varied between tungsten, manganese, magnesium, etc. It made little difference to us because filled, all the bags were heavy, and stacking them, in our physical condition, was damn hard work. It was plain to see that our future work promised not only to be tedious, but back-breaking as well.

After our tour of inspection, we returned to the first building for the remainder of our lunch period. One thing I expected—but did not hear—was griping about our new job. There was no doubt in my mind, and I am sure it was no mystery to the rest of the Yoheen gang, that leaking oxygen from the tanks was a sure way to end up doing hard, unskilled labor.

The days crept by slowly as we labored in the ore sheds. While the weather was hot, the interiors of the buildings were like ovens. As we sweated and grunted our spirits dragged more by the hour. Finally, by late November, we had filled our last bag with ore and had stacked it, only to find, since the rains had begun, all the straw sacks in the building containing the chrome ore had fallen apart because they had been piled in a part of the building without a roof. We had to painstakingly sack the ore again and transport it to the far end of the building, the end with the roof.

Our next assignment was moving 55-gallon drums a distance of about a half mile. Each man pulled a barrel off the mountainous pile of barrels, rolled it across fairly level ground to a new site—where it was stacked with the help of another prisoner—then trudged back for another.

This time of the year, the rain began coming down in earnest. If it had not been for the rain, our job would have been tolerable. We could roll the barrels at a walk, which was not as strenuous as lifting ore sacks, but all we had to keep the rain off were straw capes and coolie hats. Tacashima issued us the capes and hats each day when we arrived at work. The capes would shed water for about twenty minutes, provided they were dry when we put them on. Beyond that, as raincoats, they were useless. Unless we had a dry spell for a week or so, the capes never dried out. Everyday, all day, we were soaked to the skin. To add to our discomfort, the cold of November made us don our heavy burlap overcoats, which were not exactly water-repellent.

As a matter of fact, they were more like sponges. They held a hell of a lot of water. After working in the rain for two hours or more, the straw capes, our overcoats, and all our clothing were soaked. That added an additional ten or more pounds we had to carry around all day. Carrying ourselves was burden enough.

Wintertime in Japan, or at least on the Island of Kyushu, promises rain almost every day, or so it seemed. Sometimes when the thermometer dipped, it snowed.

If the coming winter we were facing was to be anything like the last, we could expect the temperature to drop below freezing several times before spring. Last winter was wet, but we were protected from the cold by our little stoves that we used to heat the oxygen bottles; the stoves kept us warm and dry.

After spending all day in the rain, back at camp, we would shed our clothes and wring them out to dry; however, there was no heat in the buildings, so they never did dry. Being wet, cold, and shrivelled like a prune from the rain, I did the only thing I could do to keep warm: I grabbed my towel each day and ran naked through the rain or snow to the bathhouse at the end of the street. The hot bath, like the one in Yawata, was heated almost to the boiling point by live steam. Without the hot bath to restore our body heat, a lot more of us would have perished. It was a real lifesaver.

Each day I would crawl into the scalding hot water until I was submerged to my chin. I would remain motionless, partially buoyed up by the water, and let my body suck up the heat. It warmed me all the way to the bone marrow in only a few minutes. Reluctantly, I emerged from the pool fifteen to twenty minutes later, but not before being prodded by the guards to make room for other prisoners.

In spite of the edge the bath gave us in our fight for survival, one of the Yoheen gang, Old Barney Moody of Monrovia, California, caught pneumonia and died when December 1943 was only a few days old. Barney was about forty-five years of age, very old for a prisoner of war living under these severe conditions.

Christmas day, we were still working hard on the barrels. It had been raining most of the day. Three o'clock rolled around and with it, a chilling wind from the north that changed the rain to snow. Not ordinary snowflakes, these; they were oversized, soggy and about as big as a silver dollar. The snow came thick and fast, and it was difficult to see beyond a few yards in any direction.

When the soldiers emerged out of the blanket of snow from the direction of the factory at five o'clock to escort us to the train, the snow on the ground was well over our ankles. On the train, the snow was deep, but we were made to sit down in it.

I spotted Frances Bulgardus of the Yoheen gang, from Eureka, Illinois, sitting directly across from me. He was gritting his teeth, embracing his knees drawn up under his chin, and had tears in his eyes.

"Something the matter, Bulgardus?" I asked. "Are you hurting?"

"Hurting!" he exclaimed. "I am soaked to the skin and so damn cold—if I ever get out of this alive," he cried out in anguish, "I will NEVER, NEVER, NEVER be cold again as long as I live."

I agreed with him. It was pretty miserable, but there was absolutely nothing we could do about it.

The train started moving, and as we passed over the suspension bridge, the vibrations set up by the wheels crossing over the rail joints shook the bridge and loosened a huge glob of slushy snow on the superstructure. It slipped and came plummeting down, landing with a resounding plop, completely engulfing Bulgardus.

"Jesus Christ!" he screamed, jumping to his feet.

The guard at the end of the car yelled at him to sit down, but when he saw what caused Bulgardus to break the rules, he laughed. Bulgardus shook himself and sank down into the pile of snow again, completely dejected.

I couldn't help myself. I must have been born with a mean streak, but I had to say it: "See, Frances—there's no situation so bad that it can't be worse."

His look of despair turned to disgust, "At a time like this," he sneered, "you go straight to hell." With that he ignored me. I chuckled to myself. I thought the whole episode was funny despite the grim circumstances.

The last week in December, in one of our rare visits to the equipment shed, we were in the process of eating our lunch and enjoying the heat from the stove when Cawashima and Nishi walked in. A chorus went up to Cawashima—"When are we going to burn again?"

He laughed, grinned, and waved his hands as though he were fending off a cloud of gnats, then answered, "*Mata, mata.*"

What that meant, none of us knew.

"I have a question," Nishi said, holding up his hands to quiet us down. "Is there anyone here that knows anything about welding cast iron?"

"Why do you want to know?" I asked, after no one answered for some time.

"The factory has a Chrysler marine engine," he said as he moved closer to me. "It has a crack in the block and they are hoping to salvage it."

"It can be welded," I assured him. "It is a rather complicated process."

I thought back to my school days, a particular lecture by Harry Kuhn, my instructor in the blacksmith shop at Mooseheart High School, way back in Illinois. The lecture dealt with this very thing. Harry had a small casting which he heated red-hot in the forge; he welded it while it was still red hot, then replaced the welded casting in the forge and covered it with live coals to let it cool in a dying fire. I also remember him saying, "This is only a theory, but tomorrow we will find out if it works."

I never did find out the results of his experiment because the next day, I played hooky. At that time, I was just a boy with childish ideas; none of them included welding cast iron or anything else in that line.

"Would you mind spending a few days in the machine shop to explain to those people how it is done?" Nishi asked, bringing me back from my reminiscing.

I looked at Nishi, puzzled. This was the guy I told when I first met him that I knew absolutely nothing about welding. Now he was asking me to show the Japanese how to weld cast iron. I was glad he had a short memory.

"No, I wouldn't mind at all," I assured him. Thinking to myself, if I can spend two, three, maybe four days inside, out of the rain and cold, I would do anything. I would have been happy for even one day.

"If you like," I volunteered, "I will weld it myself."

Nishi walked away and talked to Cawashima, then came back.

"Report to the machine shop in the morning; I'll see you there."

I fell in with the mechanics the next morning, and when I arrived, Nishi was waiting. He found a stool for me and bade me wait until he returned to interpret my instructions to the Japanese workmen. Before he left, he talked to the foreman and explained my presence. I sat on the stool for about two hours enjoying the warmth of the building, and watched the rain beat against the windowpanes.

During that time I observed the prisoners at work. Like the Yoheen gang, until we were assigned to the labor details, they were not killing themselves by overwork. Once I was distracted by a group of young Japanese trainees, who were outside in the rain. I could see them through the windows, in the street, practicing what appeared to be bayonet drill. What attracted me was their yelling. As I watched, they would lunge forward with their broomsticks, making a stabbing thrust, and at the same time calling out, "*Oie saw*," then take another step, thrust again, and yell, "*Yoi saw*."

Their exercise lasted about ten minutes. What impressed me most was that despite the cold and rain, they were all stripped to the waist, except for a towel around their necks. I shivered watching them.

D.B. Wilson, the marine who solved the cosmoline problem in Chinwangtao, worked here as a mechanic. He stopped beside me to ask what I was doing and to pass the time.

When the formation outside broke up, all the youngsters came into the machine shop. Obviously they worked here. One of the boys called out to Wilson as he entered the shop. D.B. waved acknowledgment. Suddenly, the youngster changed directions and came toward us with his broomstick. He placed himself squarely in front of Wilson.

"*Nihon hayti, ichi bon.*" [Japan soldier number one] He demonstrated his point with a thrust of the broomstick, his make-believe bayonet, at an imaginary enemy.

Wilson nodded in agreement. The boy, expecting an argument, was dumbfounded. He was visibly confused as he had obviously expected Wilson to defend American marines' skills. D.B. seized the opportunity to make his point.

"American *hayti* and *rekisenti* [soldiers and marines] *arimasen* [do not have]." He pointed at the end of the broomstick as he explained. The boy understood that Wilson said Americans did not use bayonets.

"*Naze?*" [Why?] He looked puzzled.

At this point, Wilson went into his act. He pantomimed holding an automatic weapon, spraying the area in front of him, including the trainee. To put the finishing touches on his act, he made a staccato sound in his throat, "Ah-ah-ah-ah-ah," like a burst of machine-gun fire.

The youth stood transfixed for a full thirty seconds, peering into Wilson's poker face. After a bit, D.B. grinned and the boy took on a sheepish look and broke away to join the rest of his companions.

Finally, Nishi showed up to act as my interpreter so I could proceed with the welding job. I told Nishi to have the Japanese workmen construct a metal box large enough to accommodate the engine block, plus clearance on all sides, top, and bottom. The steel was to be heavy enough to withstand red heat without buckling, the box to be open on top, the clearance around the engine to be at least a foot inside the box. Next, I explained how to cut slots around the bottom for draft.

The idea was simple, I thought, but something must have been lost in the translation. They didn't understand. In desperation, I asked Nishi if he could get me a piece of chalk. Nishi inquired of one of the foremen, who immediately produced a piece from his pocket. I squatted to draw the diagram on the concrete floor. I was instantly surrounded by the workmen, the foremen, and Nishi.

When I finished, the response was positive, their acknowledgment was unanimous, and the foremen mouthed an "*Ah so.*"

I drew a little oblong block inside the box I had drawn on the floor and looked up at Nishi.

"Tell them that this is the engine block."

"Engine," Nishi said, first pointing at my last drawing and then at the engine block sitting against the wall, then he grinned.

When he was sure the Japanese workmen knew what to do, Nishi departed, telling me that he would be back later in the day. I sat on my stool and watched the Japanese civilians build the box. It took them the better part of the day to weld all the seams. As they finished cutting the slots in the bottom of the box, Nishi walked in. I was about to leave because it was quitting time. Nishi stopped me. "How is the work progressing?" he asked.

"The box is finished," I said, pointing to it. "All we need now is a lot of charcoal."

I walked over to it with Nishi and he examined the box.

"I will make sure there is plenty here in the morning," he promised.

The following morning the foreman set the engine block on a bed of charcoal, then packed charcoal all around the block. Using acetylene torches, he set fire to all four sides at once, directing the flames into the draft holes at the bottom of the box.

Seated on my stool, waiting for the engine block to get red-hot, I noticed the drill detail outside going through their paces again, but there was something different in their manner from yesterday. There was none of the snap or spirit that had been evident the day before.

Wilson's friend must have told all his buddies that American soldiers don't use bayonets, but are all armed with automatic weapons. D.B., in a joking way, had completely demoralized the whole band of aspiring young trainees.

At two o'clock the block was red-hot. I motioned to the foreman that I was ready to weld. He gave me the torch, but I could not get close enough to the box because of the terrific heat emanating from it. I set the torch down and waited for Nishi to come back. He had been dropping in every few minutes since noon. Shortly, he arrived. I had him tell the foreman to cover the box with steel plates, except the part that was to be welded. With that accomplished, enough heat was blocked off to allow me to weld the crack in the block.

With the weld completed, I moved away from the box and handed the torch and goggles to the foreman. Nishi stepped up behind me, "How did it go?" he asked anxiously.

"There is no way of knowing until it cools down," I said. Then I told Nishi to ask the pusher to uncover the box so the plates he put on didn't smother the fire. "That should do it," I said.

Nishi relayed my message to the foreman, then turned sharply to me. "What do you mean, there is no way of telling?" he blurted.

"You have done this before, have you not?" he probed.

"Not me," I answered quite frankly.

"But you said you knew how to weld cast iron," he argued.

"Sorry, Nishi; I only asked, 'Why do you want to know?'" I corrected him.

"You led me to believe you knew . . ." his voice trailed off.

"All I said was, it could be done, but it was a complicated process, nothing more."

"Oh. Perhaps you have seen it done then," he said hopefully.

"Well," I answered thoughtfully, "yes and no. It was like this: I saw the welding part done, and this job looks just as good, if not better—but after it was cooled down on the dying fire, I missed that part of the experiment. It was a theory we were working out in class back in high school," I explained.

Nishi started to speak, but changed his mind. The look on his face was one of utter dismay. He backed away, took a sidelong glance at me, turned, and left by the door.

Next morning, I was the first to enter the room to examine my hand-iwork. I noticed water all over the floor. When I looked at the block, my reaction was one of shock. I could not believe what I was seeing—the block was cracked and checked all over. It was worthless, completely ruined. Someone had doused the project with water during the night.

The number-one pusher walked in, and when he saw the damage, he let out a yell that brought a soldier on the run. He came at me with a naked bayonet. I put up my hands and backed away from him as fast as I could. I hit the wall and stopped.

Nishi rushed in at that time and yelled, stopping the soldier, whose bayonet point was now pressing hard against my stomach. If Nishi had come in a few seconds later, I would have been impaled.

"What the hell is it now, Kirk?" he gasped, almost out of breath, as he came quickly toward us. "What have you done?"

"Not a damn thing, Nishi. Will you tell this guy to take his toad-sticker out of my guts before he has an accident and someone gets hurt?" I pleaded.

Nishi spoke to the soldier, who withdrew to stand off a short distance, but remained ready if needed.

"What now?" he asked again, after he got his second wind.

"I came in and found the block just as you see it." I pointed at the box with the puddles of water standing around it. "It is completely ruined, and the pusher and soldier think I did it. You can see it had to have been done hours ago, because the block is almost cold. If I had doused it now, the room would be full of steam."

Nishi considered for a moment, and went to touch the block. "It makes sense. I have to agree with you," he consoled me when he came back. "There is no way you could have done it unless you sneaked down here in the middle of the night."

"A fat chance I could have done that," I retorted.

Nishi turned away and beckoned the soldier to follow. They moved away and drew the foreman with them. After a few minutes' conversation, Nishi returned to me, still backed against the wall.

"You can relax. They agree it had to be someone other than you," he assured me.

"Thanks for the help, Nishi. I was in a hell of a spot; for a second or two, everything looked pretty bad for my future. I'm glad you showed up when you did."

"Kirk, do you have any idea why I came here early today? It was because I had my neck stuck out a mile on this project. I told my boss that I had a prisoner who knew how to weld the engine block so it would be as good as new. Needless to say, after what you said yesterday, I spent a sleepless night trying to think of something to tell him, to explain how everything went wrong. I was almost sure you had ruined that engine block."

"Nishi, you worry too much," I grinned. "If it hadn't been for that jerk who doused the block, it might have worked, and you would have been a hero. Now we'll never know."

"No, we never will, will we?" he said thoughtfully. "Seriously," Nishi confided, "I think the guy that dumped the water on that block did both of us a favor. I think he saved your hide from being burnt, not to mention my skin for having masterminded this fiasco."

13

The Bathrobe

After wearing out my welcome at the machine shop, I once again found myself facing the elements, pushing barrels across the field in the cold, wind, rain, and snow.

I began to worry about all this work with very little food to sustain me. The more I thought about it, the more I became convinced I must trade my last possession of value—my brother's bathrobe—for food. I was sure I could get a lot of rice for it from a Japanese soldier. I wrestled with the idea for about a week, then one evening after supper, with hunger gnawing at my guts, I made up my mind. I sat on the edge of the tier watching the door for a particular person to enter. Many people came in, trading beans for cigarettes, or whatever. Finally, he walked in wearing a heavy brown woolen uniform, a British soldier whose job was taking care of the Japanese mess hall. He swept the floor and washed their mess gear, for which he got what was left on their plates. I called to him: "Hey, Limey, would you come here a minute?"

He stopped, looked around, and discovered it was I who was calling him. He came over and looked up at me on the upper tier.

"Wat dah yah want, Yank?" he asked with a thick cockney accent.

"Are you the dog robber for the Japs mess?"

"A poor choice o' words, Yank," he scowled, "if yah mean ah police their mess, yer right, mate."

I paid no attention to his protest and came right to the point.

"Is it true you have been acting as a go-between in a lot of swapping deals between the prisoners and the Japs?"

"If yah mean ah arrange for parties ta meet and do business, yer right. I've done that," he answered with a grin, showing two upper teeth missing and one gone from the bottom, making a big hole in his teeth whenever he opened his mouth.

The guy was baiting me. With his attitude, it was easy to see why he had so few teeth.

"What do you get out of the deals?" I pressed him.

"The Jap blokes give me a bit o' rice if ah get 'em a good buy."

"Wait here, I will be back in a second," I said, getting up and moving to the head of my bunk. I reached under my stack of blankets and pulled out the bathrobe. I draped the robe over the end of the tier, turning it around so the Limey could see the dragons on the back. I opened the robe to show him the red satin lining.

"Blimey!" the Britisher gasped. "Wat a fancy piece!" He beamed as he ran his hand over the embroidery and across the red satin lining.

"I'd say some bloke wud like ta get 'is 'ands on that," he mused.

"I want ten mess kits full of rice and stew," I said flatly. "One a week for ten weeks."

"Ten," he echoed. "Ya'll not be getten et; most ah eva seen 'em pay fer anathing was five, an thet was a leather jacket," he paused. "Ah doan think ya'll get et," he repeated.

"That is my price," I said with finality.

The soldier continued to admire the robe. He reached out and felt the satin cuffs, then looked at me again.

"I'll take et to 'em ta see if ana of 'em want et," he offered.

"Not on your life, Limey," I remarked. "You tell them about the robe. If you can get them to come to the barracks, I will show it to them. One more thing," I cautioned. "Before you talk any of them into looking at this robe, tell them the price is ten mess kits—no less—take it or leave it. Is that clear, Limey?"

"Ah understand ya Yank, but ah doan think ya'll get et. I'll ask around." He shrugged and moved away toward the other end of the barracks.

A week passed. I had almost forgotten I had offered to sell the robe. Supper was over, and I was sitting at the end of one of the tables that occupied the center aisle that ran the length of the building. I was sipping my tea when the door opened. It was the Limey with an ugly little Japanese five-star in tow. The pair approached me.

"Ah 'ave a bloke thet wants ta look et yer fancy piece, Yank." He nodded at the mean-looking five-star, standing close beside him.

I climbed up to my bunk, brought the robe down to the floor, and unfolded it in front of the little man. The instant he saw the bathrobe as I displayed it front and back, he began to drool, his eyes opened wide, and he grinned from ear to ear.

"*Go-hon,*" [Rice] he asked excitedly, holding up seven fingers.

I turned immediately to the Limey.

"Did you tell this clown that I would not take less than ten?" I asked, very irritated. The Englishman nodded affirmatively.

"*Ju-ni,*" [Twelve] I said belligerently, confronting the Jap.

The five-star flew into a rage, came up on his toes, squealed like a stuck pig, and at the same time delivered a stinging slap to my face.

"*Numbo?*" [How many?] he shouted.

The barracks became suddenly quiet as most prisoners turned their attention to the stormy argument in progress between the officer and me.

"*Ju-shi,*" [Fourteen] I snapped. My voice sounded loud in the quiet hall.

This time the Jap looked at me in amazement. He rocked back on his heels, studied my grim face for a few moments, then broke out with a broad grin. Holding up both hands, palms toward me, in a sheepish voice, said, "*Ju* [ten], OK?"

I hesitated, still smarting from the slap on the face, not caring whether I did business with him or not. But, then I reminded myself that ten pails of rice and stew would help me through the winter. I would get the last bucket around the first of April. The weather should be warm by then. Besides, this was the only offer I had.

Prudently, I nodded yes.

He bowed and said, "*Arigato.*" [Thank you]

"Are you sure," I turned my attention back to the Briton, "he knows I want a full mess kit each week for ten weeks? Then and only then will I give him the bathrobe."

"'E knows wat kind o' deal ya want. Ah still doan know 'ow ya managed ta get all that," he said, shaking his head.

"It was easy," I answered him. "I didn't want to sell the robe in the first place, so if I couldn't get my price, I wouldn't let it go. In a way, it isn't mine. It belongs to my brother. That's why the price is so high."

The Limey looked at me, puzzled, then shrugged and walked away.

The little five-star was still examining the bathrobe, and after a few minutes he stepped back, took one more long look, then backed out the door.

Four weeks went by, and each Monday evening I received a full mess kit of rice and stew. Unlike the swill they fed us, consisting of white radishes and water, this stew was thick with chunks of meat and lots of egg noodles. The rice was all rice—no millet.

The fifth week, about the middle of February, he arrived with a pail of rice and stew, but refused to give it to me unless I gave him the bathrobe. He insisted I give him the robe and he would pay me the rest of the debt as we agreed. I answered his insistence by vigorously shaking my head no. He became furious. I was sure he was going to hit me, but he refrained. Like the first time we met, after he discovered he could not bully me, he simmered down, grinned, and handed me the mess kit full of rice and stew.

His actions were disquieting. I had provoked him to the point where any other soldier in his situation would have clobbered me. I thought about it for some time and finally, on a hunch, took the robe from under my blankets and carried it down to the Dutchman, the section leader of the third section. The Dutchman was blond with blue eyes, a heavyset man with a square jaw, while his charges, all the Javanese soldiers in the third section, were mostly dark-complexioned and slight of build. He bunked at the far end of the barracks and on the opposite side of the building, on the ground level. His bunk was further from mine than any other in the barracks.

I asked him if he would mind hiding the robe under his blankets. He looked up at me from the game of solitaire he was playing with a limp deck of cards.

"A strange request," he said. "Why do you want me to hide it?"

"I am not sure," I explained. "I have a sneaking suspicion the Jap I traded this robe to is planning to steal it from my bunk while I'm at work tomorrow. The deal I made with him was that he would pay for the robe completely before I handed it over to him. Now I think he plans to steal it so he won't have to pay me the balance. He still owes me half of what we agreed upon."

"No problem," the Dutchman said. "I'll hide it for you; I doubt that he'll ever think of searching this part of the barracks for it."

I gave the Dutchman the robe and went back to my bunk. I sat for a long time pondering what I had done. Perhaps I should've given him the robe. Maybe he would pay me the balance of rice and stew like he said. But then, what if he reneges? How would I ever get paid? If I went to the Japanese to complain, they would say I lied and kick hell out of me. What if I let him steal it? No, no, I decided against that. That would be crazy. I could really get myself into trouble. It hadn't been so long that I'd forgotten Robert Smith and the leather belt incident. Even if I could prove he had the robe, if he denied it, I would get a trouncing. The most worrisome thing about him stealing the robe, then saying he didn't have it, was—what would I do about the food I had already eaten? There was no way I could pay it back. They would probably kill me if he could convince the colonel that I'd pulled a dirty rotten trick like selling him something I didn't have . . . The hell with him, I finally decided. I would hold the robe and see what happened.

I was not surprised the following day when I returned from work to find my blankets all askew. Everything I owned, which wasn't much, was scattered all over my mat and on the mat next to mine. It had to be the work of my benefactor, I chuckled to myself. I bet he was fit to be tied because he couldn't find the bathrobe.

That evening, after the food had been dished up, I was sitting in my customary seat at the end of the table near the door. My dab of millet and some of the same old monotonous radish stew was occupying my time when the door burst open and in stormed the infuriated little five-star.

He stopped beside me. I looked up into his scowling face with a grin. He didn't say a word, just glared at me. He must have been burning ever since he failed to find the robe in my gear. Perhaps as early as this morning—undoubtedly long enough to get up a good head of steam.

"*Konbanwa*," [Good evening] I said, trying to act nonchalant, as though I was not aware of his problem, and not meaning a word of it.

"*Baka*," [Crazy] he screamed, reaching out suddenly to snatch my hat off my head. He slammed it on the floor and stomped on it.

"*Kioski!*" [Attention] he barked, becoming red in the face.

The barracks quieted down. I stood up and moved away from the table and snapped to attention. This time, I knew he was going to work me over, but he was as unpredictable as ever. He stood in front of me with a sneer on his face and his hands on his hips, looking me up and down. I could see he was fuming, but nothing happened. He turned to leave.

"*Coy*," [Come] he said, and headed for the door.

Our destination was the guardhouse. Five more surly-looking five-stars were waiting for me. I felt a sense of foreboding as I walked into their midst, like a mouse about to be torn to pieces by six angry cats.

The guardhouse, situated near the main gate, was across the street from the camp office. For furniture, the guards' shack could boast of one bench, long enough to seat six people, and a potbellied stove in the far corner of the guard room.

I stood in the middle of the room, expecting the worst. I didn't have long to wait. The largest soldier pushed me violently off the concrete floor onto the cinder-covered main street. He jerked me around, grabbed my coat, threw his hip into me, and wheeled me over his shoulder.

Intuitively, I reverted to the jujitsu training I had received years earlier. I knew exactly what to do because I had done it so many times before. While stationed at Pearl Harbor, Hawaii, I attended the martial arts course sponsored by the YMCA on Hotel Street in downtown Honolulu.

The instructor giving the course was a Japanese jujitsu black belt. For fifty cents a week, I received a three-hour lesson that taught me by degrees how to protect myself from injury in a judo fight, and how I should land on the ground without breaking any bones. I was taught the technique of how to land flat on my back without killing myself. After I mastered these lessons and a few more, I learned by observation how to protect myself in a knife or a gun attack. Then, I was turned over to the blue- and brown-belt trainees to assist in their development and to perfect what I had learned. For forty-two hours, I was slammed about at every conceivable angle, like a slab of meat on a thin straw mat with a concrete base.

I dropped the course after fourteen weeks and although I had mastered my lessons well and was to receive my blue belt, the whole idea of slamming people on the ground was not my idea of fun. There had to be a better way to spend my fifty cents.

However, now I was on my way to meet the surface of the cinder street. When you hit the ground, I recalled, land on the fleshy parts of your forearms and the balls of your feet, then let yourself down easy.

I didn't have much flesh to land on, but I prepared myself to use what I had. I could still hear the instructor yelling in his pidgin English, "Wen you wand, wet me hear you gwunt—gwunt wowed."

When I hit, I not only let out a big grunt, but I threw in a moan or two for good measure to make him think he was hurting me.

Each five-star in turn picked me up and tried desperately to slam me down hard enough to hurt me. I did as little as I could to help them in their endeavor. I went limp and became dead weight as they tried to toss me about. With my flaccid response, it made it almost impossible for them to throw me. Judo works best when your opponent fights back. You use his strength and rigidity in conjunction with your own to defeat him. My lack of cooperation caused them to tire quickly and lose interest.

The worst thing that happened to me was that I got all dirty from rolling around in the cinders, nothing more.

The five-star who had grabbed me first was the only one who showed any style, but that was because he had caught me off guard.

My little friend was still not satisfied that I had paid for my sins. He dragged me back into the guardhouse and made me kneel on my shins across the wooden bench with my hands clasped on top of my head. He disappeared for a moment, and came back with a long wooden pole about two inches in diameter.

The guard room was large enough to swing the club without hitting anything except me kneeling on the bench. The angry little man drew back and swung the club like a baseball bat. I could see he was aiming for the small of my back. I waited until the blow was about to land, then I raised up and took the impact across my buttocks. The padding was not overly thick in that area either, but it was better to absorb the blow there than to let him destroy my kidneys.

Damn—I glanced to the side—*they are all lining up to take a whack at me.*

The big guy was up next. I waited for him to try to hit me in the kidneys, but as I watched out of the corner of my eye, he fooled me. He brought the stick down across my back, broke the club, and knocked me sprawling onto the concrete floor.

My chief tormentor never gave the broken club a second thought. He had something else in store for me. He set the bench right, made me get back on it, went to the potbellied stove, pulled a white-hot poker from one of the butterfly peep holes in the door, and approached me with a devilish grin. As he moved closer, he kept the poker on a direct line with my face and stopped within six inches of my eyes.

I glanced apprehensively at the other soldiers in the guard room, hoping to find a kindred soul who would stop this idiot. The looks on their faces told me I was wasting my time. They were enjoying every minute of it. I closed my eyes as tight as I could, but still felt the intense heat and could sense light through my closed eyelids. The poker was only a few inches away.

I was scared stiff that I might lose both of my eyes, and was powerless to defend myself. If I so much as raised a hand to protect myself, I would be lucky to get out alive.

For a moment, the heat increased, enough so that I felt my eyebrows being singed. I tried to back away, but kneeling as I was on my shins made that maneuver impossible. I grimly held my ground and waited for the worst. What seemed like an eternity was only a few seconds. He withdrew the poker. I breathed easier and opened my eyes in time to catch a glimpse of him circling around the end of the bench. He approached me from the behind with the hot poker. I shuddered and visibly shook as I felt the heat of the poker come close to the back of my neck.

"*Baka*," a sudden outcry broke the tension. The camp sergeant major appeared out of nowhere. His unexpected presence and shout startled the little soldier so badly, he lost control and jabbed me in the neck, then dropped the poker. The poker hit me on the back of the leg, singed my trousers, then clattered to the floor.

All the five-stars snapped to attention. The sergeant major walked up to me. "Come," he snapped.

I gladly got off the bench and followed, thankful for the relief. My shins were raw and sore as boils. He stepped outside the guardhouse and around the corner into the shadows. I almost ran into him in my hurry to vacate the premises. He had faced about and put out his hand to stop me. "Would you treat Japanese soldier so bad if he were your prisoner?" he asked me with a quizzical expression.

Immediately, I sensed he had been watching the whole shabby affair from the office across the street. Maybe that is why he showed up when he did. The hot poker was too much, even for him.

What could I say? Considering that I had just taken a beating, and the little jerk threatened to put out my eyes and burned my neck with a red-hot poker, what did he expect me to say? In a situation like this there was no rational answer. I hesitated for a second, then blurted, "Hell, yes," I snarled, "worse."

The sergeant major smiled, shook his head, then reached down and picked up a wooden bucket full of water from under the downspout alongside the building. A sheet of ice had formed across the top from the cold weather. He broke the ice with his fist, then dumped the contents over my head.

"Ow!" I gasped from the shock of the ice water, but except for that instant outcry, I remained stoic.

"That should cool you off," he grinned.

"Now, go see your doctor. Protect yourself from pneumonia."

The mention of pneumonia sent me into a panic. No one had ever survived pneumonia in this camp. Immediately, I ran to barracks six and found Dr. Markowitz, a United States Navy lieutenant.

"Doctor," I managed to chatter between my teeth, "do you have a couple of aspirin?"

"Sorry, not for many years," he declared. "What happened to you?" he asked, concerned to see me dripping wet and shivering.

"That lousy sergeant major dumped a bucket of water over me," I stammered.

"The best thing I can suggest," Markowitz said, after considering me for a few seconds, "is to get back to your barracks, take off all those wet clothes, and rub yourself down with a towel. If you rub hard enough, the friction will bring the blood to the surface. It'll restore your circulation," he advised.

I hurried to follow the doctor's orders. The rubbing actually made me warm. I crawled between my stiff blankets naked, as I had no change of clothes. The rest of the evening I worried that someone would enter the barracks and catch me in bed, but my luck held. We had no visitors until evening roll call. I got up then and slipped into my heavy, wet overcoat. I recited my lines to the Jap "tinko" party, telling them how many men were in my section, how many were missing, and where they could be found. Through all of that, they paid no attention to my attire.

I went back to bed as soon as they left, long before lights out, but stayed awake a good part of the night thinking about this evening's events.

Was the deal off? And, if so, what was the five-star going to do about the five buckets of food he had already given me? I was sure he was going to demand reparations of some kind before the matter was settled. There was no way I could repay him, as I didn't have anything he wanted except the bathrobe, and we had already been through that—he was not going to get it until he paid in full. Maybe he was planning a few more beatings to convince me I should give it to him. All I could do was wait and see. That was my last thought before I dropped off into a troubled sleep.

I didn't see the little five-star all week, but I was sure he would be back to see me. Monday evening rolled around. I was sitting in my usual place at the end of the table, sipping my tea. The door opened, and the little man marched up and handed me the sixth payment. He held up four fingers and said, "*Moe shi?*" [Four more?]

"*Moe shi,*" I repeated and added, "*Arigato.*" [Thank you]

After he left, I opened the mess kit. On top of a full bucket of rice and stew was a whole fish, head and all—my first fish head.

Five weeks passed—the evening of the last payment, I was sitting on the robe when he entered the barracks. We made the exchange and when he got his hands on the bathrobe, he began bowing and saying, "*Arigato, arigato,*" [Thank you, thank you] With that he backed out the door.

Before he disappeared from sight, I caught one last glimpse of the beautiful robe. I sorrowed for my brother, Arthur. Now he would never know what an elegant gift I had tried to save for him. But, I was sure he would understand and approve of what I did.

14

The First Air Raid

My timing could not have been better. With the last bucket of rice and stew, the weather changed from chilly to warm and beautiful. We shed our winter wraps and looked forward to a little comfort.

One morning, about half past April, we reported for work. Lined up in front of the equipment shed, we wondered what kind of dirty job was in store for us this time. Yesterday, we had just completed a backbreaking assignment with the help of a large group of Korean men and women laborers.

We moved a railroad spur that had been used to pick up coal from a pile, now depleted. We positioned the track near a new pile of coal, as yet untouched, about a hundred yards distant. The railroad spur we had shifted was perhaps a quarter of a mile in length.

Each of us were issued a pry bar. We would slip our bars under the track between the ties and follow the procedure set down by the Koreans. We sang along with them, "*Oie saw. Yoi saw*," and moved the track assembly a little. When the track had been moved sideways some distance and any attempt to move it further caused it to spring back at us, we all moved a short way down the line and did the same thing all over again. Bit by bit, we moved the track. It took us about ten days before we had the track where they wanted it.

Cawashima finally stepped out of the shack. He looked as if he were troubled. He always looked that way before he broke the news to us of our next irksome task. This time he was taking longer than usual, and I began to suspect that this new job was really going to be a lulu; however, he said, "Today burn," and smiled from ear to ear.

We all cheered.

He added very soberly and distinctly in English, "No mischief."

"No mischief," we all repeated in unison, like a flock of birds or a school of fish that change directions with no prearranged signal.

We knew what he meant. It was my guess that Cawashima must have felt we had learned our lesson and he would not be plagued again with leaking oxygen tanks. For my part, he was right. I could not survive another winter like the last without the help of my little oxygen tank stove. I never realized how much I'd depended upon it until I had lost it.

The first winter in Japan, my stove warmed me, kept my clothes dry, and heated my food. It also converted seawater that I dipped out of the bay into salt by boiling off the water. Salt was something everyone craved, but few prisoners had access to. During my rest breaks, I picked body lice from my clothes and tossed them on the top of the stove to destroy them with a pop. There were other beneficial uses too numerous to mention.

April passed quickly now that we were back working on the scrap pile. Early in May, back at camp, we were shuffled into different living quarters. This time, all Americans—army, navy and marines—were billeted together in barracks six, across the street from the place Dr. Markowitz called home.

I didn't bother to ask anyone whether they wanted the position of boontycho. I took the job as leader of section two. I felt it was too late in the war for someone to take over a job where it was necessary to speak a few words of Japanese. The Japanese became enraged by prisoners who couldn't speak their language.

Most of the people in my section were with me in the other barracks. I did acquire one new face: a sailor named Morris H. Royten of Biloxi, Mississippi. Royten had his foot in a cast. While we were living at the citadel in Yawata, at work he had dropped an oxygen tank on his foot from the bed of a truck. The tank weighed about 150 pounds, and his foot was smashed. After six months, he was able to return to work. That same day he returned to work, he had a similar accident; he dropped another oxygen bottle on the same foot and smashed it again. His foot had been in a cast ever since.

A month following the day we moved was our day off. We had our usual shakedown and inspection, taking up most of the morning. That afternoon, Kirkpatrick entered the barracks seeking volunteers to go with "Bull," the Japanese mess sergeant, to dig up a daikon some farmer had offered the POW camp. The radish was so large the farmer could not harvest it, and he asked us to take it because we had the manpower to move it.

Six prisoners went with the "Bull" and returned in about an hour. They said the radish was a good two feet across at the top and easily as tall as a grown man. They had to dig a trench around it so they could get down in the hole and push up on the radish to break it loose from the ground. I never saw the radish, but I had no reason to doubt their story, because we had an increase of daikon in our stew that lasted a week.

Summer came. One thing was becoming apparent to all of us—the war was drawing closer every day. The increase in the number of air raid alarms told us the Americans were acquiring air bases within striking distance of Japan. Our area had not been hit, but we all knew it was only a matter of time. Whenever groups of Japanese or Koreans got together, we could hear them discussing the *B-ni-ju-kyu* (B-29). The Japanese appeared fearful, while the Koreans, who were forced laborers, seemed delighted.

A few months previous, nothing save a factory or a train whistle broke the serenity of the Japanese islands. Now, once, twice, and occasionally three times a week, a long single blast of an air raid siren shattered the calm and warned the Japanese of impending danger.

The first time we heard the sirens was in the spring of 1943 while we were at work. That time, Cawashima herded us into a shelter that had been prepared especially for us. It must have taken all of five minutes to build. A trench had been cut into a slight incline in the cinders a short distance from the water's edge of the bay. The hole was then covered with a sheet of corrugated iron and cinders pushed over the metal to form the roof. After the brief introduction to our air raid shelter, we never went back, no matter how many times the air raid siren sounded.

We, like the Japanese and Korean workers, paid little or no attention to the air raid sirens because nothing ever happened.

At camp, things were different. The soldiers forced us into the air raid shelter at night every time a siren sounded, even when it was just a warning signal. We dubbed the warning siren "Moaning Minnie." During the past few months we had spent many nights in our bamboo shelters, but we had never heard a plane go over or a bomb explode.

Our nights in the shelter were one long wait, standing erect, crammed in between the face of a hill and the bamboo enclosure about ten feet wide that followed the contour of the hill. We moved only to allow the urinal, a long, narrow cylinder like we used on the train from Tientsin to Nanking, to pass from one end of the shelter to the other.

On the fifteenth of June, a beautiful day, clear and warm, we arrived at the scrap pile about seven o'clock. We set up our equipment, kindled the fires in our stoves for the oxygen bottles, and while the tanks were heating, cleaned our torches in preparation for cutting scrap iron, making little ones out of big ones. By then it was eight o'clock.

I dragged my hoses across the scrap pile when the oxygen was hot enough, and had just settled down to cutting when the peaceful morning exploded with the wailing warning of "Moaning Minnie."

I hesitated and looked around to see if anyone was going to take cover. No one seemed concerned, so I returned to burning scrap iron.

The morning wore on uneventfully. I had almost forgotten the warning siren when a series of short blasts from the air raid siren filled the air—the attack signal! That meant we were the target. Although we had heard the "Burping Betsy" attack signal many times, we had never before been under attack—but this day I had a feeling they would come.

Everyone stopped. I stood up and scanned the skies for American planes. There was no sign of any planes, American or Japanese. Uneasy now, we all went back to work. We had our morning break, and it was almost time for lunch. "Burping Betsy" was being treated with no more respect then "Moaning Minnie." No one was being sent to the shelters.

We had knocked off for lunch when Morris Killough of Muleshoe, Texas, a typical long, tall Texan, spotted two Japanese soldiers running across the field, taking a shortcut from the factory through the cinders and slag in an apparent hurry to get to us. He called everyone's attention to them. I climbed up the scrap iron pile and from my vantage point I could see them waving and I could hear them yelling. They were too far away to make out what they were saying.

On their arrival, they ordered us to accompany them immediately back to the train. Cawashima argued to let us put our gear away first, but the soldiers would not have it. They insisted we leave, and now. We did manage to turn off our tanks, jerk the tops out of the generators, and grab our mess kits. We left everything else as it was and followed the soldiers at a dead run.

I watched the Japanese as both of them kept looking over their shoulders toward the southwest. There was a high mountain range in that direction. I glanced back; the sky was clear, not a cloud to be seen anywhere. I listened intently for the distant rumble of exploding bombs, but there was no sound.

Whatever they feared, they kept it to themselves, but they did keep prodding us with "*Hiahcoo, hiahcoo.*" [Hurry, hurry]

I checked the mountain again, and then it dawned on me why they were in such a hurry. They must have been told from what direction the planes were coming—that was the west. If our planes suddenly appeared over that range, I realized, they would be on top of us before we could travel any distance at all. And another thing popped into my head—if our planes held off until we got to the train, we could pull into the tunnel and be safe. I followed that wishful thinking with another sobering thought: The Japanese would not worry that much about saving us.

All thoughts suddenly vanished when a bomb exploded far to the west along the base of the mountain. I looked back again, but the sky was still clear of planes. We were now entering the factory proper, and there were metal buildings all around us.

Three more bombs detonated to the south. The deep rumbling sound of the large explosions, even at this distance, told me they were very heavy bombs, perhaps 500 pounds. I counted five explosions evenly spaced in the first group of bombs. They had to be from a single plane. There were no more after that one load.

We were running between two large corrugated-iron buildings; I looked back, but the sun blocked out my view of the sky, and I could see nothing. We were moving rapidly now without any urging. We passed along a loading platform that had been built as part of the structure so railroad cars could load and unload directly into the building. The soldier in the lead diverted the head of the column into the open door in the side of the building as a bomb burst directly behind us to the west. Four more bombs fell, one after another, not more than a block away and creating a hell of a racket.

I questioned the wisdom of seeking shelter inside a corrugated-iron shed; however, I had no choice but to follow where I was led. Once inside, I changed my mind. There was a gaping hole in the floor—an excavation for a piece of heavy equipment, undoubtedly—but it looked like a ready-made bomb shelter.

We had no sooner settled at the bottom of the hole, all of us except the guard bringing up the rear, when another earth-shaking explosion rocked the ground. This bomb was a little closer, but on the other side, to the north. It was followed by four more detonations, like a giant walking on the earth. The bomb must have torn hell out of something in the factory because there was a clatter of many objects falling on the roof. I began to breathe easy as the next "stick" of bombs destroyed some more of the factory, hitting further north. They had passed over this part of the target and were moving away. I sighed with relief. I had not relaxed more than a second when a terrific explosion, nearer than any before, shook the hole, causing loose dirt to fall in on us. I realized the bomb had hit west of our position. I mentally calculated the lines of impact of the previous "sticks" of bombs. I wondered if this hole would save us.

No matter—the hair stood up on the back of my neck—this could be a direct hit! It made no sense, I wanted to cry out. This bomb wasn't following the proper pattern; it should be hitting further north.

Another tremendous explosion rocked our crater, and part of the rim broke off sending rocks down on us. *Oh, God—no!* I prayed. The next bomb, for sure, was going to land in our hole. I could hear a rushing sound, like an express train highballing it through a railroad station. That must have come from the next bomb, I thought. Maybe it was from the last. They say you never hear the one that gets you. There was no place to run, no place to hide. *What should I do?* Crazy thoughts raced through my mind.

The guard who had stayed outside on the loading platform let out a yell. I looked up in time to see him leap into the hole, his form silhouetted in a blaze of yellow-orange light. Every fiber of my being went numb from the concussion of the blast. The noise was deafening. The earth buckled under me. The sides of the crater caved in burying me to my waist. Smoke and dust were so thick it was impossible to breathe. I held my breath and scrambled out of my would-be grave. Most of the men were choking, gasping, and clawing their way out with me. Still holding onto what air I had in my lungs, I waited for most of the heavy particles, like rocks and sand, to settle. Then, at the edge of the hole, I sampled the air. It was bad. It stung my nose, and I began to choke like everyone else. I climbed up on the cement floor where I could stand, and found I could breathe. I looked back in the hole. The little soldier who had jumped in on top of us was trying to pass out cigarettes. In spite of his choking from the dust, he appeared proud of what he had done. As I watched, I noticed something wrong. There was a bayonet sticking out of the shoulder of his tunic. His buddy's bayonet had penetrated his sleeve just above the elbow and exited at the shoulder next to his ear. He did not appear hurt, but he had to climb halfway out of the hole before his partner could pull it out. A few more inches in the wrong direction and he would have impaled himself on the other guard's naked blade.

Finally, the rest of the men scrambled out of the excavation for a breath of clean air. It was much lighter inside the building than it had been when we entered; most of the corrugated-iron sheeting had been blown away from the side where we came in.

Outside, we saw the same fate had befallen the building across the tracks from us—no sheeting. At the edge of the dock was a crater, right smack in the middle of the two sets of tracks. It was larger than the one we had used inside for cover. At the edge of the bomb crater, four sets of rails, twisted and gnarled, pointed skyward. The middle of the crater to the center of our hole was almost close enough to spit into—too close for comfort.

The all-clear siren sounded while we were standing outside, debating if we should return to the hole. The planes had gone as suddenly as they had appeared. We hurried to the train, now only a short distance from where we had been holed up.

Except for the damage to the railroad tracks and the buildings where the bomb hit near us, I saw no other evidence that there had been an air raid.

"Has anyone been hurt?" was the question everyone asked on the train. "No," was the answer passed up and down the line.

Eight to nine hundred prisoners of war and not one casualty. That was damn good shooting, everyone agreed.

In camp, rumors flew about that the raid was the result of the Japanese converting one of their foundries—which made castings for ships—into a plant to turn out explosive devices such as hand grenades and land mines. The prisoners who worked in that area said the building in question was flattened. It was a good story, true or not, a morale builder for the prisoners. We all felt good to think that Uncle Sam had spies working in the very heart of the Japanese Empire.

The day after the raid we stayed in camp. It began to look like a real holiday, no inspection or shakedown. The Japanese were totally unprepared; there was nowhere to send us now that the factory had been torn up, but I was sure they would think of something.

About ten o'clock in the morning they thought of something to occupy our time, their idea of a joke. Some soldiers rounded up a few prisoners and made them erect a small platform for the occasion, in the middle of the street, next to the office. That done, the camp was ordered to assemble. We all filed out in the street, where there was room, to see the colonel and the sergeant major on stage waiting to begin.

During the past week, a new prisoner had been brought to our camp—a U.S. Army captain who had been captured in the Philippines while serving as an artillery officer. The sergeant major, acting as interpreter, called him to the stand and began explaining to us that according to the Geneva Convention, officers were not required to work in factories; however, they could perform tasks in and around prison camps, making the camps more cheerful. This job they were assigning to our captain. So saying, the sergeant major reached down behind the platform, and one of the five-stars handed him a yoho pole, a long-handled dipper, and two wooden buckets. The sergeant explained to the assembly that he was to dip excrement from the toilets and pour it on the flowers that he was going to plant. Our army officer was presented with the honey-dipping outfit. He took it smiling.

I was thoroughly disgusted. I thought of Major Brown and what his reaction would have been to such a shameful and degrading exhibition. The Japanese colonel and the sergeant major would be wearing the honey buckets as hats. I would have been willing to bet on that. At least, I was sure Major Brown would have refused to allow the Japanese to ridicule him like that in front of his men.

In addition to his job as honey dipper, the captain was to represent all the prisoners in any dealings we were to have with the Japanese authorities. I didn't know much about the captain except what I had just seen, and it appeared to me that he was not going to be very effective on our behalf.

The next day we went back to work, but not in the factory. They walked us a distance of at least four miles to a huge excavation that had been abandoned for years from the looks of the erosion.

Some of us were issued yoho poles with a pair of buckets while others were handed shovels. We went down into the hole and began digging and hauling out dirt, two buckets at a time.

The new job lasted only two weeks, after which we went back to work in the factory. I would swear, with all the prisoners getting into each others' way, in all that time we moved perhaps two yards of dirt. Maybe that is why they sent us back to the factory: we were no good at unskilled labor.

1 5

B-29s and Rotten Meat

We arrived at the factory, and everything seemed to be functioning normally. We walked past the spot where the bomb had blown the tracks apart between the buildings. The hole had been filled in and the tracks were back in place. They looked as though they had never been disturbed. New corrugated-iron sheeting shone brightly in places where it had been blown away.

When time came for morning break, we had no sooner settled down, seated in a group to smoke and shoot the breeze, when Tacashima showed up. He cleared his throat to get our attention, but nobody paid him any attention.

"*Cuda,*" [Hey] he blurted, "*ma-ta-na bomboo,*" he was speaking to me, but said it loud enough for everyone to hear.

"*Ma-ta-na?*" I questioned. "*Doko?*" [Where?]

"Americano," Tacashima grinned as though he had sprung the most demoralizing blow of the war.

"*Socki?*" [Aircraft?] I asked.

"*Iie,*" [No] he answered, shaking his head and grinning ever wider.

"*Nani?*" [What?] I asked, completely baffled.

"*Gahs,*" Tacashima made a gesture with his arms indicating something large and round.

We all looked at one another, wondering if anyone understood what he meant. A couple of the prisoners mimicked Tacashima saying, "*Gahs.*"

Tacashima became exasperated, and stomped over to an oxygen tank and beat on it with his stick.

"*Gahs, gahs,*" he snapped.

"Gas," Tony LePore of Chicago, Illinois, was the first to sound off.

"A gas balloon," voiced Powney of Tampa, Florida, following Tony's contribution.

"*Bahoon, hi, hi,*" [yes, yes] Tacashima jumped on it.

"They bombed someplace in the United States called Ma-ta-na?" Ira Mason of Brooklyn, New York, said aloud.

He had no sooner had it out of his mouth when a chorus arose; "Montana."

"Hi, Matana," Tacashima tried to mimic.

Now that he knew we knew the United States had been bombed, Tacashima pressed on, "*Taksan mei shinda.*" [Many people die]

Everybody laughed, knowing Montana for its open spaces, dotted every hundred miles or so with a lone cowboy. We thought it was funny.

"*Nani* [what] ha, ha?" he asked dead serious.

"Montana, *skoshi mei,*" [few people] I explained. "*Taksan* [many] moooo." Not knowing how to say *cow* in Japanese, I did the best I could to answer him. With my deepest cow voice, I gave a long moo. All the gang joined in and again we laughed, much to Tacashima's chagrin. He backed away, pouting.

One evening a few days later, back in camp, I found myself confronted by two angry Hindu sailors and three Javanese soldiers, equally furious. They felt that I should be held accountable for the loss of their food because one of my men, Royten, had borrowed from them. All five meals he had borrowed were due and payable that evening.

I explained to them that Royten operated under the American plan—he does as he damn pleases. If their section leaders felt responsible for the actions of the men in their section, that was their problem—I did not. I also told them that, in the future, they should be more careful with whom they do business, and their beef was with Royten, not me.

I recommended they talk to Royten and if he wanted to declare bankruptcy, I would monitor the transaction. It was the least I could do to get them off Royten's back.

After a brief discussion, it was settled. Royten agreed to live by the customary rules of bankrupt dealers. He would be allowed to eat all his meals except supper every third day, which would be used to pay off his debts.

We had no sooner settled the deal, all five creditors leaving the barracks, one of them carrying off Royten's rice, when a seaman from next door entered carrying a bowl of rice. He walked down the aisle, climbed the ladder, and handed it to Royten.

I was sitting on my bunk eating my supper when I saw Royten dig into the bowl with his spoon. There was no way, I said to myself, that anyone could be indebted to Royten. This meal must be from a deal he made today and didn't bother to tell us about when we set up his bankruptcy agreement. Like the section leaders in the other barracks, I'd involved myself and I was going to end up in trouble. I promised Royten's creditors I would see to it that he stuck to his commitments.

I called to the man before he could leave the barracks, "Hey, would you come here a minute?"

He walked over to me. I was on the upper tier looking down at him.

"Did you know Royten is bankrupt?"

I knew he couldn't have known because the bankruptcy agreement had just happened, but I wanted to see his reaction.

He looked at me for an instant with a dazed expression.

"No shit," he said.

He immediately made a quick retreat, hurried back up the ladder, and grabbed the bowl out of Royten's hands.

Royten sat back, surprised.

"Damn you," I heard the man yell, and with the bowl in hand, the seaman backed down the ladder and stomped out of the barracks with only half his meal.

After supper, I crawled down to the main floor and went over to Royten's bunk. I called up to him, and when he stuck his head over the edge of the tier and saw me, he became angry.

"I'll bet you're the rotten bastard that ratted on me," he growled.

"I came to tell you that I'm going to make your bankruptcy public. You knew what the deal was. No more trading until you were completely paid off. You also agreed that I should enforce it. No one needed to know as long as you behaved yourself—that was another part of the deal. Just now you blew it. You can't be trusted."

"Kirk," he sneered, "if you do, I will beat hell out of you."

"Where are you going to find all the help," I laughed, starting back to my bunk.

"I'm warning you, goddamn it," he yelled after me.

Paying no heed to Royten's attempt to intimidate me, I climbed up on the tier, beat my mess kit on the wall, and yelled, "Attention, attention, I have an announcement." I waited until most of the noise subsided, then continued.

"Now hear this." Again I paused. By then I had everyone's attention. "For your information, Royten is bankrupt. He has an agreement with his creditors not to borrow any more meals until he is out of debt. If I catch him doing business before he completes his end of the bargain, I will dissolve the bankruptcy. What will happen to Royten then is anybody's guess. One thing is certain: He will be in no condition to be paying off any new debts. So please be advised." Then I added, "you might pass the word along to your friends in the other barracks. I'm sure they would appreciate the information."

Later that evening, I was on my way to the washroom at the other end of the barracks to get a mess kit full of water to wet the edges of my blankets. It had been discovered that the water formed a barrier that seemed to discourage the passage of bedbugs. Although we were able to keep most of them at bay with the water dam, there were a few smart ones we were unable to cope with. These crafty bugs crawled up the walls, crossed the ceiling, then dive-bombed us when they got directly over our bunks.

As I reached the clear area at the midpoint of the barracks, Royten stepped in front of me, blocking my way. Without warning he lashed out with both fists, hitting me in the chest and knocking me back into one of the tables that lined the center of the aisle. He squared off. "I warned you, Kirk. Now you're going to get it," he sneered.

Taken completely by surprise by his sudden attack, and angered beyond my ability to retain self-control, I obliged him by wading in swinging. I could never box. All I knew about fighting was to stand toe-to-toe and slug—the first man down was out. To my surprise, he was not where I thought he should have been, and for my troubles he gave me a clout on the ear.

Royten was a southpaw. He also appeared much taller than I remembered; most of the time I had seen him lying down. In addition, even with his foot in a cast, he was quite agile. The way he was forcing the fight, I got the idea he felt he had nothing to fear from me.

His blow to my ear hurt and did very little to soothe my ruffled ego. I went at him again like a charging bull, and he rewarded me by stepping aside and giving me another bang on the ear. The blood started running down the side of my neck and onto my clothes. Now, I was beginning to understand why he was so confident. He had more than just a nodding acquaintance with the Marquis of Queensbury rules. He handled himself like a pro.

From the age of three, I lived in an orphanage where my mother worked. My siblings and I all lived as the other orphans did. I had bouts with my brother orphans when all reason failed to put my point of view across; fists were the only way I could make them understand. We had rules we observed—the fight was over if one was knocked down and chose not to get up, or a nose was bloodied. I can't remember anything about a bloody ear, so as far as I was concerned, I was still in the fight.

I charged him again hoping to get in just one lick, and again he was not where I hoped he would be, and once more he smashed me on the ear. I must have looked terrible with blood all over me, and since his last punch to my ear, I was bleeding more than ever. Royten was delighted, staying out of reach and laughing at me. He was having his way.

I knew I would have to do something different or he would soon make me look like a complete fool. I calmed down, realizing that my rushing him was playing right into his hands. Royten was ready to belt me again; he knew exactly what I was going to do if I followed the same pattern as before. I decided it was time for a little deception, or he would make good on his promise to whip me. I concluded Royten was no dummy, so I put on an act. I even roared a bit to distract him and started to wade in as before. This time, instead of following through, I stopped, stepped back, and watched him take the bait. Up to now, the contest had become routine for Royten. This time, however, when his fist went out where my ear should have been, I was not there and his guard was down.

I brought my right fist in from the basement in a good, old-fashioned haymaker, hit him square on the side of the jaw, and spun him around. My fist, wrist, forearm, elbow, and shoulder stung from the impact of the blow.

Royten appeared to recover quickly, but he did not press the fight; he stood with his guard down, his arms hanging loosely at his sides, and with a peculiar look in his eyes.

I must have hurt him, I told myself. The way my right arm aches, he has got to be hurting. I watched him for a moment. He had not moved since I had hit him. I sensed he was exhausted; however, my condition was not much better. I could hardly lift my left arm, and my right was useless; it pained terribly from the shock of the blow I had landed.

On a hunch that he had had enough, I took a step toward him. He backed away, lost his balance, but saved himself from falling by bumping into the ladder that led to the upper tier.

"Come on, Royten," I gasped, "Let's get on with it. You started the fight," I puffed, "now you are going to do battle, or I will be forced to kick the hell out of you."

Royten, with a blank look on his face, slid down into a sitting position with his back against the ladder.

"Are you going to get up?" I paused to take a deep breath, trying to catch my second wind. "Have you had enough?" I gasped. My lungs ached.

Royten nodded.

That was the best news I had had all year. If Royten had shaken his head no, I would have declared him the winner.

I looked around to find something to sit on; a bench was directly behind me. With the greatest effort, I wobbled across the short distance and plopped down just before I was about to collapse. Never in my life had I been so wrung out, especially over such a short fight and with so little exertion. I sat on the bench for a long time, trying to regain my strength. Royten had slumped over on one of the mats and appeared to be asleep. When I did move, every bone in my body ached.

I decided to forego the water for the bedbugs until later. I gathered up my mess kit and made it back to my bunk and flopped on it. To hell with the water—the bugs could feast tonight.

Later, I somehow managed to wake up, wipe the blood off with spit and a towel, stand roll call, and go right back to bed and sleep immediately thereafter.

I awakened again during the night with a strange feeling that something was wrong. I propped myself up on one elbow and looked about. Although it was dark in the barracks, I soon became aware that I was alone. There was no one in the barracks except me. Then I heard what had probably awakened me—the sound of bombs exploding in the distance. I had slept through the air raid siren and all the noise that goes with evacuating the prisoners from the barracks. Perhaps I was a little overtired.

I heard two soldiers talking outside my window and crawled over to it and looked out. Toward the northwest, orange flashes lit up the night sky. Searchlights streaked back and forth across the heavens.

The two soldiers were standing near the corner of the building just below me. I could not make out what they were saying until one said in a loud voice, "*Nani skoki?*" [What or whose aircraft?]

"*Wakaron,*" [I do not know] the other replied.

I looked up to see if I could spot the plane. There it was! One searchlight beam had suddenly locked onto it, then two, then three beams began tracking it.

"*B-ni-ju-kyu,*" [B-29] both soldiers cried at the same time.

I watched the B-29 glide like a white ghost against the black sky until my vision was blocked by the overhanging eaves of the barracks. I listened apprehensively for the crack of anti-aircraft batteries, but there was only silence.

They had no idea whose planes were flying overhead, I chuckled to myself as I crawled back under my blankets with all the bedbugs. How can the war possibly last much longer? With a warm and contented feeling, I slipped into the realm of pleasant dreams.

November crowded October off the calender, and as November wore away, the rain, wind, and cold were on us again. I began to worry once again about the lack of food and heat, plus the danger of pneumonia. I had made up my mind that I was going to do something about the heat this year. If we had heat, the need for food would not be so critical. I would go straight to the Japanese colonel and demand wood and charcoal to burn in the pits already built into each barracks. What could he do to me except slap me around a bit and then say no. There was no way of knowing if they would give us wood, unless we asked.

A week before our day off, I talked D.B. Wilson into going along with me. As I put it to him, "All the Jap colonel can do is say no. What have we got to lose?"

We discussed going through the army captain to have him do it for us, but we rejected the idea after recalling his lack of manliness when he let the Japanese crown him chief shit merchant of camp. We concluded it would be a waste of our time.

A week later, on our day off, our numbers had increased to eight marines. After a tiring inspection and shakedown, we lined up outside our barracks and marched straight up the street to the office. We halted opposite the window where the sergeant major usually sat to watch the traffic passing in the street and through the compound gate.

At my command, we executed a smart right face. The sergeant had seen us coming and had raised the sash. He was leaning over the sill.

"What do you want?" he demanded.

179

"Sergeant major," I answered in a loud voice, "request permission to speak to the colonel."

"What for?" he asked suspiciously.

The colonel must have heard my request, for he came into the room behind the sergeant and spoke to him. The sergeant spun around and snapped to attention. The two engaged in a rapid conversation that lasted only a few seconds. The sergeant turned back to me. "The colonel will hear you," he said with doubt in his voice.

"Sir," I began, as the colonel stepped out from behind the sergeant, "we represent all the prisoners. We are cold. Would it be possible for the Japanese army to furnish us with wood and charcoal to heat our barracks so that we may keep warm this winter? There are three pits in each barracks already for that purpose."

The sergeant major began translating, but the colonel broke out into a chuckle long before the sergeant had gotten under way. I suspected the colonel had understood every word. As the translation continued, the colonel's chuckle turned into a belly laugh. The longer he regarded us standing at attention in the street, the harder he laughed. Finally, he found a chair and sat down to keep from falling over. Maybe my request translated into Japanese sounded like a big joke.

I wished I knew what was so damn funny. His laugh was beginning to rankle me. With a laugh like that and a red suit with white trim, he could pass for Santa Claus. He even had the build for the job, short and plump.

It took considerable time for the colonel to simmer down enough to tell the sergeant what he wanted done with us. After a few curt remarks, the sergeant emerged from the office and, beginning at the far end of the line, proceeded to slap each man in turn. When he stopped in front of me, he said, "You again," and shook his head.

My feelings were mutual—if I never ran into him again, it would be too soon. He remembered the bucket of water he had dumped over me about a year ago. I would have liked to do the same to him.

He must have read my mind because he belted me twice, once on each cheek. He then backed off one step and barked, "Right face . . . forward march."

We dissolved our formation long before we reached the barracks. Once inside, I sought my bunk where I lay down to reflect on what we had done. Actually, we had accomplished nothing except to raise a little hell with the established procedures. We had the audacity to bypass their chain of command and go directly to see the head man. If any Japanese soldier, or group of soldiers, had tried anything like that—to usurp anyone's authority—they would have been beaten to a pulp, probably killed. Now it was my turn to chuckle.

I reconsidered that insidious laughing by the colonel. For the life of me, I couldn't see what was so damn funny about asking for wood and charcoal. I could be certain he had no intention of giving us any.

A week passed, and we heard no more about our trip to see the colonel. During that time I received another letter from Aunt Bessy. Bessy's letter was full of weather reports, all bad, and her children were sick again. I studied the new letter carefully for some time for a hidden message. I went to the cardboard box that held all my treasures— a spoon, a rusty razor blade, a little box of salt I had extracted from the water dipped from the bay, and Aunt Bessy's letters. Now I had three of them, and they were all the same except the measles, chicken pox, mumps, colds, sniffles, and whooping cough were being swapped back and forth among the kids. I was sure it was some kind of code, like the seaman's letter from his brother about the battle of Midway. The bad weather she spoke of could mean the Japs were losing, or perhaps it was the other way around, but the kids and their diseases—that had to be a code.

I decided to take the letters to the British sergeant; he was still a section leader in my old barracks where he remained after the Americans were moved out. He knew the customs of Bessy's country. Maybe he could make something out of them.

I found the sergeant with the Dutchman, the soldier who had been kind enough to hide my bathrobe to prevent the little five-star from stealing it. The Dutchman had also stayed behind when we moved. He was telling the Limey's fortune with that same old deck of cards; they were as limp as cabbage leaves.

"Limey," I interrupted, "will you do me a favor?"

"Depends." He glanced up at me from the Dutchman's bunk and saw the letters in my hand.

"Wat ya got there?"

"Some letters from a gal in England who claims to be my aunt. I was not aware I had an aunt until she informed me in her letter about a year ago. She says a lot of strange things that could have a hidden meaning, like the guy's letter in barracks five a while back that told about the battle of Midway. You speak the language; I thought maybe you could interpret what she is saying."

"Wat da ya mean, I speak the bloody language?" he demanded with indignation.

"Relax, Sarge," I cautioned. "What I meant was, you are from that country, knowing the people and customs; you may see something in these letters that I could never see."

"Oh," he acknowledged, putting out his hand for the letters.

"I'll 'ave a sufty."

"A what?" I questioned, perplexed.

"I'll 'ave a look et 'em."

"Take your time," I said, "I'm in no hurry." I handed him the packet of letters.

"All right," he said, stuffing them into his shirt pocket.

It was two weeks before I saw him again. One evening after evening chow he came to return the letters.

"Sorry, Yank," he began, "there ain't a bloody thing in 'em. She sez they 'ave lots o' rotten weather. Ah been ta Glasgow, an ah agree. It's all bloody baud, like she sez. As fer younguns, ya never see sicker, white-faced mites anawhere in the world."

"That is too bad," I remarked. "With all that writing I could have sworn there was something in there somewhere."

"Nothing there, mate," he said as he turned to go.

What kind of talk is that—ya never see sicker, white-faced mites—I reflected as I watched him step outside. Well, so much for the coded letters.

It was now late November. The next day, following the strikeout with my coded letters, the cowboy driving the engine on the way from work was extra rough. I was rubbing my slightly bruised posterior, but soon forgot everything when I stuck my head above the edge of the gondola car and got a whiff of something bad. The putrid odor that hit me in the face told me that something was dead, long dead and close by. We were a half mile from camp and the breeze was coming from that direction. As we headed into the wind the stench became stronger and more dense. The closer we came to our compound, the more convinced I became that it was coming from there. Once inside the walls, whatever it was boiled around us, making the buildings dance like a mirage. It was so thick it could easily have been sliced with a knife.

I walked into the barracks to be greeted by a familiar sight—Royten, perched on his bunk with his foot still in a cast.

"Royten," I yelled, "what is that awful stench?"

"Rotten whale meat," he called out in a loud voice so everyone could hear. "Rotten whale meat that we're having for supper."

"You are kidding," I answered in disbelief.

"Nope, rotten whale meat," he shouted above the din as the barracks rapidly filled with returning prisoners.

I went to Royten's bunk to hear the story, and learned that a phone call had come from the docks at Moji, asking if the prisoners would like to have some whale meat. Bull immediately accepted the offer and took a detail of prisoners to truck it back. He was given two wooden barrels of meat. The wooden casks, even though sealed tight, reeked of something dead—right through the barrel staves. The Bull took the whale meat anyway and brought it back for our supper.

When the buckets of stew were brought into the barracks, I had to admit, I had never seen so much meat in any one stew. The Bull must have used both barrels for this one meal. The stinking smell convinced him that this was the last chance. If he didn't get rid of it today, tomorrow he would be forced to bury it.

Dipping the stew from the buckets intensified the stench, like someone stirring an outhouse with a stick—but worse.

Soon the whole barracks reeked so badly my eyes watered.

I considered the ration of stew before me. It was full of meat. The meat was red and had streaks of what looked like gristle throughout. There was no escaping the full force of the nauseating stench sitting under my nose. I had my doubts that I would be able to eat it. All around me, other prisoners were spooning up the stew as though they were enjoying it. There were a few, like myself, having difficulty convincing themselves that this was good for them, this foul-smelling bowl of gunk. Halfway down the barracks on the upper tier of my side of the hall, one character was eating his whale meat while holding his nose. That seemed to be the answer to my problem. Maybe, if I could get by the awful smell, I could get it down. I tried and almost vomited, but kept it down by sheer willpower.

The next morning, we heard that two prisoners in the hospital died during the night. Rumors had it that the stew killed them. I couldn't put much credence in that, because if they were that close to death, they couldn't have been eating anything. However, there was a possibility, someone else suggested, that they died from the smell. I couldn't argue that theory one way or the other.

November winked out. December moved along into its last week, and purely by accident our day off came on Christmas. We went through the usual day-off routine in the morning, standing inspection and submitting to shakedown, but that afternoon there was something new.

A truck came down the street and stopped at each barracks to dump a bundle of kindling and a bag of charcoal. Everyone was elated.

At last, we were going to have some heat, a real Christmas present from our captors.

Three fire details quickly formed, one for each pit, and they went to work with exuberance. The kindling and charcoal were evenly divided among them. A search for paper turned up a Bible, which was donated by a slightly frigid prisoner. His remarks were, " 'Tis better, at this time, to be warm than holy; besides, I read the book many times."

It took the fire crews no time at all to lay the fires in the pits. In about a half hour, a soldier came into the barracks with a piece of burning rope and lit all three fires, then hurried next door to do the same for the others.

The kindling caught fire immediately. In less than five minutes the building was filled with dense smoke, and in another three minutes the barracks were empty. Everyone was outside in the street, coughing and gasping for air. We found we were not alone; people were boiling out of all the other barracks with the same problem—smoke. There was only one course of action: to put out the fires and open all the windows in the barracks to flush out the smoke and fumes.

With the air clean again and the windows closed, now everyone was freezing. The open windows had let out the accumulation of body heat generated by a barracks full of men. Sometimes, the smell that accompanied the body heat left a lot to be desired, but in our situation, nobody cared—especially when it was twenty degrees warmer inside than it was out in the weather.

Wrapped in my overcoat, I sat down on my mat and leaned back against my blankets, thinking about the colonel and his hysterics a month ago when we had asked him for wood and charcoal. He must have known what would happen. How could we have been so stupid? He saw the flaw in our plan and on Christmas Day, he smoked us out. Santa Claus turned out to be a joker.

I chose not to remind anyone that I had had anything to do with this fiasco. I had had no idea it would turn out this way. Charcoal fires are not supposed to smoke, but I forgot about the kindling.

A few days after Christmas, some kid was caught coming through the gate for work carrying a sack of beans. Because of the young fellow's sickly condition, Max Neuse, a North China Marine, stepped out and informed the soldiers that the beans were his. Max felt he could take the beating and the trip on the dead run a lot better than the kid. After Max was beaten, the soldiers poured a bucket of ice water over him and then stood him in a cistern in the icy water for three hours. Max came down with a case of pneumonia; two days later Max Neuse was dead.

16

Death, Roots, and Espionage

January came cold, and with it, for me, an increasing hunger. I had nothing left to trade and only one small hope. One day on the job some time back, I was moving scrap iron and uncovered a spoon. I traded it for a few beans in camp. Now, my breaks and part of my lunch period were spent searching for something, anything, to trade for food.

On one of these quests for treasure, I noticed a broadleaf plant growing in the cinders at my feet. There was nothing else thriving in the area except these plants. I pulled one; it had a root shaped like a carrot. Its interior, like its exterior, was also white, but for a red ring running throughout its center. Sliced crosswise, it looked like a piece of Christmas candy.

Wondering if it were poison, I cut one with a sharpened piece of scrap iron and licked it. The root was neither bitter nor sweet. It had a peculiar taste, somewhere between the two, with a little bite to it.

I pulled a few more, sliced them into my mess kit, added water, and placed them on the stove to boil. After an hour they had become soft. I ate a small piece, then went back to work, waiting to become sick, but nothing happened. Before the day was over, I had eaten five whole roots. I awoke the next morning no worse for having eaten them.

After that, I made a daily trip to the root patch to supplement my diet. The only scare I had that our new food source was in jeopardy was the time Bernstein cooked up a batch and took a full mess kit into camp and tried to peddle them for beans. Had he been successful, our patch of roots most certainly would have been depleted. It was not to be; the roots cooked up had a gray appearance, and either cooked or raw, had a bite to them something like a radish. Bernstein had no luck trading them, and after his try, no one else made any attempt to swap the roots.

The roots remained plentiful during the winter months for any-one who wanted them. They grew best when there was an abundance of rain. The rain stopped with the coming of spring, and the plants shriveled and died. Perhaps it was because they were growing in cin-ders where there was no soil to sustain them.

Plants were not the only living things that died in the spring. Pris-oners kept dying also. One morning shortly after the roots dried up, I crawled out of my sack and was in the process of folding my blan-kets when a shout arose from section one, directly below our tier. "This guy is dead! Hey, Woodie! Conway is dead!"

Woodie Woodall was the section leader, but there was nothing he could do at that instant, because the door opened, admitting the tinko (roll call) party. Woodie, a U.S. Army sergeant, did what came naturally.

The tinko party stopped in front of him to receive his morning re-port. He began with his usual aplomb, but when he got to the part of his recital where he was to tell where the missing men were, he placed one in the galley, another in the hospital, and then he hesitated—but only for an instant—before saying, "*Ichi mei shinda.*" [One man dead]

"What do you mean, one man dead?" the sergeant major squealed.

Woodie must have pointed to the man laying on his bunk, because one of the sergeant's escorts ran to see. I imagined he went to verify that the man really was dead.

"Men do not die in their quarters. They must go to the hospital to die," the sergeant stormed at Woodie.

"But nobody told him," Woodie replied frankly, without giving a thought to what he was saying.

Immediately, realizing what he had just said, Woodie laughed in-voluntarily.

Standing above the two, I watched the sergeant and listened to Woodie. The Japanese sergeant had no sense of humor, and registered his displeasure by slapping Woodie soundly across the face. The slap should have had a sobering effect, but it had just the opposite. Woodie lost complete control and laughed unabashedly. The sergeant major struck him again, this time with his fist, knocking Woodie down on his mat where he lay, holding his sides, laughing and crying hysterically.

The sergeant watched him for a moment, then shook his head. I detected a faint smile which quickly turned to a frown as he uttered, "*Baka.*" [Crazy]

Conway was a United States Navy man. No one seemed to know what caused his death. I noticed him naked on the cart ready for the run to the crematorium as I reported to the sick bay with malaria that morning. There was a Hindu on the cart with him, and from the looks of both of them, they had starved to death.

The Japanese doctor verified that I was having another malaria attack, and issued me a certificate assuring me three days to shake the fever and two more to recuperate, so I could find my way back to work on the sixth day.

Once any prisoner contracted malaria, he was on his own. It was strictly up to our bodies to shake it. They never gave us anything to fight the fever. We just had to sweat it out.

The day I returned to work, Nishi stopped by the scrap pile to see me. "I heard you had another attack of malaria. Is that right?"

"Yeah," I said, "it gets worse each time. The next siege, I may not make it back."

"Kirk," Nishi said quietly, "I know a doctor, a friend, who has been working on a serum to cure malaria. The last time I talked with him, only a few weeks ago, he said his lab tests had all been successful and now he was looking for human guinea pigs." He looked at me inquiringly. "Would you be interested?"

"You betcha," I replied, without giving it a second thought, "lead the way."

"All right," Nishi said. "First I will have to get permission from the army. As soon as I have taken care of that, I will be back to get you and take you to him."

Two weeks later, about the middle of May, Nishi pedaled out on his bike from the factory to see me.

"The army has given its consent," were his first words. "Are you still interested in getting that malaria shot?"

"I'm ready," I answered without hesitation.

"Before we go," Nishi cautioned, "my friend, the doctor, asked me to warn you that this is new medicine and it has had a rather violent effect on those who have received injections thus far. Also, I am to tell you that there are no guarantees it will work at all. There is also a remote possibility that it may kill you, although, he said, no one has died from it yet. All he can promise is that those who have taken the serum so far have not had a recurrence of malaria. He wants to impress upon you that because the serum is new, it is too soon to know what, if any, the long-term effects on your body will be. After knowing all this, he says, if you still want to take a chance, you are welcome to try it."

"Lead the way, Nishi," I said, indifferent to his warning. "I have everything to gain, and as far as my life being in jeopardy, the way I look at it, one or two more bouts with malaria and I am a goner anyway. Who knows—this might be the cure."

I couldn't help thinking of all the guys I knew who had died of malaria and all those who died of it that I did not know.

"Wait a second," he said. "I'll tell Cawashima I am taking you to the hospital. I'll be right back."

We were on the road; Nishi was pedaling his bike and I was walking alongside him. I wore go-aheads, or flip flops, I had cobbled together from scraps. My split-toed sneakers had given out. It was a beautiful day, and I was grateful for the change. I said as much to Nishi.

That started Nishi talking. As we moved along slowly, I discovered he was a native of California. In fact, he was born and raised near San Francisco. He grew up on beefsteak and apple pie, he said. Rice, according to him, was all right, but not for a steady diet. I asked him, Why, if he liked the United States as much as he claimed, why was he in Japan? Nishi said he had been duped into coming to Japan and once here, he, like me, was a prisoner.

A year before the war began, he explained, he received a telegram, supposedly from his dying grandmother. It was her deathbed wish to see her grandson, who lived in America. Included with the telegram was enough money to book passage aboard a ship to Japan, he said. He accepted the news as factual, and since he had no reason to suspect foul play, he embarked on a free trip to Japan—home of his ancestors.

Upon his arrival in Yokohama, he was promptly pressed into the military service. The telegram turned out to be a hoax to get him to Japan, where his particular talents could serve the Japanese Empire. Since he was educated in the United States, they figured they could use him some way to help in their war effort. It was obvious he harbored an underlying and bitter resentment, especially for the deception that separated him from his family.

A half hour later we came to the hospital. Except for the citadel, where we were housed in Yawata, this was the largest structure I had seen in the area.

Once inside, Nishi guided me through long corridors to a door with a frosted glass panel that was adorned with Japanese characters. Without knocking, Nishi ushered me in. A pretty young women in a nurse's uniform arose from behind a desk and confronted us. Nishi talked to her, explaining our presence. The nurse looked at me and pointed to a bench against the wall behind us.

"She wants you to wait there until the doctor is ready for you," Nishi explained.

They both left the room by the door behind the desk. I was alone, the first time since I was captured at Chinwangtao. Except for the desk, the bench I was sitting on, and the doors, the room was piled from floor to ceiling with medicine cabinets full of bottles of various sizes, all filled with many colored chemicals.

I waited, contemplating my surroundings. The entire place was spotless and had a smell of alcohol. The dainty little nurse in her starched white uniform, white stockings, and shoes, with a white cap to match, was also aseptic. Everything about the place was clinically sterile. I looked down at my own filthy rags, all the seams crawling with body lice. My trousers and jacket were made of burlap that at one time had been new and clean. Now, they were dirty and torn. My shoes were a couple of pieces of wood I'd found in the scrap heap. For straps to hold them in place, I used two short lengths of my Marine Corps fair-leather belt. The Japanese had long since stopped issuing us footwear back in 1943. With all this cleanliness about me, I was beginning to feel like a toad that had just crawled out of the muck and was perched on a snowy white pillow.

To hell with it. I became angry for feeling self-conscious about something over which I had no control. One bar of soap every three to six months, and sometimes not even then, does not stretch very far. I had no choice but to use the soap they gave me to wash my body. As it was, my skin itched, scabbed, and peeled off all over my body. It would have been stupid to use the soap for my clothes, especially when the dirt was the only bond that held them together.

The nurse appeared in the doorway and beckoned to me. I entered the adjoining room, where there were many more glass cases, bottles, and chemicals. Nishi was talking to a short, stocky Japanese with large horn-rimmed glasses. He wore a white smock with a stethoscope dangling from his side pocket. I assumed he must be the doctor, Nishi's friend.

The doctor bowed to me and sucked in air through his teeth. I returned the bow, the least I could do for what he was going to do for me. Whatever he had planned, he was ready, for on a small porcelain table in the middle of the room, laid out on a towel, was a horse-sized hypodermic syringe like the one used on me by the doctor back in Yawata, when he gave me a shot for dengue fever.

Maybe they had never heard of anything but large-sized hypos in Japan, I speculated.

There were two stools near the table, and the doctor motioned to me to sit on one of them. With no further ado, he took the stool opposite me, swabbed my right forearm with alcohol, picked up the hypo, and expertly slid the needle into a vein.

He made a comment in Japanese. Nishi translated for me, saying, "If you feel like passing out after the injection, feel free to do so." Nishi chuckled.

"That will be the day," I said, laughing as I watched the doctor expel the bright red fluid into my arm. He was in no hurry, and by the time he finished, my arm felt quite warm. After withdrawing the needle, he sat quietly for a moment watching me, as if he expected me to explode.

"Do you feel all right?" Nishi asked with concern. "Can you travel?"

"Sure," I answered. "I feel great. The only thing is, my arm, where he gave me that shot, is all warm."

"Let us go then," Nishi said.

I got up from the stool, then thought I would be polite and bow again and tell the doctor thanks, but as I bent forward, a great surge of heat swept over me, accompanied by a blinding flash.

I awoke stretched out on a gurney. The doctor had his stethoscope on my chest, the nurse was holding my hand feeling for a pulse, and Nishi was off to the side with a worried look.

I was on fire, and at the same time, wringing wet with sweat. It felt like I was having a giant-sized attack of malaria. In a few minutes, the fire went out and I stopped perspiring. I felt better almost immediately and was able to stand. Soon, I was walking beside Nishi's bike on the road back, completely recovered.

It was then that I got this crazy idea to ask Nishi to help me do something I had been thinking about for months. I wanted to get some pictures of the sick and dying prisoners, so someday all Americans could see how the Japanese had treated American prisoners of war. As I toyed with the idea of asking him, I thought, first of all, from what he had told me on the way to the hospital, he was more American than he was Japanese. Just now, he had gone out of his way to see that I was inoculated against a dreaded killer, malaria. The life-giving serum may be new and unproven, but I was sure it would end my malaria attacks. If he would do this to save my life, I was almost certain he would not turn me over to the authorities to be killed for what I was about to ask him.

It troubled me to think of a good way to ask without sounding ridiculous, so as we moved along, I formulated and rejected four or five different approaches to present to him. Finally, I put it to him this way: "Nishi, have you ever been to see the men in our hospital in camp?"

"Once or twice," he answered. "Why?"

"Then you know the lousy medical treatment—or lack of it—the prisoners are receiving, and why so many of them are dying," I said.

Nishi nodded, but said nothing.

"These prisoners who are dying are not ordinary men. They are soldiers, sailors, and marines. When captured, they were perfect physical specimens—the flower of their country's youth, so to speak. I think someone should be held accountable for their slaughter. What do you think, Nishi?"

"Maybe they will someday," he commented.

"Not without proof," I countered.

"Proof?" he echoed. "What kind of proof?"

"Photographs of the sick and dying men," I offered simply.

"Who is going to take these pictures?" Nishi said, looking at me suspiciously.

"Not you, Nishi; I will do it."

"You want me to get you a camera and film?" He searched my face in amazement.

"I am glad you brought that up," I said. "I can take pictures without a camera—that is, without a conventional camera. All I need is a few photographic plates."

"What good are plates without a camera?" he asked, puzzled.

"It's simple, Nishi. I can build a pinhole camera with materials available in camp. All I need are plates to fit the camera," I explained.

Nishi said nothing for some time. He just pedaled slowly, wrestling with his conscience and looking straight ahead. Finally, he stopped and straddled his bike and looked at me, stark and staring. His face appeared thinner and his skin paler, set off by his jet-black hair showing around the edges of his military cap.

"Do you have any idea what the army will do to you if they catch you taking pictures in a prison camp?" he asked incredulously, not really believing I was serious.

"They would probably shoot me," I answered frankly, "what else?"

"You know damn well they will, and me too for being mixed up in this," he blurted. "Kirk, you are out of your mind, and I am just as crazy for standing here talking to you about it." He paused, looking hard into my eyes. "You are really serious!" He searched my face with a distressed expression.

"You know I am, Nishi," I answered, clearly and resolutely.

"Why me?" A pained look crossed Nishi's face.

"You are the only one that can pull it off. That is, if you had a mind to," I coaxed.

"What good will pictures do, even if you are able to get them?" he asked, still fighting with his conscience for a valid reason to get involved, or stay out altogether.

"Photographs," I argued, "will be the whole case, Nishi. One picture of a starving man or a poor soul swelled up with beriberi will tell a hell of a lot more than trying to describe what they looked like."

"That would be undeniable," Nishi agreed.

"What's more," I went on, "it will be hard evidence that these men did exist. By the time this war is over, all, or most of these poor slobs in the hospital right now, will be long dead. I am sure you are aware of that. You also know what happens to the prisoners who die. They are cremated. It would be impossible to look into a crock of ashes and say this guy died of starvation, beatings, or disease. It will be indisputable proof that our captors, the Japs, were nothing more than cruel and in-human beasts."

There was another long period of silence, marked by a lot of soul-searching.

"If I go along with this plan of yours," Nishi asked, "when do you intend to take the pictures?"

"On our next day off, which should come around again in twenty days. That is, if there are no changes in our schedule," I told him.

"I am not sure," Nishi said thoughtfully. "This is pretty risky busi-ness. How big is the camera?"

"The camera has to be built. When I do, it will be made for four-by-five plates. If you are worrying about the soldiers seeing the cam-era and knowing what it is, forget it. It will be nothing more than two innocent-looking black boxes, in which I will store my toothbrushes and tooth powder. With just a little luck, we can pull this off and no-body will be the wiser."

"Luck?" Nishi moaned. "With my past history of luck, they may let me use your blindfold after they make me take it off your bullet-riddled body."

We traveled down the road for a long time before Nishi spoke. "My better judgment tells me to stay out of this, but I will give it con-siderable thought, then do what my conscience dictates."

We reached the scrap pile. I thanked Nishi for taking me to get the malaria treatment.

It was exactly two weeks later that Nishi showed up at the scrap pile. He stopped to talk to Cawashima for a few minutes, then came crawling over the scrap iron carrying his briefcase. It was not unusual to see him with a briefcase. He always had one in hand or strapped to his bike.

He stopped beside me and set the case down alongside the oxygen tank. I was sitting on the tank with my torch all apart, cleaning out the gas ports. Nishi looked around at the Japanese workmen and the other prisoners. Satisfied that no one was paying any attention to us, he said out of the corner of his mouth, "Kirk, if you still want those photographic plates, they are in the briefcase at your feet. There is nobody watching; take them now," he urged.

I reached down into the case and removed a tightly sealed box. I recognized the package with the familiar Japanese characters. I had used the same type of glass plates for copying line drawings in the photo lab while stationed in Tientsin, China. It was a very fast photographic material, good for a pinhole camera, maybe a little too much contrast. There were six 8x10-inch plates. I slipped the box under the oxygen bottle and covered it with a few handfuls of cinders. I looked up at Nishi and said, "I have a problem."

"What is it now?" he asked quickly.

"The camera I built is a 4x5. I can't use these plates unless I cut them. There is only one way I can do that—with a diamond glass cutter."

"You built the camera already?" Nishi raised his eyebrows. "You were pretty sure of yourself. Now you'll have to build another camera for not waiting to find out what size plates I could get."

"Nishi," I appealed, "there is nothing I would like better than to take 8x10 photographs, but under the circumstances, that size plate is too fragile. In addition, it's going to be difficult enough to conceal a 4x5 camera. I am sure the first soldier who spots me carrying a great big 8x10 box will stop me to find out what it is. Even if I could find the material large enough to build the 8x10 camera, I have run out of time. I could never finish it before our day off."

"OK, I see your point. I guess it will have to be a 4x5," he conceded. "Now, tell me why you can't use a regular glass cutter. It would be easier to find."

"Because," I explained, "if my cuts on the plates aren't clean, sharp, and deep, I'll end up with jagged edges on the sides of the plates and won't be able to fit them into the camera."

"This gets more complicated all the time," Nishi complained. "I'll see what I can do. By the way," Nishi growled, changing the subject, "if anyone asks what we were talking about, I told Cawashima I wanted to check with you on the malaria serum reaction. You might tell your friends the same. The fewer people who know about these pictures, the safer it will be."

"No need to worry about that, Nishi; I have no intention of letting any more people know than I think necessary," I assured him. "And you can tell your doctor friend to chalk up another cure. I am long past due for another attack of malaria."

"I doubt that it'll surprise him," Nishi said, and with that, he picked up his briefcase and departed.

During lunch period I scrounged around for a piece of string, but had no luck. In desperation, I removed two of the braided straw ties from one of the raincoats to fashion a harness to hold the box of plates in the small of my back to pack them into camp.

That evening, I informed Dr. Markowitz about what I intended to do. He promised to give me full cooperation. Next, I enlisted Martin A. Gatewood, of Chillicothe, Texas, one of the gallant defenders of Wake Island. He set up a security for me while I was making the exposures, to prevent the Japanese from interrupting me.

I had one more problem to solve, and then I would be all set: I needed a darkroom where I could change the plates. Because this pinhole camera was only one shot at a time, I had to reload with a fresh plate for each picture. I thought of using my blankets. They were stiff enough to stand up by themselves to allow working room beneath them. There was a big "but" to this method, however; if a soldier should happen to enter the barracks, I could ruin all the plates trying to hide them, not to mention being caught breaking one of their rules—blankets are supposed to be folded and placed at the head of each bunk except during sleeping hours. Regardless of the chances I was taking, if I could not find a more suitable place, I would be forced to use my blankets.

That night, after I crawled into bed, I tried to think of some alternative method, until I was overcome with drowsiness and went to sleep. Again, during the night in the air raid shelter, I racked my brain, but kept coming up with a blank.

The next day, true to his word, Nishi showed up on the job and slipped me a diamond glass cutter. "Remember where you got that. I want it back," he said emphatically. "I borrowed it. I'll see you the day after the break for the cutter and the exposed plates."

"What do you mean, the exposed plates?" I demanded. "I had planned to stash them until after the war, then develop them myself."

"Not a good idea," Nishi argued. "You may be forced to move about and they could be ruined. Then all this would be for nothing."

I considered my options for a moment and decided I had very few. He was right. The undeveloped plates could easily be damaged in any number of ways.

"You have a point, Nishi," I agreed. "I'll see you the day after the break."

"Lots of luck," he offered sincerely as he left.

That evening, on my way to the bath, I noticed the door to the Japanese soldiers' bath standing slightly ajar. I detoured to have a look inside. It was a small room with a concrete tank sunk in the middle of the floor, about the size of a freshly dug grave, but not so deep. There was a lip all around the edge of the tub and a piece of plywood leaning against the wall that appeared to be the right size to cover the hole. I hung up my towel on a nail and dragged the plywood over to the tub and tried it. It was a perfect fit. I lifted the board and crawled under it, then let the plywood down over me. The tank was lighttight. This was just what I needed! I became excited. All I had to do now was find someone who knew when the Japanese used this bath—or if they ever did.

Later in the evening, I waited for Kirkpatrick to come in from his job in the galley, located next door to the bathhouse. I called to him as he entered the barracks. "Moose, could I have a word with you?"

"What's on your mind, Terence?" He looked up at me from the floor with his winsome smile.

"I was wondering if the Japs ever use that bath beside the galley. Would you know?"

"Yeah," he said, "they use it every day. They fill the tub about eight o'clock, then turn the steam on, and by lights-out the water is hot and then they bathe." He looked at me, perplexed. "Why, Terence?"

"Oh, no good reason," I lied. "I just wanted to know if the Japs ever took a bath."

"I know you, Terence. You're up to no good. You had better be careful or you'll be in a heap of trouble."

"OK, Moose," I grinned, "I can't hide anything from you. I was actually planning to dynamite their bath sometime when they were all in it, and I would rather not be caught setting the charges."

With that, Kirkpatrick shook his head and continued on his way toward his bunk. I leaned back against my blankets feeling smug about the latest development—now, I had a darkroom. With the last obstacle out of the way, the photographic mission should go off without a hitch. Our day off came right on schedule. I endured the inspection. We were told we had to attack the bedbugs again. They said there were too many of them. One bedbug was too many, but there was only one way to get rid of them—burn the buildings down. Even then, we were not too sure that would do it. There were probably enough of them in each barracks to stomp out the fire.

Next, during the shakedown, I had the camera in plain view. The camera consisted of two cardboard boxes, each open at one end. One of the boxes was slightly smaller than the other so it would slip snugly inside the larger, making the camera lighttight except for the pinhole in the end of the smaller box. The pinhole at present was covered by a piece of black tape. The two halves were separated on my shelf above my bunk. In one, I had some Jap-issue toothbrushes, and in the other, a spoon and a box of tooth powder, just as I had promised Nishi. The Jap soldier picked up both parts of the camera, looked in them and set them down again. The rest of the soldiers pulled my blankets back and I held my breath because the plates I had hidden under my mat had raised the mat about a half inch above normal. Thankfully, he did not notice.

That day, inspection and shakedown finished early. I was ready to begin the operation as soon as I could get my camera loaded. Gatewood and his security guards fanned out all over camp to watch for guards. Meanwhile, I went to the hospital to alert Dr. Markowitz that I was ready. When I returned to the barracks, Gatewood gave me the green light to begin.

I collected everything I would need: my camera, the plates, two templates I had made, and the diamond glass cutter. When the coast was clear, I ducked into the Jap bathhouse.

In the bath and under the plywood, I opened the box of photographic plates after I was sure there was no light leaking around the edges of the tub. I placed a plate on the lid of the carton and with the 5x8 template aligned to the eight-inch side of the plate, I scored the glass with the diamond along the edge of the template. A light tap with the cutter and the glass separated into two 5x8 pieces. Next, using the 4x5 template, I reduced the two 5x8s to four 4x5s. I removed one more 8x10 plate and cut it into four additional 4x5s.

Now, I had eight 4x5 plates. I felt that many would be enough. If I could get in and out of this bathhouse that many times without someone spotting me and wondering what I was doing, I would be pushing my luck to the hilt.

It was also time to quit because I was beginning to perspire. Perspiration had a tendency to leave nasty fingerprints on photographic materials.

I dropped a plate in the large half of the camera with the emulsion side up and slid the smaller half in place. With the camera loaded, I ventured forth to make my first exposure.

The doctor was ready for me. He had his patients waiting in the sun between the barracks and the hospital building. I set the camera down on the edge of a concrete cistern to steady it, and aimed the camera at the sick men standing in a row. I removed the patch from the pinhole after asking them to hold still as long as I had the patch in my hand, and then I began counting. One second, two seconds, three seconds, and so on, up to ten seconds. Then I replaced the patch over the pinhole.

I returned to the bath whenever it was safe to do so, and reloaded. Each time I came back with a loaded camera, Dr. Markowitz and his two corpsmen had a group of sick men waiting to be photographed. In the last picture, two of the men were too weak to stand by themselves. The two corpsmen stood behind them and held them up. After I had taken three more pictures, I felt I had made my point. I then photographed the doctor and his two corpsmen.

Better than an hour was required to complete four exposures. The problem was that a good part of the time was spent dodging the guards. There was no way I could have possibly done it without Gatewood and his lookouts.

Four unexposed plates remained of the original eight. The Japanese had all gone to chow by this time, so I set the camera in the doorway of the bathhouse and took a picture of the main street.

There was one more picture I had to have: a shot of the hydroelectric plant next to our camp. To me, it was a prime military target, and here we were practically nestled under its eaves—as if the Japanese were saying, "If you knock out our plant, you will kill your own men to do it."

There was only one way I could get a picture, and that was from one of the gun towers. The best tower for that coverage was the one on the east wall. The platform was high enough to allow me to bring in a little of the camp buildings in the foreground of my picture.

I changed plates, found Gatewood, and told him what I was going to do. He ran off to tell his men while I went directly to the tower. The ladder to the tower was anchored to the east wall. I climbed with one hand while holding the camera in the other. On the platform, I bellied along the catwalk to the northwest corner of the tower and pointed the camera at the hydroelectric plant.

A shrill whistle! The prearranged signal that the soldiers were in the area.

I peeled off the black tape from the pinhole and started counting: one second, two seconds, three seconds, four seconds, five . . .

Two shrill whistles!! The soldiers were not only close, but they were heading in my direction!

. . . seconds, six seconds, seven seconds, eight . . .

That should do it, I said to myself; I had better get the hell out of here.

With the black tape in hand, I reached around the front of the camera, holding the box still, but my hand shook so badly I missed the hole. I pulled it off and made another try.

With the patch in place to protect the plate from damage, I grabbed the box, scooted back to the ladder, and practically dropped to the ground from a height of about twenty feet.

Gatewood, standing at the north end of the hospital building, beckoned excitedly for me to hurry. I scampered across the open space, and ducked in beside him just as the guard detail turned the far corner of the hospital building and marched to the guard tower to post a guard.

I picked my way to the back door of the barracks and once inside, sat down at the nearest table to catch my breath and to gather my wits. That last picture was too close for comfort. After a rest, I got to my feet, and when my knees stopped shaking, I hurried to remove the exposed plate. As I stepped outside the front door of the barracks into the main street, I got another shock. All the sentries were back on their posts, and one who had not been there before lunch was now pacing back and forth in front of the bathhouse. I hoped he would find no reason to look into the bathtub. If he did, we would have the damnedest shakedown this camp had ever seen.

There were a few prisoners wandering about on the street. I didn't feel I would be conspicuous, so I sat down with my back to the wall of the barracks and placed the camera between my legs to wait. In a few minutes the guard left and walked toward the far corner of the prisoners' bath, which extended about forty feet beyond the soldiers' bathhouse. The instant he disappeared, I made a dash for the darkroom.

Quickly, I unloaded the camera and wrapped all the exposed plates together with paper from the original plates. I picked up the camera and gathered up all the spare plates. I never considered reloading the camera again; I had had enough. The enemy traffic was becoming too heavy. I reached up to lift the plywood cover . . .

I froze! A Japanese spoke in the room above me . . . then another voice. My heart began pounding. I held my breath, afraid they would hear me, but I could not control it. I began to wheeze. My face felt flushed. I put my head against the cold concrete on the side of the tub to cool down. They won't do anything to me even if they do catch me, I consoled myself. Maybe a little slapping around, nothing more.

It was no good. I knew I was telling myself a damn lie. The longer I squatted in the tank, thinking about my situation, the more terrified I became. If a guard should lift the cover and see me with all this photographic material, he would shoot me without batting an eye.

The sound of their voices quieted a little. I realized then they were not inside, but standing in the doorway. A few minutes passed and all was quiet. I relaxed and began chastising myself for having that emotional outbreak of fright.

All was quiet for another few minutes, then I lifted the plywood cover to peer through the crack. There was no sound nor anyone in the doorway. I climbed out noiselessly and ran to the door. There were no guards anywhere. Gatewood was standing in the doorway of our barracks; when he saw me, he began frantically giving me the hand and arm signals for double time. I ran, and he held the door open for me as I covered the distance in a wink.

"I thought you were a goner," he said. "One of those Japs had a towel around his neck, and I think he was planning to take a bath. You were lucky that sentry came around the corner when he did to stop him, or that Jap would have gone into the bathhouse. They both talked by the door for a while, then the guy with the towel went back down the street. I would like to have known what he said to that guy to make him change his mind," Gatewood wondered out loud.

"I know," I said. "He told him the bath was closed until after dark."

"How did you know that?" he asked, surprised.

"It was easy," I laughed, remembering what Kirkpatrick had told me about their bath schedule. "I speak Japanese," I fibbed.

I destroyed the camera, dumped the surplus plates in the toilet, fashioned a small package from the original box, and carefully packed the exposed plates to protect them from damage.

The next day at work, Nishi came by to ask me how the malaria serum was affecting me. When I was sure no one was watching, I dropped the box of plates and the diamond cutter into his open brief-case, which he had conveniently placed alongside my oxygen tank.

One week later, Nishi delivered the developed plates and thirty prints, five of each picture. I hid them quickly in the scrap pile, then returned to my equipment and Nishi. "Will you tell me something, Nishi?" I asked.

"Perhaps," he said. "What is it?"

"What made you do it? I doubted at first that you would go through with the plan."

Nishi studied me thoughtfully for a few moments and then shrugged.

"I really do not know," he answered slowly. "Maybe it was because I was raised in the States. We think a lot differently in America than people elsewhere on earth. Most of us become angry with the villain who makes anyone suffer, no matter who they are. Somewhere in my growing up, maybe it was the Saturday-afternoon matinee, I learned to root for the underdog, especially when the odds were against him. Perhaps I wanted to be the all-American boy, do something gutsy, or be a hero.

"The point you made—that somebody should pay for this— brought me into agreement with you. That, and a little score of my own

I felt should be settled over the shabby trick they pulled on me. Then again, maybe I did it just for the hell of it. Then, too, as long as you were sticking your neck out a mile, and I was already committed, the least I could do was to help get us both killed," he said with a laugh.

"Whatever your reason, Nishi, I will see to it that you are given the credit due you," I said.

The Last Air Raid

The pictures were spread out under my sleeping mat, well hidden, so there were no telltale lumps or bumps to give them away. I resigned myself to the fact that they would stay there until the end of the war.

June passed; our day off came late in July. In the afternoon of that day, the three other section leaders in the barracks, along with an ad hoc committee that had been formed specifically to take over the food distribution, came to see me. I had been administering the food since I organized the system in the barracks across the street the day we arrived from Yawata. This committee had somehow convinced the other section leaders and many followers that they had a better method to dispense the food. They promised that their system would mean more food for everyone. My past experience made me skeptical, but how can you argue with hungry men when someone tells them there is a way for them to have more food? I made no effort to dissuade them, and even offered to give them my records to help if they wanted. They declined.

Following the first meal under the new management, Gatewood came to me.

"Those guys are padding their own buckets," he told me. "I have been watching them. They're pretty slick, but I know," he assured me.

Gatewood had been the rice paddle man ever since I took over the food in the other barracks. No one had ever accused him of being dishonest, so this whole matter was a personal affront to him and he was bothered by it.

To me, it was a relief. I had not realized how much time it had demanded of me and the worry it caused to see that for every meal, everyone in the barracks got an equal share of rice. This had been a self-appointed job that I had held for better than two years. I welcomed the rest.

The new committee's system was used to serve the meals that evening and the following morning—an actual total of three meals, because they also dished out the noon meal with the morning chow, which everyone took to work in their mess kits.

The next evening, Gatewood, at my suggestion, had informed the other section leaders as to what was happening. All the leaders watched the new dealers dish out the chow at a discreet distance, mindful of what Gatewood had told them, until all the rice (millet) had been distributed in the various section buckets.

Before the food could be taken away, the leaders gave me the high sign to reveal the fraud. I stepped forward to the edge of the tier as spokesman for the barracks, and explained to all hands what had just happened.

Gatewood then proceeded to paddle the rice back into the original buckets as everyone gathered to watch. When he had finished dishing out equal amounts from each section's bucket, the committee's section's share was better than an eighth of a bucket more.

All the prisoners were furious. It was suggested that the members of the committee be shoved headfirst into the ten-hole at the back of the barracks and be made to swim around in the excrement for an hour. Others proposed they be flogged; however, sanity prevailed, and everyone agreed the punishment meted out was worse than any other that could have been contrived. The three members of the committee were put on half rations for eight consecutive meals to make up for what they had stolen.

The section leaders asked me to take my old job back administering the chow, but I declined, giving them two reasons.

"There must have been doubt in your minds," I told them, "before this happened, or that ad hoc committee could not have convinced you so easily. Now, I am afraid there will always be doubt. My second reason," I continued, "is that I like my newfound freedom from worry. However, I can recommend a good man to take my place. Tony the Greek in the third section has substituted for me many times when I had malaria. I'll turn the books over to him if you say the word."

The section leaders agreed. Tony got the job taking care of the food, and Gatewood returned to his job as the paddle man.

August arrived, and with it a worrisome problem for me. I was off my feed. That is exactly what it was—horse feed. The millet the Japs had been substituting for rice since way back in the spring of 1943, when we were in Yawata, had slowly been increased in our diet and like amounts of rice decreased. Now, we were living on 100 percent millet—a level teacup each meal.

Millet is great for horses, I think, but it raises hell with the intestines of a human being. In order to digest it, we would need another fifty feet of intestines. It is easy to see why the whole camp had the trots, and had had for years. As long as we had nothing else to eat except horse feed, it would be impossible to cure our diarrhea.

I called upon Dr. Markowitz, knowing full well I was wasting my time—except for that glimmer of hope within every human, even in the worst of times. Like Foots Anderson used to say, "There will be a better day tomorrow."

In this case, I hoped that the Japanese may have broken down and given the doctor something to help us.

"Sorry," he sympathized, "all I have is charcoal."

"Not that junk," I groaned. "Doctor, I have been taking charcoal for years, and to date, it has done absolutely nothing for me."

"If you like," the doctor suggested, "I can give you a chit to include you in the white rice diet." Then he added, "There's not much food value in the rice because it is mostly water, but it will be easier on your intestines," he promised.

I tried the white rice, and as the doctor had predicted, it contained very little nourishment—although it did slow my diarrhea some. I began to lose weight, which was bad because I had very little to spare.

On the morning of the eighth of August, I trudged wearily out the gate to the train, and then hiked from the train to the scrap pile. The majority of the prisoners were totally ineffective in their jobs. Most were too weak to work at all because of the lack of proper food, and too tired to care from lack of sleep. Almost every night for the past three months, bombers had come on their midnight visits. We spent sleepless nights standing two, three, and sometimes four hours packed together in our bamboo air raid shelter.

This morning differed very little from any other morning, until the lament of "Moaning Minnie" shattered the serenity of the valley so early in the day. Although the air raid siren warned us of impending danger, our Japanese escorts paid no attention. We had not had a daylight raid since the fifteenth of June last year. Despite the fact that we spent most of our nights in the air raid shelter and heard the rumble of bombs exploding in the distance, from all outward appearances, we lived in a peaceful valley, untouched by war.

I set up my cutting equipment and perched on a large slab of steel. I chose this particular one because it was about five inches thick; it had enough mass so I could sit in one place and burn for an hour without having to move.

The last thing in the world I wanted to do was to be the first to begin working, so I squatted on the slab and broke down my torch to inspect the gas ports. Soon, the Japanese burners were all cutting along with a few of the prisoners. As I picked up my spark lighter to ignite my torch, I was startled by the raucous voice of "Burping Betsy," and dropped the lighter.

It was unusual to have the attack signal come so close behind the warning siren. I gazed at the clear blue sky and scanned the mountaintops that ringed our little valley. It was just another beautiful day. The heavens were clear and a deep blue. I glanced at the other prisoners and Japanese workers. No one seemed the least bit concerned.

I turned back to my work, lit the torch, and applied the flame to the slab. I began cutting a wide slot in the rusty steel plate so the molten metal would fall out the bottom and not puddle up and blow back at me. I became mesmerized by the blue cutting flame of the torch as it ate its way slowly through the thick piece of steel.

I had cut about halfway across the four-foot chunk of steel when I was jolted back to reality by a strange sound, a racket like hailstones hitting a tin roof. I looked up and saw hundreds of smoking white sticks dropping out of the sky and showering the nearest factory building about a quarter of a mile away. It was the rolling mills, where many prisoners worked.

I jumped to my feet, dropped my torch, and faced the west. There I beheld the most overwhelming sight I had ever seen in my life. Formation after formation of four-engine bombers were topping the rim of the western mountains and slipping quietly into the valley. It was strange. There was no sound from their engines that I could hear. The bombers were a study of silver pendants gliding ghostlike across a background of a blue-velvet sky, stretching across the mountains from north to south. I watched agog as the bombers drew closer. They were so low I could see them opening their bomb bay doors. Next, great black canisters the size of boxcars began falling from their bellies. A short distance from the planes, the canisters literally flew apart, scattering hundreds and hundreds of small, white cylindrical sticks in all directions. Each stick was a firebomb that came plummeting to earth and left a trail of white smoke behind it.

I have no idea how long I stood transfixed, gaping at the awesome spectacle, but I snapped back to my senses when a firebomb hit the ground a short distance away. I looked about; there was not a soul in sight. Everyone had obviously sought the shelters at the first sight of the planes.

I jumped off the slab and threaded my way through the pile of scrap iron to the railroad track. I started running toward the shelter on the beach, located several hundred yards to the west in the direction of the oncoming B-29s. I had not taken more than a dozen steps when I remembered I had left my go-aheads (wooden shoes) behind. I retraced my steps, gingerly now, realizing I was barefoot.

The bombs were falling off to my right into the heart of the factory, and further along the mountain to the south in the city of Yawata. I picked up my go-aheads and noticed the torch was still burning.

I turned it off and tucked it under the heavy piece of scrap iron I had been cutting so it would not get broken by a bomb.

I must be out of my mind, it came to me in a flash; *my life is in peril. What am I doing? I had better get the hell out of here.*

As I turned to go, an anti-aircraft battery opened fire on the B-29s from the mountaintop to the north, across the bay, pumping flack into the formations of bombers. Like hawks, three small planes swooped down out of the blue; thin streaks of white smoke jutted from each plane straight at the gun position. Suddenly, the whole top of the mountain seemed to erupt in one terrific explosion. There was no more action from the mountaintop gun. None of the B-29s appeared to have been harmed.

I hurried back to the track. When I reached the point where I had stopped to go back for my shoes, I found the area strewn with brightly burning firebombs. They were as close as two feet to each other, but not more than three feet apart. When I saw the firebombs, I detoured over the scrap pile without thinking, taking the most direct route to the shelter. Within a few minutes, I panted up to the air raid shelter still carrying my go-aheads in my hand. I had just run barefoot over the scrap iron pile and didn't get a scratch.

All the prisoners were in the hole when I arrived. The shelter had not changed since the time we visited it more than two years before, except for a few cinders that had settled in. We crowded inside and waited for the guards to come get us as they had done on the last raid, but nobody came; even the pushers had deserted us. Perhaps they went to a safer shelter. I could not blame them; anything would be better than this, even a hole in the ground. Corrugated-iron sheeting is not much protection against a bomb, or even a firebomb.

There was a feeling of elation at first. At last, Uncle Sam was giving them hell. I felt it was long overdue. As time went by, the earth rumbled as bombs lay waste to the land, its buildings, and its people. The sounds were strange to our ears: rushing noises, like the blowing of a strong wind; crackling, like electricity or wood splitting and breaking; the familiar speeding freight train sound of heavy bombs, like those used in the first raid, followed by deep rumbling as the earth quaked. There was no pattern to these heavy bombs. They seemed to be dropping them everywhere at random. No bombs had landed near us; it sounded like they were exploding in the direction of the factory, the city of Yawata, or further away to the east.

The light coming through the entrance of the shelter was beginning to fade. In about an hour, it was quite dark outside. During the whole time, the bombers had been hammering relentlessly at everything in the area. As we seemed to be out of their target zone, I decided to venture outside to have a look.

I left the shelter and walked to the water's edge, noting the fires burning directly to the south, west, and east of our position. Directly across from us, over a narrow inlet from the bay, an oil storage tank was erupting violently. Great billows of black smoke were passing over us and out over the bay. That was part of the reason it was so dark. In all directions except due north, fires were raging out of control and adding to the ever-darkening pall now engulfing the valley that, but a few hours earlier, had basked complacently in the noonday sun. To the north, the only clear spot—a small fishing village nestled between the bay and the base of the mountain—was untouched, still shining brightly in the sun.

They have escaped destruction, I thought as I watched. But no, at that very moment a flurry of firebombs began dropping out of the overhanging smoke into the water just offshore from where I was standing and marched across the bay toward the village. The white cylinders trailing smoke moved up out of the water, over the fishing boats, up on the docks, into the village, and on into the forest beyond. I watched the smoke begin to rise from the docks and boats; next came the flames, and within minutes, the boats, docks, village, and forest were all a roaring inferno.

It was an odd sight to see the firebombs that had landed in the bay shining upward through the murky waters. Magnesium firebombs require no oxygen to burn. They develop their own oxidizing agent once they are ignited. There is no way to extinguish the bombs; they must burn themselves out. While they are in the process, they ignite anything flammable in contact with or near them. At this moment, the people in the village were fighting a losing battle against the bombs.

I decided to return to the shelter in case another bomber had the same target in mind. The next bombardier may loose his bombs a tad earlier, which would put me in the target area.

Back at the shelter, I learned that Frank Siejack of Baltimore, Maryland, and Powney had braved the firebomb storm to get our mess kits from the tin shack on the other side of the scrap pile where we had left them this morning. I polished off my white rice; that is, I drank it. It was like thin soup.

I sat in the entrance for some time watching the light fade. It was now twilight. I became restless again and decided to take another tour. This time, I went further along the beach in the direction I had gone before. The fishing village was still burning, but not as violently. The docks were gone along with some of the boats, while a few of the larger boats were adrift and burning. I could not see if the forest was still afire for all the smoke from the village. It was dark everywhere now, even over the fishing village—dark like dusk. Ashes were falling about me like snowflakes.

I selected a high spot at the point where the inlet and the bay met, hoping to get a better view of the factory. Suddenly, everything blacked out. As I returned to semiconsciousness, I gasped for air. I could not get my breath. I felt as if I were being smothered in a feather bed. I was falling, twisting, and somersaulting as if in a dream.

When my world finally returned to normal, I found myself lying flat on my back, some distance down the hill from where I had been standing. I lay quiet for a short time, mentally checking every part of my body for damage. I could feel no pain. Everything appeared to be attached in its proper place, so I got slowly to my feet. Standing quietly for a moment, I again checked for holes and bleeding, but found everything satisfactory. As I started to move, I experienced a slight dizziness that caused me to wobble when I took my first step. I stumbled a few times on my way back to the air raid shelter, but I attributed that to the darkness. I crawled in and leaned against the wall in the shelter. I still was not sure what had happened to me out there. Whatever the explosion was, I neither heard nor saw a thing before it blew. I promised myself that after the smoke cleared a little, I would go back out there to see if I could determine what had caused it.

It could have been a delayed-action bomb, I surmised. Maybe it had been buried out there for a long time. It had to have been buried deep, because if it had been near the surface, that blast would have blown me to kingdom come. That was the only answer I could come up with—that the force of the blast was funneled straight up instead of sideways, because the bomb had been buried deep in the loose cinders.

Something wet trickled down the side of my face under my left ear. I reached my hand up and came away with wet fingers—slick at first, then, in a moment, they became sticky. Blood, I suspected; I must have scratched myself.

I felt drowsy. I glanced at the entrance, noting the degree of darkness. It would be a long time before the smoke cleared, I thought. I would just close my eyes and rest a bit.

"Wake up, wake up," someone said, shaking me, "the guards are here."

I must have dozed off, I thought. I shook my head to clear away the confusion, then crawled out of the shelter.

Outside, it was dark. Not black as it was earlier, but overcast and smoky everywhere. Visibility was down to a few hundred feet or less.

"What time is it?" I asked Langston as I lined up in ranks beside him.

"About five, I think," he answered.

"When did the raid stop?"

"What do you mean, when did it stop?" He looked puzzled. "Where have you been?"

"Asleep, I guess," I answered sheepishly.

"Asleep," he echoed. "How could you sleep through all that racket?" Then he added, "As close as I can figure, the bombing stopped about a half hour ago."

My mind was still foggy, but there were two things I was sure of: my left ear hurt like hell, and I had slept away a part of my life I had not wanted to miss. I would have liked to determine what caused that blast. If there was a hole out there, that would tell me a lot. I would know it had been a delayed bomb buried deep in the cinders.

We stood waiting while the Japs counted us to make sure we were all present, which seemed to take them more time than usual. The soldiers seemed to be acting strange, glancing here and there as if expecting some unwanted visitors. Perhaps after the drubbing they had just taken, they feared for our lives—or maybe theirs, if they tried to protect us from the possible angry mobs.

I wondered if we were going to collect our equipment that we had left out on the scrap pile and return it to the shed. The question was answered even as I formed the thought. One of the guards started running toward the factory, calling over his shoulder, "*Hiahcoo, hiahcoo!*" [Hurry, hurry!]

We passed the equipment shed at a run. The door to the corrugated shack was wide open, and all the pushers and Japanese workmen were gone. No one could be seen anywhere. I wondered what could have happened to them. As we ran, I got the feeling that except for this small group of prisoners of war and the two soldiers, there was not another living soul on earth. It was spooky running through the semidarkness; we saw switch engines, stopped dead on their tracks with fires still burning in their boilers, but no engineers or brakemen could be seen anywhere to tend them. Shop doors stood ajar, but no people nor any sounds except the clatter of our wooden shoes and the incessant cries of *Hiahcoo* from the guards greeted the strange stillness.

The all-clear sounded. That made me feel better. We were not alone after all—someone had to activate the siren.

Compared to the raid a year ago, this run through the factory was a lot different; there was a lot of evidence of destruction. Large pieces of metal were laying about; buildings had burnt to the ground with only a telltale pile of glowing embers to mark the place where once an office building stood. There were an untold number of factory buildings with their sides blown in. Smoke still drifted from open scars in the buildings. To me, it looked as if it would be a long time before this plant would be open for business again.

We arrived at the train and there, heard the bad news. A prisoner who worked in the rolling mills had been killed by a firebomb that came right through the roof. He took a direct hit on the back of his head—he never knew what hit him. Another prisoner of the same crew had his forearm torn off at the elbow by a firebomb. It occurred just as the raid had begun, probably when I first heard the clatter and looked up to see the hundreds of firebombs hitting the rolling mills. It had been a good six hours since the bombing started, and as yet, the prisoner who had lost his arm had not received any medical attention. One of his buddies had tied a rag around the stump to keep him from bleeding to death. The man was in shock and needed medical attention badly.

A rumor quickly spread through the train that the firebombs had caused a firestorm in the city of Yawata, and the death toll was more than 65,000. Someone also passed on the information that the citadel had burnt to the ground. Wishful thinking, I was sure; there was nothing in that building that could burn except the straw mats on the iron bunks.

The firestorm in Yawata accounts for not having seen anyone; the workmen and pushers must have all gone home to find out what was left of their homes and families, and to pick up the pieces. After having seen the bamboo, straw, and rice-paper houses packed together with not enough room between them to swing a cat, plus the narrow streets, a firestorm would have a high mortality.

When the prisoner who had lost his arm reached camp, Dr. Markowitz took over and did a satisfactory repair job on the man's stump. He used a few surgical implements donated by the prisoners, like a rusty hacksaw blade, a pocketknife, and one he had himself, a red-hot poker from the stove. To say the good doctor worked under a handicap was an understatement. Surgical equipment was nonexistent. Except for charcoal—which was plentiful in our ill-equipped hospital—there was nothing to save lives.

18

The Fat Man

Following the big raid on the eighth of August, with all its excitement, we were herded again at midnight to stand for hours in our bamboo air raid shelter and listen to the bombs exploding on some distant target.

Finally, back on my mat, I dozed off at about 3 A.M. While I slept, a B-29 named *Bock's Car* was winging its way across the Pacific toward Japan and me. It had an atomic bomb in its belly. Its destination was the arsenal at Kokura on the northeast coast of the island of Kyushu. There were no towns, buildings, or farms, only a hydroelectric plant and a prisoner of war camp. It was a military area with an arsenal somewhere close at hand.

This bomb in the belly of *Bock's Car* was ten feet, eight inches long and five feet in diameter, and was intended to destroy the stockpile of military arms and equipment stored in the arsenal at Kokura. Unknown to the crew, there was also a prison camp with 670-some wretched, starving Allied prisoners of war.

However, it was not meant to be; with mechanical failure, human error, and God's help, we survived.

Before takeoff, a crewman discovered a malfunctioning fuel pump that served an auxiliary fuel tank containing 600 gallons of gasoline. The captain decided that gasoline was nonessential because there was an adequate supply and more in the other tanks to make the trip from Tinian to Japan, and then to the American-held base on Iwo Jima.

When *Bock's Car* reached Yakushima, an island off the south coast of Kyushu, at 8:09 A.M. Tokyo time, to rendezvous with its escorts, only the instrument plane, *The Great Artiste*, was on station. The other aircraft, the photographic plane, was late.

While *Bock's Car* and *The Great Artiste* circled at the rendezvous area waiting for the photo plane, the skipper of *Bock's Car* received a weather report from an advanced scout plane that the target area was clear. *Bock's Car* was ready for the bombing run, but the skipper decided to wait another thirty-five or forty minutes, hoping the photo plane would show.

At that time, the photo plane was hopelessly lost, flying far to the north in a wide circle searching for *Bock's Car*, and worse, it had taken off without the photographer, who had stepped off the plane and run to his tent to get his parachute.

Meanwhile, back in Kokura, the weather was changing. A northeaster was beginning to blow the smoke from the air raid of the day before back to Japan. A blanket of haze, thick in places, was spreading over the land.

Bock's Car finally arrived over Kokura to drop the "Fat Man" (the plutonium bomb). The bombardier had specific orders not to drop the weapon except on visual targets. *Bock's Car* plied back and forth over Kokura while the bombardier searched anxiously for a hole in our protective mantle below. After the third pass, the anti-aircraft batteries were beginning to get the range. Not only was the ack-ack a worry, but spending so much time over the target was inviting fighters. They were trying to climb to the high altitude of the B-29s. Worst of all, fuel was running out because of the bad pump that denied them the use of the 600 gallons in their reserve tank.

The skipper gave the word to abort the Kokura mission, and *Bock's Car* changed course toward Nagasaki.

19

The Bountiful B-29s

I was awakened after only a short nap by the Japanese bugler blowing the Japanese version of reveille. Today was the ninth of August. I got up wishing I could go back to bed. These all-night stands in the air raid shelter were killing me for lack of sleep.

I waited for roll call, pondering the outcome of this day. I remembered the raid of a year ago. There had been no work in the factory for two weeks. Instead, we worked in the excavation near camp digging and carrying dirt out of the hole on yoho poles. I dreaded the thought of having to go back to that again. It was damn hard work, and my physical condition this year, compared to last, was very poor. I doubted that I could do it.

Breakfast came around and with it, millet for the noon meal. That was an indication that we would not be in camp for lunch. As the clock moved on to eight o'clock, we were still waiting to go to work.

This raid, I concluded, must have upset them again, just as the last raid had done. They were not sure what to do with us.

The weather was clear and warm, and it felt good in the sunshine. The prisoners began drifting into the main street with their mess kits, fully expecting to be called for work. As the minutes ticked by eight o'clock, the sky began to cloud over, and in fifteen to twenty minutes, smoke started blowing in from the sea, covering the land with haze. The smoke, residue of yesterday's bombing raid, increased as time passed. Dark clouds at times blotted out the sun. It was an eerie sight for this time of day, changing from sunlight to twilight from minute to minute.

Thinking of the raid, I unconsciously put my hand to my left ear. I was thankful it had stopped hurting. Nine o'clock came and went. Finally, a soldier entered the barracks and announced that there would be no work today. We must spend our time killing bedbugs.

The merchant seamen living in the barracks next to ours, beside the galley, passed the word that we were having fish for supper. This was a first; they'd never before fed us fish. This fish, they said, had been cooked early this morning at the same time they prepared our breakfast. After the millet and stew were taken from the bins and distributed to the barracks, the fish was placed there to await our supper. The fish, they said, was covered with flies.

That evening we had fish, the same fish the merchant seamen had reported seeing nine hours earlier. Needless to say, the mackerel were alive with maggots. I placed my fish on the lid of my bento (lunch) box that I still had from Yawata, while I ate my rice and stew. For a moment, I could have sworn I saw the fish move. It was then I decided to take it outside and scrape off the maggots to keep the fish from walking away. When I got around to eating it, I found it very tasty (yuck). I could not bring myself to do as some of the others had done; they ate fish, maggots and all. They said that everything tasted just like fish.

The second day in camp was no different than the first. We killed bedbugs all day so we could sleep at night. There were no more air raid sirens. We speculated that there was nothing left worth bombing. Whatever the reason, we were all thankful for small favors.

Five days later, August fifteenth dawned. The morning passed like it had the last few days, but late in the afternoon a soldier came into the barracks and ordered everyone outside to assemble in the quadrangle near the Japanese soldiers' billet. Except for the main street, the quadrangle was the largest open space in camp. Even at that, there was not enough room for all the prisoners to assemble. Some had to find standing room on the main street so they could hear what was being said.

The Japanese colonel came out of the office and mounted a stepladder held for him by the sergeant major. The colonel looked around into the eyes of the prisoners for a full minute; then, without the aid of an interpreter he blurted, "The war is over," in flawless English. He paused, perhaps expecting some kind of reaction from the men standing in front of him.

There was no sound or change of expression from the prisoners. All he got was a deadpan stare from 670 tired, bone-weary, starving men.

"Japan is a poor nation. We have lost the war," he said, with a hurried delivery.

I could see he was having difficulty maintaining his composure. I could feel absolutely no sympathy for him.

"We would be grateful to you if you would leave your clothes behind when you go. I am sure this coming winter is going to be long, hard, and cold for the Japanese people." Again, he paused to search the faces of the men before him. Not one, if they felt as I did, would have given an ounce of compassion for the whole Japanese race; no doubt he saw it in our faces.

The colonel climbed down the ladder and disappeared among his soldiers, who were standing, facing us, armed to the teeth. The crowd broke up and the men drifted back to their barracks to consider what they had just heard, not quite believing it. As for me, after forty-five months in prison and still seeing armed guards with fixed bayonets walking post, I, too, was having difficulty accepting it as the truth.

The only change that took place in camp that night was all hands dragged their blankets outside after shaking off the bedbugs in the barracks, and then slept on the ground. All the barracks were surrendered to the blood-sucking bedbugs. Although the ground was hard, there was very little difference between it and the straw mats.

"The Japs are gone! The Japs are gone!" someone yelled, running through the prone figures stretched out all over the street, and managing to arouse the whole camp.

During the midnight hours, the Japanese had packed up their gear, picked up their weapons, and—without so much as a good-bye, kiss my ass, or go to hell—like thieves, they sneaked away in the night.

Within an hour, the marines had taken over the duties of security of the compound by establishing a guard and posting sentries. We were still in a hostile country; it was our duty. There were six Roman swords in the guardhouse, left behind by the Japanese in their hurry to vacate the camp. The marines adopted and used the swords to arm the guards.

It was anyone's guess what would happen to us now that we had been left to fend for ourselves. Kirkpatrick had taken over the galley and had assured everyone there was enough food to keep us for a week.

Our new commanding officer, Major W. O. Dorris of the United States Army, cautioned us to sit tight until the American forces made contact.

Two days passed before we saw any planes, but even then, they were too high and too far away for us to signal them.

Late on the third day, a Japanese gendarme came to the gate and informed us that there had been a food drop west of Kokura. Fourteen volunteers, myself included, went out to retrieve the food.

We commandeered a truck from the power plant next door, much to the displeasure of the local maintenance crew.

D.B. Wilson drove the vehicle out to the designated area, which turned out to be an abandoned Jap army base. The food had landed outside the fence and was scattered over ten acres. It was canned goods, and practically all of it had burst on impact. There was very little we could salvage.

Early the next morning, the marines, with the help of everyone in camp, started a project at the water's edge on the beach north of camp. All the white rags and white clothing in camp were collected and laid out in a panel on the sand, spelling POW in 20-foot letters. A long white arrow pointed directly at our compound. The sign was all completed by 9 A.M.

Less than an hour went by when a small combat plane, flying north about a quarter of a mile west of camp, spotted the panel. A lot of skywatchers were on hand, and they saw the plane veer sharply and head straight for us. A shout went up: "He's seen us!" they cried, "he's seen us!"

The plane flew low over the beach waggling his wings, and passed out of sight behind the small hill at the northeast corner of camp. In about three minutes he came at us from the south at rooftop level and roared over camp, going like a bat out of hell. He cleared the barracks peaks by inches, and the thundering of his engine shook every lousy bedbug from its hiding place. As he ripped past the north edge of the compound, he swooped into a vertical climb, again waggling his square-cut wings. He continued straight for the stars until he appeared to be hanging on his propeller, then he winged over and came at us in a power dive, pulling out at the last instant in a deafening roar, missing the peaks of the buildings with no more clearance than a sheet of tissue paper, while the backwash from his prop ruffled the roofs of the barracks.

God, I thrilled. A lump welled up in my throat.

"I am proud to be an American," I shouted, trying to add a little more noise to the din. "That is how we won this goddamn war—sheer guts!" I yelled after him waving my arms.

The pilot brought his plane up to a few thousand feet and leveled off, heading south. Three hours passed and he was back, leading a flight of B-29s. There were six of them. Before the bombers arrived over camp, the fighter whipped in ahead, circled, and dropped something on the beach.

Everyone, except the two guys who went to look for whatever it was the pilot dropped, was standing in the street watching the oncoming bombers. As the B-29s reached the outer boundary of our camp, they were so low I could count the rivets on their skins. Their bomb bay doors were wide open. The lead plane disgorged four or five pallets with brightly colored parachutes attached, one at each corner of the pallets. The idea, I think, was for all four chutes to open simultaneously and lower the pallet slowly to the ground. Only a second lieutenant could be given credit for a brainstorm like that.

When the first pallet dropped from the plane, only one chute opened and the pallet dumped its load.

"TAKE COVER!" everyone yelled.

Like magic, everybody vanished. We hadn't gotten out of the way one instant too soon, as cases of canned food began marching up the main street, exploding on impact.

After the bombers had passed, it was a minute or two before any-one ventured from their hiding places.

Bombing us with food was more frightening than the real thing. During the war everyone took their chances; all offerings were marked TO WHOM IT MAY CONCERN. Here and now, however, all packages were addressed to us. How could they miss with their experience?

Miraculously, there were no casualties; a survey of the damage fol-lowing the food drop was in itself incredible. Only one structure had suffered. Our bamboo air raid shelter had been completely demol-ished by three cases of peaches. As for the rest of the compound, where the cases of food walked up the main street, chicken noodles were splattered all over the fronts of the barracks and hanging from the electric wires like tinsel.

The bulk of the cardboard cartons and cases fell behind camp on the beach. The cushioning effect of the sand saved most of the food from damage.

The two men who retrieved the item dropped from the fighter plane returned. One of them was carrying a monkey wrench with a note attached. "You people were lucky," the handwritten message read, "you were scheduled for THE BOMB."

Not knowing what was meant by THE BOMB, the information was meaningless.

Without waiting for someone to decide what should be done with the food and whatever else was in the drop, I told the corporal of the guard to send his men out and escort all cases and cartons to the empty barracks next to the guardhouse.

There, I supervised the handling of all supplies. No one questioned my authority or right to do so. First of all, I was a marine; marines had taken complete control of everything in the compound—except the hospital, of course, which was Dr. Markowitz's domain. My reputation for fairness and honesty was thus far unblemished in spite of the at-tempt by the ad hoc committee over the food a while back.

With the help of Courtney and a curly-headed kid named Roberts—both submarine sailors from the Grenadier and members of Woodie Woodall's section—we were able to establish a smoothly running commissary store.

One of the packers bringing in the cases of food reported a Japanese civilian killed during the food drop. The slain man, he said, was in a corrugated-iron building behind the power plant.

I went over to check out his story. It was true. A case of peaches had smashed through the roof, leaving a gaping hole. Had the Japanese workman been anywhere else in the building at that time, instead of sitting at the little table eating his lunch, he could have had peaches for lunch instead of the other way around.

I reported the death to the Japanese in the power plant, then returned to camp. Kirkpatrick was in the commissary with his crew. Roberts was loading him down with all kinds of canned food for our supper. Courtney was busy issuing chocolate bars and cigarettes to the section leaders. It was a pleasure to see all the happy faces for a change, as the section leaders from each barracks waited to receive their share of the treasure.

"Only one chocolate bar per man per day," Courtney was telling them. "Just like it says on the wrapper."

That evening, we had soup that would have made a gourmet drool. It was loaded with noodles, meatballs, tomatoes, and everything the cooks could use to make it taste *gooood*. For the first time in years, we had all we wanted to eat. Unfortunately, our stomachs had shrunk so small that two bowls of soup was too much. The millet went begging. It ended up as garbage, which was a real problem. It was also a first; we had never had garbage before and had no idea what to do with it. Eventually, it was dumped into one of the barracks toilets, just where it belonged.

A week passed, and we still had a lot of food in the commissary from the original food drop when another flight of B-29s was spotted heading our way. Immediately, everyone panicked and ran out of camp and onto the beach. The flight of nine four-engine giants passed low over us and continued on. This time their bomb bay doors were closed.

I wondered if they were passing over just to pay their respects, or if they intended to double back and bomb us again with food.

We watched as they flew out to sea. About a mile out, one of the planes broke away from the formation and circled to the west, rounded the power plant, and made a direct run toward the beach. The single B-29 came in at treetop level. The plane was equipped with a very powerful public address system, and when the giant reached a point directly overhead, a voice like the crack of doom shook the sandy beach: "Get off the beach, get off the beach, get off the beach . . ." The voice faded away in the noise of the engines as the plane passed out of range.

The marine guards herded everyone back to the compound wall. After allowing a few minutes for us to clear the beach, the planes came in one at a time, each in turn depositing a long cylinder on the beach that buried itself about three-quarters of its length in the sand.

After the last plane released its cylinder, the whole camp went out to carry in the treasure. The nine cylinders, we learned, were made of six 55-gallon drums each, welded end-to-end with the tops and bottoms cut out, except for the bottom barrel, making one long container. The Army Air Force had filled the cylinders with food, clothing, cigarettes, toilet articles, etc., then tacked a thin metal plate over the open end with an arc welder. The canisters were not too difficult to break into. We used the monkey wrench provided us by the fighter pilot.

Before the day was over, everyone in camp had a new U.S. Army uniform, including underwear and socks. There was a slight problem fitting the whole camp with shoes. When the popular sizes ran out, we had to issue sizes two, three, and four sizes too large. Nobody complained; any size shoe was better than wooden shoes, or no shoes at all.

Among the many good things we received that day were medicines and medical supplies. We hurried them to the hospital where they might still save a life or ease a pain. We were supplied with more canned and packaged foods like bacon, hams, flour, canned milk, raisins, all kinds of dried fruit, more chocolate bars, and a variety of candy bars—almost everything anyone could imagine that could be packaged dry or in cans. In addition, we were provided with ciga-rettes—Lucky Strikes, Camels, and Chesterfields, by the cases. There were many choices of cigars, pipes, pipe tobacco, snuff, and chewing tobacco. It was as if they had sent us a complete commissary and post exchange.

Included in the drop were back issues of *Life* magazine and a num-ber of copies of *The Honolulu Advertiser*, a newspaper. It was through these publications we learned about the atom bomb and the part it played in ending the war. I, for one, really did not care how they did it, as long as the war was over.

During the next two weeks there was very little activity about camp. Everyone was relaxing and putting on weight. I must have gained ten pounds or more. There was no way of knowing, but I was sure I weighed at least 110 pounds, maybe even 120. We lolled around all day and slept under the stars at night, still keeping away from the barracks full of bedbugs. They were getting more voracious every day. Now, they were out in the daylight searching for blood. You took your life in your hands if you dared enter their domain.

There was nothing to do but wait—wait for our representatives of the United States government to come rescue us and take us home. It had been more than three weeks since the Japanese colonel had in-formed us the war had ended. The train that ran past our front gate about every four hours was always loaded with Japanese soldiers and civilians. They were hanging on anywhere they could find a hand-hold; some even rode the cowcatcher. It was obvious to us that they were all heading home.

It may have been that notion—that all the Japanese were going home—that prompted a dozen or so of our more adventurous souls to throw caution to the winds and join them. In each case, our ex-POWs walked out on the tracks in groups of two or three, dressed in their new khaki uniforms, and waved to the oncoming train. The engineer would stop and let them climb aboard.

These fearless men, who would not wait any longer for the Americans to come, stepped out to face the unknown. They all stopped by the commissary for food to tide them over until they reached Tokyo, their destination, they said. Courtney, Roberts, and I loaded them down with chocolate bars, cigarettes, and anything they wanted. More than once I had the urge to go with them, but instead, I wished them Godspeed and a safe journey home. Somehow, I felt it was my duty to care for the food, a crazy idea that my services were needed here.

I whiled away part of my time as a member of the guard. We had two guard posts, the front and the rear gates to the compound. With a total of thirty-six marines, my tour of duty came around every four days. I had performed duties as corporal of the guard three times, and never during that thirty-six hours while I was on my post did one person come to the main gate—not even a Japanese.

Except for the brave souls who left camp to catch the train for home, no one passed through the gate. The other corporals of the guard had similar lackluster tours during their watches; as one pointed out to me, "There is nothing out there for us except hostility."

On the ninth of September, I decided to get a release for the pictures I had taken during the war. Someday, if I were so inclined, I would have them published. I picked up a set from their hiding place under my sleeping mat and took them to Major Dorris, the senior military officer in camp. The major agreed I should have every right to do with them as I chose, and issued me a release.

On the thirteenth of September, there was still no word from our armed forces. After breakfast, I went to the commissary to see if Courtney and Roberts needed any help. They assured me they had everything under control. As I stood in the midst of all that food, cases filling both upper and lower tiers, I suddenly got a craving for only one thing—an egg. A fresh egg.

"Do you think," I asked Courtney, "that I could swap a chocolate bar for an egg with one of the local natives?"

"I don't see why not," he agreed. "There is a lot more food value in the chocolate bar than there is in an egg; however, you have a problem." He sounded skeptical. "Where can you find an egg?"

"Wherever the chickens are. Where else?"

"Have you seen any chickens lately? For that matter, have you seen any chickens since you have been in Japan? Furthermore, can you ever remember hearing a rooster crow?"

He was right. Except for the chicken's head Langston had fished out of the bay, as far as I knew, chickens were nonexistent. I decided to forget the egg for the time being.

I went back to the barracks, fought my way through the bedbugs, and got a set of the pictures I had promised Dr. Markowitz, and took them to the hospital.

After delivering them, on my way out, I stopped short. There, stretched out on an army cot, was none other than Ras. His bony feet were protruding beyond the end of the small cot into the aisle. His stomach was bloated from wet beriberi. His arms and legs were nothing but bones with loose skin hanging from them. The color of his body was sickly yellow, and his deeply sunken eyes made his head look more like a skull than that of a living man. What was worse for him, he must have been suffering terribly. Why Grim Death had chosen to pass him by each day for the past few weeks could only be due to his indomitable spirit.

I was aghast. I could hardly believe that a man as strong and as robust as Ras had been the day he buffaloed his way into our room in Yawata, only two years ago, could be reduced to such a wretched being as this.

Ras sensed what was on my mind; he glared at me, his lips parted. "Get lost, you lousy son of a bitch," he growled, barely able to speak. Nevertheless, with great effort, he managed to make his sentiments known to me.

The compassion I had been feeling for him at that moment promptly vanished.

"Ras," I said, unable to suppress a grin, "you are just as ornery now as the first time we met. Remember how you told the whole room that whenever everyone was doing without, Ras was going to have his? It looks like you got it all."

Ras did not try to answer. He just peeled his lips back in a deathly sneer.

"I hope you make it," I said, waving to him as I left.

He is as hateful as ever, I thought to myself. In his shape I doubted if even the good food would help. He had been eating it now for at least three weeks. He looked too far gone, but then who knew—only the good die young.

Back at the commissary, after lunch, I made up my mind I was going to search for that egg. Since I'd first had the idea, it had been gnawing at me, and now, it had become an obsession—I must find an egg.

2 0

The Quest

With two chocolate bars in the shirt pocket of my new army uniform, I walked out the gate, over the railroad tracks, and straight south along a dirt road. There was nothing on either side except fields choked with weeds. There were no houses or chickens.

Fifteen minutes later, two miles or more, I came to a crossroad. It appeared to have had more traffic than the one I was using, and it also looked like a better road, so I turned west hoping to see some people. Up until this point, I had not seen a soul. Another mile or so in my new direction, I noticed some activity way off to the left in a field. I found a footpath and followed it through waist-high weeds until I came to a dwelling—I should say, a hovel.

Everyone had disappeared by the time I arrived. I promptly knocked and just as quickly, as though they had seen me and were waiting, the door opened.

A very old Korean, bent with age, bowed even lower and stepped aside with a gesture that I enter. Inside, the room was dark; only a small rice-paper window on the opposite wall provided lighting. I tried to straighten up, only to bump my head on the ceiling. As my eyes became accustomed to the semidarkness, I could see the room was full of men—perhaps eight. It was too dark to be sure. They were all squatting on their haunches in a circle facing a small, low, square table. There were bowls on the table that contained what appeared to be milk, except it looked a lot thicker. My host bade me join the group, indicating an open space between two men, probably his place. I moved to the spot and assumed the squatting position. The old Korean brought me a crock containing the same thick, milky substance as in the other bowls on the table. I accepted his offering, and holding the bowl in both hands, I nodded to the old man. Close inspection revealed it had the smell of fermentation. I followed the lead of the other men and

took a big swallow. Immediately, I regretted it. I became slightly nauseated, but managed to suppress any outward signs.

I set the bowl on the table like the others had done and proceeded
with my quest for the egg. I tried communicating with the men facing me by using what little Japanese I knew. It took no time at all to
determine that we had no common language between us, but in spite
of the language barrier, I felt there had to be a way to get my idea
across. My next attempt was sign language. When all else fails, use that
universal language to communicate. I made an oval with my thumb
and forefinger, pointing out to my audience the shape of the object I
sought, and to identify it further in relation to a chicken, I clucked like
a hen: "Puck, puck, puck ta pucket," in a falsetto voice.

My technique must have been bad because all I drew was a blank
response from some and a quizzical expression from the others. I tried
tucking my hands under my armpits and flapping my elbows up and
down, repeating my imitation of a hen that had just laid an egg. Again,
I got absolutely no recognition, but this time there were a few smiles.

Maybe because they were poor they had never owned a chicken,
but they must have known what a rooster sounds like. Everyone has
heard a rooster crow, I reasoned. With that conviction, I tried my best
rooster call.

That did it. They all laughed and clapped their hands. I was at a
loss. I had not the foggiest notion what they thought I was trying to
tell them. Perhaps they thought if all Americans who were coming
soon were like this one, life hereabouts was going to be hilarious.

I could see I was getting nowhere. I reached in my pocket, removed one of the chocolate bars, and placed it on the table. I got up
and bowed. "Thank you," I said and backed to the door. Everyone got
to their feet and bowed in turn.

Outside and back on the road again, the way in front of me was
level and no buildings were in sight. I was still heading west a half
hour later and beginning to get a little discouraged. I made up my
mind to turn back when I spotted a lone bicycle rider bearing down

on me from the direction I was heading. Perhaps there is something further ahead, I decided. I would walk a bit further. The lone rider must have been coming from somewhere.

The cyclist was dressed in a long black coat split up both sides, black trousers, and a black, broad-brimmed hat. We were on a collision course. If I refused to move out of his way, he would surely run me down. Knowing what I did about these people, his arrogance disturbed me. I moved over to allow him to pass, but even as he came near and abreast of me, I had no idea what I was going to do until I had done it. On a sudden impulse, I reached out, grabbed the handlebar and jerked the bicycle from under the unsuspecting rider. He tumbled into the ditch alongside the road and ended up on his back, looking up at me with a dazed expression.

I bowed, smiled, and used an expression I thought I would never use on these people: "Vae victis." [Woe to the vanquished]

The teenager stared wide-eyed, but made no move to recover his property. I got on the bike and called over my shoulder, "Arigato gasaimos." [Thank you very much]

I pumped the bicycle along effortlessly, and in no time, I had covered a great distance—miles. I tried every path and byway searching for people, but every trail proved fruitless.

I became aware, in spite of my continuous exertion pedaling the bike, of a feeling of vitality surging through me that I had not felt in years, almost like in the race back in Yawata. As I reflected on the wonder of the strength it took to jerk the bike from under the boy, it became obvious: I had been eating good, solid American-style food for better than three weeks. I had gained a lot of weight and filled in a few muscles. I must have weighed at least 125 pounds, maybe more. Best of all, I hadn't had diarrhea since the first B-29s showered us with happiness.

I continued on until I was about to conclude that this road too was taking me nowhere. I pedaled up a small rise, and as I came over the rim, there before me was complete and utter devastation. The remains of a small town stretched out and ended abruptly at the base of a small knoll a quarter of a mile away. I looked for signs of life, but could see nothing stirring.

Where do all the people go when their homes are burned? I wondered.

The roadway was mostly clear of debris, so I pedaled through the distressed area. There were no bodies or stench of rotting flesh, just ashes where a town had once stood. At the far side of the field of ashes, where the town had nestled against the hill, the road vanished around a turn, and to the left of that was a clump of trees. As I drew near, I could see a house hidden among the trees.

That looked to be a likely place to find chickens. My hopes soared. As I approached, I noted people moving about outside the house. There appeared to be more than a family. The two-story structure was too large for a Japanese family dwelling. When I drew close enough to make out who the people were, and discovered they were all women, I concluded, by their hairdos and brightly colored dresses, they were geisha girls.

That did it. I felt like cursing. A geisha house had to be the least likely place in Japan where one would find someone tending chickens.

With this last disappointment, I let myself be persuaded that I was wasting my time. If all Japan was like what I had just seen over the past three hours, there is very little of anything left in the whole country, let alone chickens. Maybe the Japanese colonel was right when he said the Japanese were in for a long, hard, cold winter.

It must have been five o'clock when I crossed the tracks in front of camp and coasted down the slight incline from the railroad bed. I noticed a small group of people near the gate of the stockade. That was unusual. Something important must have happened. As I pulled up, five of them, Japanese gendarmes, spread out across the entrance to block my way. The honey-dipping captain was standing behind them. Off to the side, I recognized the kid in black, the owner of the bike.

I had come to a stop and put both feet on the ground, still astraddle the bike, when the bravest of the Japanese police rushed forward and grabbed my left arm and tried to throw me to the ground. A surge of anger gripped me as I jerked my arm free of his grasp. I seethed with rage to think these people still thought they reserved the right to exercise their brutality on anyone they chose.

It is said that one's entire life passes before them in a wink when they are about to die or be killed. So also, did I glimpse the past forty-five months of vivid hell they had made for me. Seeing Butcher being burned to a crisp on a needlessly cruel electric fence; Riddle murdered in cold blood in the prime of his life; Big Red crying to live, but being denied the proper food that would have saved him; Killebrew, for the want of a little medicine; Neuse, another murder; each day an average of three bodies laid out on the dead-run cart having died from pneumonia or starvation. All this because the Japs had a stupid belief that because we had surrendered, we were cowards and had no right to live.

Now that they had waved the white flag, by their own standards, they had become worse than cowards. We never, ever claimed to be something we were not.

Here before me, my antagonist reached to lay his hands on me again. I countered with a left jab to his shoulder to square him away for what was coming.

Looking back at the starvation, cruelty, and other abuses—both physical and mental—that the Japanese captors had meted out to me, I channeled every ounce of hate and vengeance I could muster into my fist and smashed him in the face. The force of the blow knocked him off his feet and flat on his back. He was back up instantly, bleeding from his nose and pulling a short sword from a scabbard at his hip. Before he could attack, his four buddies grabbed and held him.

I picked up the bike, carried it to the young Japanese, and pushed it at him. He took hold and started to step backward. I let go, and he tripped and fell with the bicycle on top of him. Once again, there he lay, flat on his back, wide-eyed, looking up at me.

"Thank you," I said, turning to face the gendarme. I singled out the Japanese with the sword and started directly for him. *This is a hell of a way to go*, I thought, *but I will be damned if I am backing down from any of these little bastards again.* I had run out of cheeks.

As I closed in on the little guy with the sword, he dropped it and he and the rest of the little yellow bastards gave way and let me walk right through them—no guts. I was about five steps past when I heard, "I am going to put you on report for what you just did"—this from the shit-dipping captain. These were the first words he had uttered since I had arrived at the gate. He was going to stand there and do nothing while those bastards worked me over.

"What the hell do you mean," I snarled as I whipped around, "you are going to put me on report? We won this goddamned war, or haven't you heard?" I glared at him. "To the victor go the spoils," I said sarcastically, and with that, I turned my back on him.

In five or six light steps I was in the commissary. I felt great.

I had just gotten one lick in on this war, such as it was, even if it was a little late. Courtney looked up from a stack of cases he was setting in a pile for Kirkpatrick, I guessed.

"Any luck on the eggs?"

I shook my head.

"Courtney," I said flatly, "I'm leaving on the next train for the States. There, I know I can find an egg. You people can run this place without me. You have been running it ever since the first food drop."

Courtney abandoned his pile of food and called to Roberts, who was working down the line among the cases and cartons. When Roberts arrived, Courtney asked, "Mind if we tag along?"

"We both figured it wouldn't be long before you decided to head for home. You have been acting restless lately, especially each time someone walks out to catch a train for home."

"Suit yourselves," I said. "I'm leaving as soon as I collect my gear from the barracks. I'll stop by the galley and tell Kirkpatrick that we are leaving, so he can find someone to take care of this place. I will be leaving in about a half hour. Will you be ready?"

"Hell," Courtney laughed, "I'm ready now. What you see is what I own."

"That goes for me too," Roberts chimed in.

"I still have one candy bar." I said, "Get me another and a couple packs of cigarettes. We may need some trading material."

I picked up my pictures and a few papers I was sure I would need someday, shook hands with some of my buddies, and made it over to the galley in about ten minutes.

Moose was stirring a large pot of stew with a wooden paddle.

"I came to say good-bye and to tell you that you'll have to get someone to watch the food. I'm leaving, and my helpers are going with me."

Kirkpatrick put his paddle down, reached over, and patted me on the shoulder.

"Do you think you should, Terence? I heard about your row at the gate."

"News travels fast," I commented.

"Terence, if you go out there among the Japs, there is bound to be trouble. I know you. You can't control your temper. Damn it, Terence, you will start this war all over again," he said with a twinkle in his eye.

I refused to listen and backed away for the door.

"If I don't see you again, Terence, have a long and happy life," he called after me.

"I hope you have the same, Moose," I answered as I stepped outside.

Courtney and Roberts were standing in front of the commissary when I came by. We left camp together and walked up on the railroad tracks.

2 1

Beyond the Point of No Return

Our timing was lousy. We must have just missed the train. It was getting dark and almost three hours had passed before one finally came along. We all began waving our arms, hoping the engineer would see us. He did; the train ground to a halt beside us and the engineer motioned to us to climb on the cowcatcher.

We pulled into Moji station about fifteen minutes later. We got off the front of the locomotive onto the platform and began wading through throngs of people like salmon fighting their way upstream. Our objective was to get a seat on one of the coaches. Everyone was carrying a bundle, especially the women; all those bundles didn't make our progress any easier. The soldiers were still armed with rifles and bayonets, only this time, their bayonets were encased in scabbards at their sides. We seemed to be the only ones going against the grain, but we persisted until we reached the coaches. All passengers were getting off the train, so we waited for an opportunity, then boarded.

There were plenty of seats. As a matter of fact, we had the entire coach to ourselves. It didn't seem quite right, but we were not going to knock our good fortune. We sat waiting for the train to move. In a few minutes, the conductor appeared in the doorway at the far end of the car and called out, "*Moji Co.*"

"OK, Moji Co," I acknowledged. He shook his head and left. Presently, the train began to move. When we cleared the station, I noted it was pitch-black outside.

"Where is Moji Co?" Courtney asked after a long silence.

"Your guess is as good as mine," I grinned.

"But I thought you knew," Courtney said, completely baffled.

"There is no way I could know," I remarked, "but if we wait, I'm sure we will soon be there."

I had no sooner gotten the words out of my mouth when our car began to clatter over numerous railroad switches.

"I know where we are," I laughed.

"So do I," Roberts declared, "we are in a railroad yard."

Finally, the train came to a stop, we climbed down out of the car, and started walking back toward Moji. We were miles from the station. Nothing was moving in the railroad yard, which eliminated the danger of being run over. We picked the shiniest set of tracks that reflected light from the poles in the yard, and hoped they would lead us back to Moji.

We had not traveled far when an engine's headlight loomed up ahead, on this same track. We waited until the train was close enough so the engineer could see us in his headlight and began jumping up and down and waving our arms in an effort to attract his attention. The driver brought the engine in close and stopped.

We walked alongside the giant engine. I never realized how large these Japanese locomotives were until now. The drive wheels were taller than I could reach. Even in the United States, I cannot remember see ing locomotives this huge. We stopped directly under the cab. It must have been two stories off the ground. The driver leaned out the window.

"Moji," I yelled to the engineer and pointed in the direction he had come. "Tobacco *kudasai*." [give]

"*Nani?*" [What?] he called down above the rush of the engine.

"Moji, *itteh* [go], Americano tobacco kudasai," I yelled, holding up a pack of Chesterfields.

The only lighting in the yard was from floodlights on high poles spaced every hundred yards or so, none of them very close, but even in the dim light he recognized the package as cigarettes.

He understood my request, for he put his hand down to accept my offer. I tossed and he caught the pack. After examining them carefully, he pointed toward the front of the locomotive. We crawled up on the cowcatcher, and the engineer backed the locomotive all the way back to Moji Station.

We got off on the platform and stopped beside the cab and thanked him. He smiled and waved as he puffed on one of the cigarettes while he pushed the lever that chugged his engine from the station into the darkness.

We moved along the loading platform looking for a place to sit down. We saw many small groups of Japanese sitting on their baggage, but there did not seem to be any benches for the convenience of the passengers. As we drifted along the edge of the platform, I spotted a man dressed as a conductor coming toward us. People were stopping him and asking questions. As he came abreast of us, I asked. "Yoko-hama, *nanji*?" [what time?]

He answered very rapidly over his shoulder as he passed. All I got from his response was, "San." [Three] He was gone before I could ask him to repeat.

We were not totally in the dark. At least we were in the right station, and the train for Yokohama was due sometime between three and four o'clock in the morning. The station clock in the middle of the long platform told us it was eleven o'clock, which meant we had over four hours to kill.

We finally sat down on the edge of the platform and hung our legs over the tracks. None of us had eaten since noon, so we each broke out a chocolate bar and nursed them while we waited.

At 3:15 A.M., I was beginning to wonder if I had heard the station-master correctly, but even as I wondered, he came by again calling out the names of cities. As he ran through them, I picked out Yokohama and Tokyo. It was then I assumed we would not have long to wait.

The people began lining up in queues at marks along the platform, and we quickly got in one of them hoping to get a seat. I doubted that we would because I remembered all the cars being filled to over-flowing with travelers during the past three weeks as they passed our prison camp.

The train rumbled into the station at 3:20. Quickly, all those getting off spilled out of the open doors onto the platform, and just as promptly, all the people waiting in lines boarded. There was no wasted time; the train could not have delayed more than three or four minutes and it was on its way again.

We crowded into the coach; there was standing room only and not much of that. I stopped by the first seat on the right as we entered the coach. There were three Japanese soldiers seated there. Each was armed with a rifle and bayonet.

To the victor go the spoils, ran through my head.

"Hey," I barked, loud enough to be heard at the other end of the car. The three soldiers looked up at me.

"Out," I commanded sharply, cocking my thumb over my shoulder.

Instantly, without hesitation, the three obediently got to their feet and moved past us down the aisle.

A hush fell over the coach. I took the seat nearest the window, and Courtney and Roberts seated themselves beside me. The quiet soon passed, and soon everyone was chattering again.

I had had a busy day and a long one. The turmoil did not bother me, now that I was actually on my way home. I didn't care if the Japanese were talking about us. We had won the war. A feeling of warmth and contentment settled over me in spite of my rotten luck in not finding an egg, and my unpleasant meeting with that captain. The hum of voices soon lulled me to sleep.

I awoke with the sun shining in my face. I looked out at the picturesque landscape. A green carpet sloped away from the train for miles, with a gentle slant that gradually became steeper, and finally turned up sharply into a range of fairyland mountain ridges standing out like a storybook picture against a deep blue sky. Little trails or roads leading into the mountain passes led my eyes to darkened areas that once had been villages nestled in the canyons; now, they were nothing but burned scars on the landscape.

As I watched the scene unfold before me, I began to notice an inconsistency about the rural buildings and dwellings we were passing. Most of the roofs were badly in need of repair. This was not like the

Japanese people. As a rule, everything was very tidy. As we proceeded, the damage became worse. Soon, we saw a few outbuildings that were laying flat, and some homes appeared to have been pushed over as if by hurricane-force winds. Next, parts of buildings were strewn about everywhere. After that, we entered an area where everything was burned, like the little town I had seen yesterday on my quest for the egg. The train slowed to a crawl. The conductor stepped into the coach from behind us and called out, "Hiroshima."

We finally stopped. I watched with interest as a man with an extra-long-handled shovel and an equally long rake picked up a rusty tin can and deposited it in a 55-gallon drum. He treated it as if it were hot, but I knew different. Why he didn't pick it up with his hand and put it in the barrel was beyond me.

Another strange sight caught my eye: a row of cornstalks behind the man with the shovel were bright green and taller than the man.

That is odd, I thought; I wonder why the corn was spared when everything else was burned up in the fire. Except for the cornstalks, there was nothing but desolation as far as I could see on my side of the train; nothing standing except a lone smokestack.

Stopping every few minutes, at every town along the tracks, used up most of the day. It was nearing four o'clock when we rolled into Yokohama. We got off the train because everyone else was getting off. Maybe we had to change trains here for Tokyo. We followed the traffic, not sure what to do next.

Courtney was taller and could see over the heads of most Japanese. He was first to spot the MP.

"Hey, look," he pointed, "an American MP."

Almost at the same instant the crowd thinned and the military policeman spotted us. He hurried toward us and when he got within range, he boomed, "Where the hell did you guys come from? This is a restricted area."

"We are POWs," I answered as he came up to us. "We came in on this train from Kyushu."

"Where the hell is that?"

"It's the southern island," I explained. "It is part of Japan."

"You mean, you came all the way across Japan, on this train, without weapons?" he asked disbelievingly.

"Weapons?" I laughed. "Whatever you guys did to the Japs, it worked, because they are all tame," I said.

"What service do you belong to? I see you are wearing army uniforms."

"Marine Corps," I answered, and at the same time, Courtney and Roberts spoke up: "Navy."

The MP guided us to a call box on one of the stanchions nearby. He picked up the receiver as the train started to move, and his voice was lost in the rumble of the wheels. The soldier talked briefly, then hung up the receiver and turned to us. "The Navy is on its way. They will be here in a minute."

It was less than a minute when all three of us spotted a sailor in whites running toward us against the traffic. When he reached us, he shook hands.

"Glad to have you back," he puffed, nearly out of breath. I could see he genuinely meant it. He was beaming from ear to ear.

"Follow me. I will take you to Navy headquarters. Do you want to get there in a hurry?" He laughed. We all voiced a joyous approval, bade the MP good-bye, and followed the young sailor at a run. Once outside the station, we piled into a jeep for a short ride to the docks.

At Navy headquarters, more sailors greeted us, patted us on our backs, shook our hands, and told us how glad they were that we had made it back alive. We were escorted into the warehouse where we were each issued a new set of navy dungarees.

Next, they introduced us to a shower. After we had bathed and were dressed in our new navy outfits, we were taken into a warehouse next door. As we entered, the odor of frying steaks smacked us right in the face, a memento of the past, and definitely an essence one was not likely to forget.

We sat down at a mess table with white sheets spread over it. This meal was being prepared especially for the three of us. They must have started preparing it when they'd heard we had arrived. No sooner had we seated ourselves when a young sailor approached us carrying three plates. He placed one in front of each of us.

"See if you can get around that," he said with enthusiasm.

I looked down at the most beautiful T-bone steak I had ever seen. It completely filled my plate. I was overwhelmed. There were many times in the past few years when I'd doubted I would ever see this day. Mortimer, the interpreter, promised I never would. *I had really made it back*, I thought, as a lump welled up in my throat.

I peered up at the sailor who seemed to be waiting for a comment. My eyes, slightly glazed as I stubbornly fought back a tear, told him all he wanted to know. The sailor turned away quickly to let me have my moment of joy.

I attacked the steak, but could only eat a small portion before my stomach began to hurt; its capacity was too small to accept normal quantities of food.

After the meal, we were questioned by two groups of officers, first the Army, then the Navy. I gave each a set of my pictures and explained how I got them with Nishi's help, furnishing me the photographic plates and the processing. I detailed how I'd made the pinhole camera, and also gave them Nishi's address at the factory so they could verify the authenticity of the prints.

Next we were taken to the docks and there boarded a lighter (motorized barge). There were POWs already on board. As we proceeded across Yokohama Bay, dodging sunken ships with their masts sticking out of the water, I discovered Major Brown among the POWs. We shook hands and congratulated each other for having survived. When he told me he had been sent to Zenzugi, I was not a bit surprised. That was a special camp, exclusively for officers the Japanese could not handle. If I knew the major, he was in their hair at every turn.

We reached the other side of the bay around seven o'clock, and found a transport plane standing on the runway waiting for us with its propellers turning. We quickly boarded and the plane took off.

I never looked back at that land of sorrow, tears, and pain; where the whole country smelled of human waste and the flowers, if any can be found, are odorless; where I never heard a bird sing; where women are treated as chattel or worse; where men have no honor and are cruel and vicious. There were about twenty POWs in our group. All of us had given up the security of our stockades for a breath of fresh air and to seek out the conquering Americans. The crewmen of the transport told us that we were the third group of American POWs to leave Japan.

It was dark when we settled down in a smooth landing on an island in the Pacific. We were taken to a mess tent and treated to a meal of S.O.S. (chipped beef on toast). It was delicious, what little I could eat. At that time, everything tasted good.

During the meal, a Marine Corps captain informed us that the name of this island was Iwo Jima. He said that nearly 4,000 marines were lost taking this piece of volcanic rock from a garrison of 40,000 Japs. When the battle was over, only 129 Japanese had survived.

A few of us ventured out onto the beach after supper. As I walked, I sank into volcanic ash up to my ankles. The granulated pumice had the consistency of quicksand, pulling at my feet with every step. I shuddered to think of what the marines who landed here under fire had to go through. It must have been a nightmare trying to move from place to place, like the devil himself was holding onto their feet.

The next morning, bright and early, we were off again, and landed on Guam by noon. Everyone was taken to the naval hospital. I was assigned to a ward that was equipped with a perpetual snack bar. It was open twenty-four hours a day, with a built-in short-order cook. The nurses encouraged us to eat as often as we could, but not to overeat. First off, I ordered a fried egg, then a poached egg. Later in the day I had one scrambled and one boiled. All of them tasted better than I had dreamed.

The following morning, I awoke with a fever. At first I thought it was dengue fever, because it did not act like malaria. The doctor checked me over and said it was cat fever. I had had cat fever once before, back in 1938 when I was stationed at Pearl Harbor. It was strictly tropical and caused me to run a high fever for a course of five days. It left me feeling weak as a kitten.

That same morning, all the POWs who had come in with me, left by plane for Hawaii. Seeing them go did absolutely nothing for my morale.

During the next five days, a few more POWs arrived from Japan, only to leave the following day for the States. These five days were the longest days I had ever spent in my life.

The morning I was pronounced well, I was the first one on the plane and the only POW. The flight took us across the Pacific to Hawaii, with a touchdown on Johnson Island for a few minutes to refuel.

My left ear bothered me on the trip from Guam. When they dropped me off at the naval hospital in Hawaii, I went directly to the sick bay for treatment. I chose not to tell the doctor what had caused my ear trouble. I did not want to admit to the stupidity of walking around in a bombing raid. Whatever the trouble, the doctor fixed me up with a few drops of medicine in my ear. After that there was no more pain.

I slept in the hospital that night. The bunk was almost as hard as the straw mats I had been sleeping on for the past forty-five months.

After breakfast the next morning, a corpsman gave me a physical examination. When he weighed me, he said, "You should eat more—you're about forty-five pounds underweight."

At ten o'clock I began looking for something to eat. I walked all over the hospital in search of a snack bar like the one back on Guam, but all I could find was a hamburger stand run by the Post Exchange. I was penniless. I went back to the ward and asked the nurse if there was any way I could get some money. She went to the desk, picked up the phone, talked to the person at the other end of the line, then turned to me and asked, "How much do you want?"

"Oh, five will do fine," I said. She passed on my request and hung up the receiver. "The paymaster will be up this afternoon," she promised.

I went back to my bunk to wait for lunch. I began reading the local newspaper when a voice interrupted me.

"I understand you were a prisoner of war?"

I nodded.

"Would you like to have a photograph of yourself?"

"Sure. Why not?" I answered. "How is this?" I held up a newspaper and pointed at the headline, STRIP JAPS' STRENGTH.

"Hold it just like that," he agreed. The photographer focused his camera and fired off a flash.

"I'll bring you a copy as soon as I run them off," he promised, and was gone.

At 2:30 in the afternoon, I was still waiting for my five dollars when the photographer returned and handed me an 8x10 print of the picture he had taken. I thanked him and had just slipped it under my pillow when a petty officer with a briefcase approached.

"Are you Terence S. Kirk, the ex-POW?" he asked, very businesslike.

"Yes I am," I answered. "Why?"

"You requested some cash, is that right?"

I nodded.

"Do you have any identification?"

"Only this." I pulled a slip of paper out of my shirt pocket and handed it to him. "This is what they gave me when I reported in to the Navy in Yokohama. A temporary ID, they said."

"What about dog tags?"

"What are dog tags?" I questioned with a puzzled expression.

"If you don't know," he looked at me curiously, "I guess you don't have any. I'll have to accept your temporary ID."

The chief opened his briefcase and brought out a stack of green-backs which he set on the bed. Next, he handed me a form.

"Sign your name at the 'X,' along with your rank and serial number."

I took his pen and signed the form while he counted out twenties into five piles, five in each pile. When he had finished, he put the rest of the money back into his briefcase. He looked at me. "Is the count right?"

All I could do was nod. I was dumbfounded. I had asked for five dollars so I could buy a two-bit hamburger and maybe a nickel candy bar, and the Navy had given me $500.

The chief folded up his case and walked away, leaving me standing there gazing at all that money piled on my bunk.

I recovered quickly from my shock because of the gnawing in my stomach, telling me I needed some nourishment. I gathered the money, stuffed it in my pockets, and headed for the Post Exchange. I bought a hamburger, but found I could eat only half of it; my stomach hurt.

Hours later, after supper, I took off my clothes and lay on my bed. It was still early, but I thought if I could go to sleep, the time would pass more swiftly. I had no idea when they had me scheduled to leave for the States. Maybe I would go tomorrow. I must have been tired, for I dropped off to sleep as soon as my head touched the pillow.

"Kirk, Kirk." Someone was shaking my bunk.

"What?" I sat up quickly to see a corpsman standing alongside my bunk.

"A plane is leaving for the States in an hour," he said anxiously. "Would you like to be on it?"

"You betcha!" I exclaimed, full of excitement. I was on the floor slipping into my clothes. *Home at last*, raced through my mind.

I picked up my treasures, my total worldly possessions in one hand, and hurried out of the hospital into a waiting jeep. The driver whisked me away to Pearl Harbor where I boarded a huge Mars flying boat.

I had no sooner fastened my seat belt when the giant plane's four engines began to rumble. It picked up speed, and in a few seconds was racing across the waters of Pearl Harbor throwing spray high in the air and leaving a frothy wake behind. Slowly, the flying boat lifted out of the water and soared over Barbers Point. I looked down into the twilight to see the Marine Corps Rifle Range, where I had qualified my first time as a marksman, so many years ago.

We leveled off and swung around onto an easterly course, straight for the good old United States of America, to home and my wonderful mother.

As we flew into the gathering darkness, I unhooked my seat belt and got up to look over the huge ship. I found it very empty. There were only seven passengers, including myself and a crew of five, making a total of twelve men. The size of the aircraft made it seem like a flying barn. There were more than fifty seats. This plane could easily carry fifty combat troops with all their gear, plus a few special weapons to boot. Like myself, the passengers and crew had little or no baggage.

There was a small room on the same level, behind the pilot's cabin. The other six passengers had gravitated there because it had a table and one of the passengers had a deck of cards. They invited me to join them in a friendly game of draw poker to while away the hours.

The passengers were all marine officers—lieutenants and captains. From their conversation, I learned they were all veteran combat pilots. Their presence on this plane was due to their having amassed many points, which made them eligible to return to the States. Although they must have flown many combat missions to get all these points, not once was there any mention made of the war.

Lady Luck was smiling on me; by midnight I had won thirty-six dollars. I picked up the cards to deal.

"Gentlemen," a voice said. The crew chief, a chief petty officer, was standing in the doorway. "The skipper has asked me to inform all of you that our outboard engine has been slowly losing oil pressure for the past twenty minutes. He says he will be forced to shut it down soon. He says we are an hour from the point of no return. He also wants to remind you of something you may already be aware of—that all the airplane mechanics left Hawaii on the first available transportation the week after the war ended. If we turn back, he says, there is no guarantee . . ."

"Come to the point, Chief," voiced a tall, hawk-faced captain, sounding irritated. "We would like to get on with the game."

"OK," the chief blurted, "the skipper wants to know if you want to go on with three engines, or turn back?"

"That doesn't make a hell of a lot of sense," said the youngest pilot, a first lieutenant; the others called him Larry.

"We will be flying back to Hawaii on three engines, damn near as far."

"Press on, of course."

"Does anyone want to go back?" the chief asked. "How about you?" He looked at me.

"What do I know?" I shrugged. "I'll go on three; let's not turn back, I want to get home."

The chief left. I started to deal, then stopped and began to wonder about the consequences of the loss of an engine.

"Hey, deal the cards." This from the irate captain.

He brought me out of my trance and also caused the conversation to resume. I proceeded with the deal. This devil-may-care attitude of all these combat pilots must be rubbing off on me, I thought. Considering all their combat time, they must have been in worse situations than this. The feeling of confidence they had given me is what I needed at a time like this, with one engine down and only three left to fly better than halfway across the Pacific.

In spite of my newfound assurance that everything was going to be all right, I kept my ear tuned to the sound of the engines. As the crew chief had informed us, the outboard, starboard engine was put to rest. The only difference I could detect was a slight decrease in the overall noise level.

An hour passed, and nothing was said about the lifeless engine. The conversation was back on the point system again. I didn't understand what they were talking about and couldn't have cared less. My mind was on the dead engine out there on the wing.

Finally, a lull in the conversation gave me an opportunity to break into the discussion. "It's a good thing this is a flying boat," I said with certainty. "With one engine gone, if we are forced down into the sea, at least we'll float."

My statement, I thought, was ignored. There was silence; everyone seemed preoccupied with his poker hand.

"I can't imagine why you would say that," Larry said at last. "To my knowledge, none of these so-called seaplanes that have set down on the ocean has floated yet," he said as though he meant it.

"You are pulling my leg," I said hopefully.

"Now, why would I do a thing like that? Why, I don't even know you," he said with a puzzled expression.

I was sure he was joking. I studied him for a moment; except for myself, he was the only winner. He was a good poker player, and I could never tell when he was bluffing, even now.

There is a remote possibility that he is serious, but that would be ridiculous, I told myself. Since this war began, I have spent one hell of a time getting this far. Now, that I am almost home, I can't appreciate anyone joking about me ending up at the bottom of the ocean. Abruptly, I lost my desire for poker. I stood up and collected my winnings.

"I think I'll go back to my seat and get a little shut-eye," I said. "Thanks for the donations."

The plane was a little chilly outside the room. I slipped into the combat jacket I had left hanging on the back of my seat. I sat with my arms folded to keep warm. Outside the porthole was nothing but blackness below and only stars above. I could see the outline of the wing where it blocked out the stars. I shivered and snuggled down in my coat. Momentarily, the chill subsided, and warmth overtook me—along with a merciful sleep to soothe my weary and troubled mind.

I awakened with a shudder. Something was amiss! I sat upright pulling against my seat belt. There was no telling how long I had been out. A dim light was easing its way through the porthole, and the sky was beginning to lighten to the northeast and ahead of us.

I unhooked my seat belt and made my way back to the poker room.

"If you can't win when you're dealing, there ain't no use playing," one of the players remarked as I stepped into the room.

"Come back to let us win our money back?" Larry laughed when he saw me come in.

"What is wrong with the plane?" I asked anxiously, coming right to the point. "It doesn't sound right."

"Oh, that," he said, trying to pass it off as if it were nothing. "We lost the other outboard engine a while back." Noting the expression of alarm on my face, he was quick to add, "Not to worry." He grinned. "These damn planes are supposed to remain aloft on only one engine. Only one, mind you. We still have two left."

None of the other pilots showed the least concern. Damn, I thought, these guys have ice water in their veins instead of blood. I turned away to return to my seat.

"Come on, deal the cards," one of the players complained.

I got back to my seat and noticed the sky was getting lighter by the minute. The outboard engine was silhouetted against the morning light, its propeller feathered, offering little or no resistance, quietly coming along for the ride. Not so the two inboard engines. They seemed to be running a lot faster and harder than normal.

"Kirk." The crew chief was standing in front of me. "The skipper wants to see you."

I climbed up to the cockpit and stood in the narrow space between the pilot and copilot.

"There's the California coast," the pilot said, sweeping his hand across the windshield. "How long has it been?" he asked.

"Many, many years," I answered mechanically as I peered to the coast, shrouded in the mist of Indian summer. Only straight ahead could I make out landfall.

"Will we see the Golden Gate?" I asked hopefully.

"Yep," he assured me, "it's coming right up. We'll be setting down in San Francisco Bay in a few minutes."

"We have lost oil pressure on starboard engine!" the copilot interrupted. He turned his head to look back at the engine on the wing.

"We're on fire," he reported calmly, with the same cool as portrayed by the fighter pilots.

It must be one of their rules, I thought; among all Navy and Marine Corps flyers, no matter what—nobody panics.

"Kill the engine. Hit the extinguisher," the pilot ordered with deliberate finesse, as though this were a routine drill. Then he held his face mask to his mouth, "Mayday, mayday," he repeated over and over.

The copilot was busy throwing switches, pushing and pulling levers.

"You had better go strap yourself in," the skipper said, turning to me. "This could get rough."

I turned away in anguish to retrace my steps slowly down the ladder. At each step, his voice rang in my ears. "Our position, two miles due west of the Golden Gate Bridge. Mayday, mayday."

By the time I got back to my seat, the six combat pilots were all strapped in their seats. I found Larry; he had been watching me.

He winked and smiled, but I could see his smile was not genuine. He had finally broken down. He was scared too, but that didn't make me feel a damn bit better.

I buckled my seat belt and turned my head to the porthole in time to catch a glimpse of the underside of the Golden Gate Bridge as it flashed by. It looked the same in the dawn's early light as it had at dusk, eight years and seventeen days ago when I'd sailed under the bridge aboard the USS *Henderson*, bound for Hawaii, the Philippines, and the Orient.

I looked down; the water was getting closer, coming up fast. I turned and faced forward, fixed my eyes on the small ladder leading to the skippers' cabin, gripped the sides of my seat with all my might, and listened to the last surviving engine screaming its heart out as it tried to keep this monster in the air.

I waited.

For what?—Only God could know.

THE END

Afterword

T hough it was frightening to come into San Francisco Bay on one
engine, the huge plane sat down smoothly. The crash boats were
waiting for us and the Navy corpsmen whisked me off to Oak Knoll
Naval Hospital in Oakland, California.

After my release from the hospital, the Corps gave me liberty to
go home. They gave me two options for travel: plane or train. At the
time, POWs had priority over anyone else to travel, so I chose the
train. After all, I had had enough of flying for a while.

I arrived at Mooseheart, a child city of the Loyal Order of Moose. It
was the orphanage where I grew up and where my mother still worked
as a house mother in one of the cottages. She told me that Mooseheart
had given her the honor of ringing the liberty bell there on VJ day.
Mother hugged me and cried. I thought she would never stop.

Since I was still in the Corps, I reported to the Great Lakes Navel
Training Station Hospital just north of Chicago. There the doctors
were supposed to watch us to see if we were going to fall apart. After
about a month, I was given six months leave. When I came back I was
offered any station I wanted if I would reenlist in the Corps. I signed
up and took another three months leave. This time when I came back,
the first sergeant said, "Don't unpack your bags, you're going to Wash-
ington, D.C." I complained because when I had reenlisted I had requested Great Lakes Training Station. His remark was, "You're here
aren't you? Well, you're leaving for D.C. in the morning!" Oh well,
that's the Corps.

After two years' duty, I was transferred to Camp Pendelton and assigned to Able Company, 1st Marines, 1st Marine Division. During
the next two years I did extensive combat training of the troops and
was promoted to Master Gunnery Sergeant. In my last two years in

the Corps, looking ahead, I could see I lacked skills to make a living with when I retired. Electronics looked like a good field, so I enrolled in a correspondence course with DeVry Institute. The day after I retired from the Corps, I went to work for Convair in their test lab. Later I worked for Karr Electronics, building ship to shore transceivers. Two years later Karr Electronics went belly up. (It wasn't my fault.) My next job was with the Federal Aviation Administration as an electronic engineering technician. I retired seven and a half years later as a Proficiency Development Evaluation Officer.

This time I really retired. I went to work on my farm, built a huge barn, planted apple trees, and have been working more than ever before.

Back in 1945, as I was routed through Guam on my way home from Japan, a government-issued gag order was produced for me to sign. It stated that I was not to tell *anyone* what I knew about Japanese prisoner of war camps. Like a good Marine, I did what I was told. I never breathed a word to my mother or anyone else for thirty-eight years. During that time I was married for eighteen years and my wife and two children never knew I was a POW.

What had happened to my pictures? The pictures I had risked my life—and the lives of the other brave Marines and Allied POWs who helped me—to take? It was my goal when I took the pictures that all the world should see them. Especially Americans, so they could know how their sons, brothers, fathers, and friends had died. But the U.S. government did not share my goals.

After thirty-eight years, I could wait no longer. Surely in that time, all the people who had initiated that gag order had died. So, I published the forbidden pictures in the first edition of this book, *The Secret Camera*, in 1982. I received the Purple Heart in November of 2004.

ABOUT THE MEN

James D. McBrayer was one of the Marines who escaped from the train en route from Woosung to Mudken. He is now in his nineties and ranks as a general.

Moose Kirkpatrick was my best friend. We worked as telephone linemen together in Tientsin. Moose went on to serve in Korea as a telephone lineman. He was killed in action by sniper fire at Inchon Landing. Recently, he has been nominated to receive the Medal of Honor for his actions while in Woosung.

Wilbur Ditewig was a North China Marine POW. Ironically, he had a brother who was also a POW in Mudken, and another brother killed in action flying over the English Channel.

Nishi left Japan after the war and went to live in Chile.

By the way, I learned that Aunt Bessie was truly my mother's sister.

Of the 203 North China Marines, thirty-one are still living at the time of this printing. We still meet annually for a reunion. This year being the sixtieth anniversary of VJ Day, the gathering will be especially memorable. If not for the bombing of Hiroshima and Nagasaki, we would have met certain death.

—*Terence Sumner Kirk,*
Summer 2005

The Yoheen Gang

BERNSTINE BLESSENGER BULGARDUS ELLIOT GUSHWA

HAHNE HARRIS KILLOUGH KIRK LANGSTON

LAPORT LEE MASON MOODY POWNEY

RICHY SCOTT SIEJACK WALKER WILLIAMS

Prison Camp—Company Street

Allied Prisoners of War, Malnutrition Cases

ALLIED PRISONERS OF WAR, MALNUTRITION CASES

Drain Hole Patch, Beriberi Cases (Center man is supported by corpsman behind him.)

THE HYDROELECTRIC PLANT AT KOKURA, JAPAN

福岡俘虜收容所俘虜通信用箋

HEADQUARTERS CAMP NUMBER THREE
Fukuoka, Japan.

September 9, 1945.

Subject: Publication of Photographs.

To: Whom it may concern.

　　1. I hereby release five (5) photographs taken in
prisoner of war camp no. 3, Fukuoka, Japan, of patients
and others in the above camp.

　　2. Corporal Terrence S. Kirk, 260583, U.S. Marine
Corps, the photographer, has permission to publish the
photographs at his own discretion.

　　3. The photographs were taken with a camera made
from a cardboard box.

W. O. DORRIS,
Major, U.S. Army,
Commanding.

PHOTO RELEASE

Terence Sumner Kirk